100 MENTAL MATHS

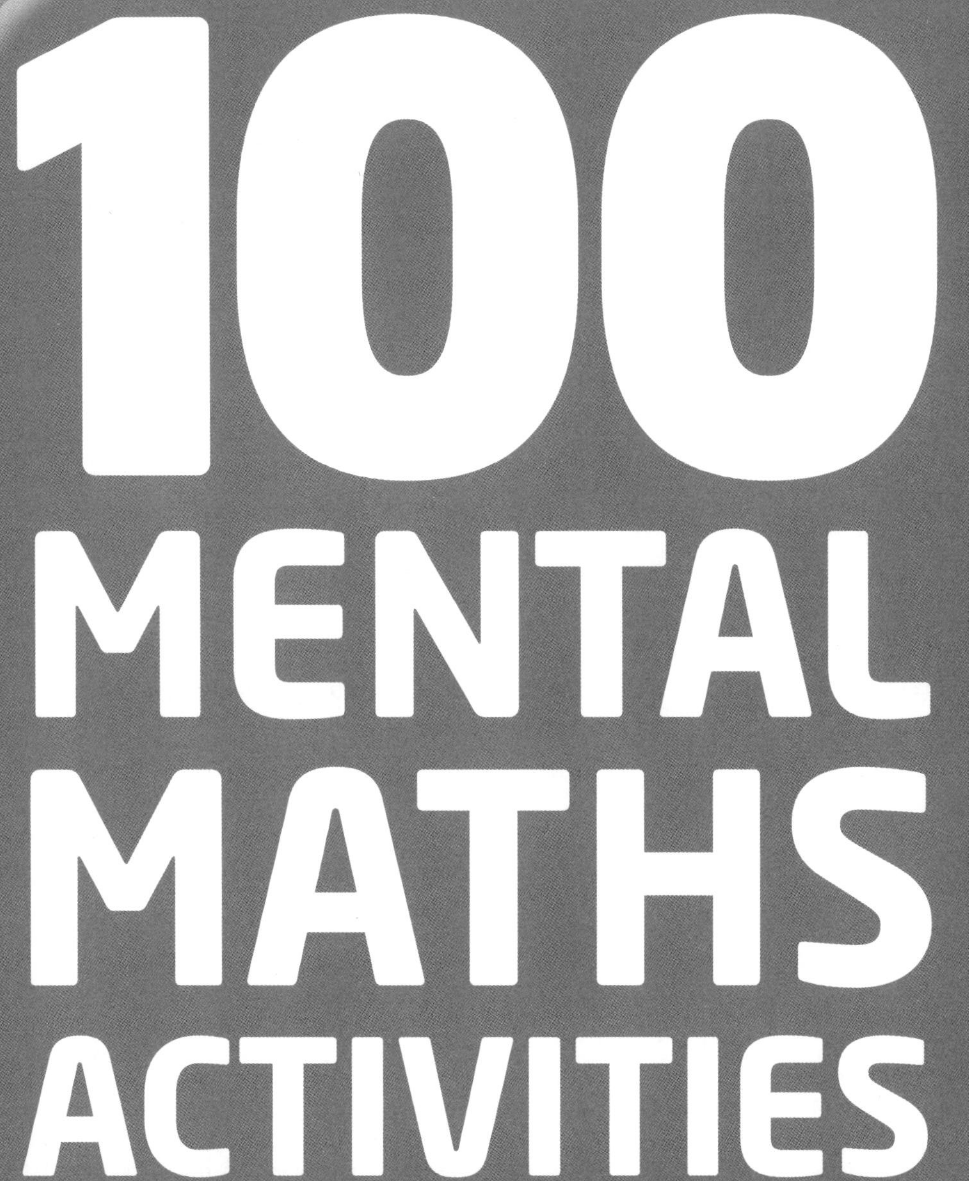

100 MENTAL MATHS ACTIVITIES

YEAR 6

John Davis and
Margaret Gronow

Authors
John Davis
Margaret Gronow

Illustrations
Mick Davies

Series Designer
Sonja Bagley

Designer
Quadrum

British Library Cataloguing-in-Publication Data
A catalogue record for this book is available from the British Library.

ISBN 978-1407-11420-0

Designed using Adobe InDesign

Published by Scholastic Ltd
Book End
Range Road
Witney
Oxfordshire OX29 0YD

www.scholastic.co.uk

Printed by Bell and Bain Ltd, Glasgow

1 2 3 4 5 6 7 8 9 0 1 2 3 4 5 6 7 8 9

CONTENTS

Introduction **4-5**

Activity blocks

Block A

Overview grid **6-7**

Activities **8-20**

Block B

Overview grid **21-22**

Activities **23-39**

Block C

Overview grid **40-41**

Activities **42-56**

Block D

Overview grid **57-58**

Activities **59-69**

Block E

Overview grid **70-71**

Activities **72-87**

Photocopiable resources **88-95**

Oral assessments

Oral and mental maths assessments - Level 4 .... **96-100**

Oral and mental maths assessments - Level 5 .... **101-110**

Mental maths teacher record sheet **111**

Introduction

About the series

100 Mental Maths Activities is a series of six photocopiable teachers' resource books, one for each of Years 1–6. Each book offers a bank of mental maths activities, each designed to last between five and ten minutes. The activities are designed to fit the planning guidelines of the *Renewed Framework for Teaching Mathematics* (2007) and are therefore divided into five Blocks with three Units of work in each Block.

This series provides a valuable accompaniment to *100 Maths Framework Lessons* (Scholastic, 2007). The mental maths activities are designed to accompany lessons in the framework series and grids are provided at the start of each Block to indicate the lesson and page numbers of the associated lesson plans in the relevant *100 Maths Framework Lessons* book. Used together, the teacher will have a rich bank of resources, activities and questions, offering greater choice and variety, while keeping to a closely similar mathematical content and progression. It is for the teacher to decide when to repeat an activity and when to move on: the exact mix of consolidation and progression needed will vary from one class to another. However, the series is also wholly appropriate for independent use alongside any maths scheme of work.

The six Rs of oral and mental work

In addition to matching the content of the Renewed Framework, this series also reflects the six features of children's mathematical learning that oral and mental work can support identified by the Primary National Strategy when renewing the Framework. The 'six Rs' provide a valuable guide to the purposes of each starter and a 'type of starter' is offered alongside each of the activities in this book.

The six types of starter include:

- rehearse: practising and consolidating known skills
- recall: securing knowledge of facts – usually number facts
- refresh: drawing on, revisiting or assessing previous knowledge and skills
- refine: sharpening methods and procedures (eg mental strategies)
- read: using mathematical vocabulary and interpreting mathematical images, diagrams and vocabulary correctly
- reason: using and applying acquired knowledge and skills; using reasoning to draw conclusions.

For further information on the 'six Rs' visit the National Strategies website: *www.nationalstrategies.standards.dcsf.gov.uk.*

About the book

Each book provides support for teachers through 15 Units of mental maths, developing and practising skills that will have been introduced, explained and explored in your main maths lesson time. Few resources are needed, and the questions for each activity are provided in full. The books are complete with answers, ready for you to pick up and use.

The activities are suitable for use with single- or mixed-ability groups and single- or mixed-age classes, as much emphasis has been placed on the use of differentiated and open-ended questions. Differentiated questions ensure that all the children can be included in each lesson and have the chance to succeed; suitable questions can be directed at chosen individuals, almost guaranteeing success and thus increased confidence.

Several essential photocopiable resource pages are also included (see pages 88-95). These resources are listed alongside each activity where required and should be prepared in advance of each mental maths session.

Each activity in this book has one or more learning objective based on the Year 6 teaching programme in the Renewed Framework. Curriculum grids are presented at the start of each Block to assist teachers with their planning and to highlight links with the related *100 Maths Framework Lessons* title. Alongside the activity description, required resources are highlighted, as well as the 'type of starter' (see above for further information). Where appropriate a 'mental strategy' for solving a number sentence or problem is suggested. Discussion of the children's methods is encouraged, since this will help the children to develop mathematical language skills: to appreciate that no single method is necessarily 'correct' and that a flexible repertoire of approaches is useful; to improve their overall confidence as they come to realise that all responses have value. Strategies are encouraged that will enable the children to progress from the known to the unknown number facts, thus developing their ability to select and use methods of mental calculation.

In Year 6, emphasis is placed on using strategies and skills developed in earlier years. Opportunities are provided to help consolidate (and combine) calculation strategies, including the relationships between the four operations. The children's understanding of place value is reinforced, and practice is given in using factors, multiples and doubles. Practice is also provided to encourage the children's understanding of the relationship between fraction, decimal and percentage forms of 'less than one'. In the final lessons on this topic, the calculation of prices and discounts provides a real-life connection to this potentially difficult part of the syllabus.

The children are challenged to select appropriate operations (and combinations of operations) to solve word problems involving number, money, time and measures. This provides both a sound basis for work at the secondary level and an introduction to the use of arithmetical techniques in real life. Games are included to provide variety and generate enthusiasm for numbers. Open-ended questions are used to challenge the children and extend their thinking, while pair and group activities encourage mathematical discussion and give the children opportunities to explain the outcome to the class as a whole.

Transitional assessments

Transition is a time when, historically, children dip in their performance. Why this occurs is open to discussion but schools are increasingly aware of the need to accurately track children during these periods in order to ensure, as far as possible, a smooth learning journey. Transitional assessment is therefore important not just as a tool for summative judgements at the end of a school year, but also for communicating with teaching colleagues across the school.

100 Mental Maths Activities Year 6 includes three photocopiable single-level transitional assessments for levels 4 and 5, which will provide evidence of where children have reached in relation to national standards. Printable tests, mark schemes and answer sheets are available on pages 96-111.

BLOCK A

Unit 1

100 Mental Maths Starters				100 Maths Lessons		
Page	Objective	Activity title	Starter type	Unit	Lesson	Page
8	Find the difference between a positive and a negative integer, in context.	1 Positive and negative	Rehearse	1	4	11, 12
9	Find the difference between two negative integers, in context.	2 Double negative	Rehearse	1	6	12, 13
10	Use decimal notation for tenths, hundredths and thousandths.	3 Equivalent fractions and decimals	Recall	1	7	13, 14
11	Use decimal notation for tenths, hundredths and thousandths; partition, round and order decimals with up to three places, and position them on the number line.	4 Where decimals lie	Read	1	9	15
12	Use place value and multiplication facts to 10 × 10 to derive related division facts involving decimals.	5 Decimal division	Refine	1	3	11
13	Calculate mentally with integers and decimals: U.t ± U.t, TU × U, TU ÷ U, U.t × U, U.t ÷ U.	6 Double decimals	Recall	1	10	15, 16

Unit 2

100 Mental Maths Starters				100 Maths Lessons		
Page	Objective	Activity title	Starter type	Unit	Lesson	Page
14	Use decimal notation for tenths, hundredths and thousandths; round decimals with up to three places.	7 Round up	Reason	2	7	26
15	Use knowledge of place value and multiplication facts to 10 × 10 to derive related multiplication facts involving decimals.	8 Related multiplications	Refine	2	2	22
15	Calculate mentally with integers and decimals: U.t ± U.t, TU × U, TU ÷ U, U.t × U, U.t ÷ U.	9 Decimal targets: addition and subtraction	Recall	2	3	22, 23
16	Calculate mentally with integers and decimals: U.t ± U.t, TU × U, TU ÷ U, U.t × U, U.t ÷ U.	10 Doubles and halves	Recall	2	4	23
17	Calculate mentally with integers and decimals: U.t ± U.t, TU × U, TU ÷ U, U.t × U, U.t ÷ U.	11 Products	Rehearse	2	6	25
17	Use inverse operations to check results.	12 Check time	Reason	2	10	28, 29

BLOCK A

Unit 3

100 Mental Maths Starters				100 Maths Lessons		
Page	**Objective**	**Activity title**	**Starter type**	**Unit**	**Lesson**	**Page**
18	Use decimal notation for tenths, hundredths and thousandths; partition decimals with up to three places.	(13) Circle time	Recall	3	4	36
18	Use decimal notation for tenths and hundredths; order decimals with up to three places.	(14) Washing line	Rehearse	3	8	39
19	Calculate mentally with integers and decimals: U.t ± U.t, TU × U, TU ÷ U, U.t × U, U.t ÷ U.	(15) Over the top - decimal doubles	Recall	3	2	34, 35
19	Calculate mentally with integers and decimals: U.t ± U.t, TU × U, TU ÷ U, U.t × U, U.t ÷ U.	(16) Add what?	Refine	3	3	35
20	Calculate mentally with integers and decimals: U.t ± U.t, TU × U, TU ÷ U, U.t × U, U.t ÷ U.	(17) Division bingo	Recall	3	9	40
20	Calculate mentally with integers and decimals: U.t ± U.t, TU × U, TU ÷ U, U.t × U, U.t ÷ U.	(18) Match up	Rehearse	3	10	41

1 Positive and negative

Resources
'Positive/negative number line' (from photocopiable page 88), one per child

Learning objective
Find the difference between a positive and a negative integer, in context.

Type of starter
Rehearse

Mental strategy
Remind children that when finding the difference between a positive number and a negative number, the two numbers should be added.

Answers

1. 6
2. 7
3. 11
4. 13
5. 11
6. 15
7. 14
8. 17
9. 21
10. 16
11. 6
12. 10
13. 15
14. 15
15. 13
16. 17
17. 13
18. 18
19. 18
20. 14

Ask children to find the difference between these recorded temperatures in 'Chilltown' and 'Hotsville'. All temperatures given are in degrees Celsius.

1. -1 and 5
2. -4 and 3
3. -7 and 4
4. -3 and 10
5. -2 and 9
6. -10 and 5
7. -8 and 6
8. -4 and 13
9. -7 and 14
10. -5 and 11

Now switch the towns so that 'Hotsville' comes first.

11. 4 and -2
12. 6 and -4
13. 5 and -10
14. 7 and -8
15. 10 and -3
16. 15 and -2
17. 9 and -4
18. 11 and -7
19. 5 and -13
20. 6 and -8

Double negative

Learning objective
Find the difference between two negative numbers, in context.

Type of starter
Rehearse

Mental strategy
This time, because both numbers are negative, the answers are found by subtracting the smaller number from the larger.

Resources
'Positive/negative number line' (from photocopiable page 88), one per child

Explain to the children that during the winter in 'Chilltown', the temperature rises each day between 6am and 11am, but even then it still stays below freezing point.

Ask them to find the difference between these daily lows and highs - both are negative numbers. All temperatures are given in degrees Celsius.

1. -10 and -2
2. -8 and -1
3. -15 and -4
4. -7 and -2
5. -11 and -5
6. -12 and -3
7. -10 and -6
8. -7 and -1
9. -8 and -3
10. -14 and -6
11. -9 and -3
12. -15 and -6

Answers

1. 8
2. 7
3. 11
4. 5
5. 6
6. 9
7. 4
8. 6
9. 5
10. 8
11. 6
12. 9

BLOCK A

3 Equivalent fractions and decimals

Resources
None

Learning objective
Use decimal notation for tenths, hundredths and thousandths.

Type of starter
Recall

Answers

1. 0.5
2. 0.1
3. 0.4
4. 0.7
5. 0.3
6. 0.25
7. 0.75
8. 0.63
9. 0.01
10. 0.07
11. $^{9}/_{10}$
12. $^{2}/_{10}$ or $^{1}/_{5}$
13. $^{37}/_{100}$
14. $^{9}/_{100}$
15. $^{25}/_{100}$ or $^{1}/_{4}$
16. $^{75}/_{100}$ or $^{3}/_{4}$
17. $^{5}/_{10}$ or $^{1}/_{2}$
18. $^{125}/_{1000}$ or $^{1}/_{8}$
19. $^{83}/_{100}$
20. $^{3}/_{100}$

Give the equivalent decimal for each fraction.

1. $^{1}/_{2}$
2. $^{1}/_{10}$
3. $^{4}/_{10}$
4. $^{7}/_{10}$
5. $^{3}/_{10}$
6. $^{1}/_{4}$
7. $^{3}/_{4}$
8. $^{63}/_{100}$
9. $^{1}/_{100}$
10. $^{7}/_{100}$

Give the equivalent fraction for each decimal.

11. 0.9
12. 0.2
13. 0.37
14. 0.09
15. 0.25
16. 0.75
17. 0.5
18. 0.125
19. 0.83
20. 0.03

4 Where decimals lie

Learning objective
Use decimal notation for tenths, hundredths and thousandths; partition, round and order decimals with up to three places, and position them on the number line.

Type of starter
Read

Resources
A board or flipchart

On the board or flipchart, draw a number line from 1.5 to 4.5, marked off in tenths, with every 0.5 labelled (see below).

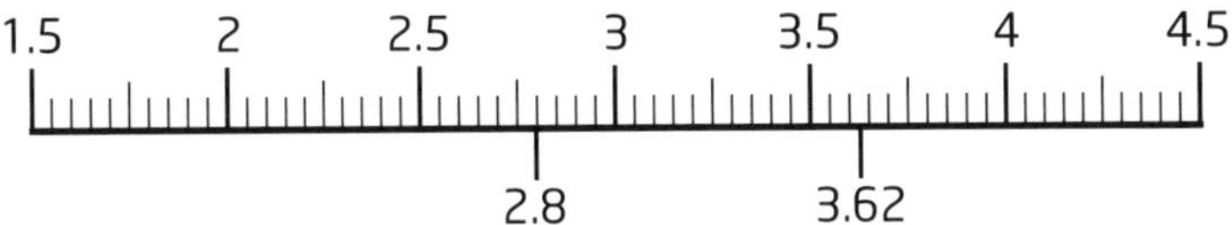

Ask individuals to draw a line showing the position of each given number and state where it lies (eg 2.8 lies between 2.7 and 2.9, 3.62 lies between 3.6 and 3.7).

Show the positions of these numbers on the number line.

1. 2.3
2. 3.8
3. 1.65
4. 3.02
5. 4.39
6. 2.7
7. 3.32
8. 2.1
9. 4.15
10. 3.56
11. 2.41
12. 3.95
13. 2.88
14. 1.82
15. 2.52

Answers

Between:

1. 2.2 and 2.4
2. 3.7 and 3.9
3. 1.6 and 1.7
4. 3.0 and 3.1
5. 4.3 and 4.4
6. 2.6 and 2.8
7. 3.3 and 3.4
8. 2.0 and 2.2
9. 4.1 and 4.2
10. 3.5 and 3.6
11. 2.4 and 2.5
12. 3.9 and 4.0
13. 2.8 and 2.9
14. 1.8 and 1.9
15. 2.5 and 2.6

BLOCK A

5 Decimal division

Resources
None

Learning objective
Use place value and multiplication facts to 10 × 10 to derive related division facts involving decimals.

Type of starter
Refine

Mental strategy
Ensure that the children understand that the two sets of answers will have the same digits but that when 2.4 is divided by each factor, a decimal point will need to be placed between the digits.

Ask the children to provide the division facts related to the factors of the number 24.

1. 24 ÷ 1
2. 24 ÷ 2
3. 24 ÷ 3
4. 24 ÷ 4
5. 24 ÷ 6
6. 24 ÷ 8
7. 24 ÷ 12
8. 24 ÷ 24

Then, ask the children to provide related division facts based on the decimal number 2.4.

9. 2.4 ÷ 1
10. 2.4 ÷ 2
11. 2.4 ÷ 3
12. 2.4 ÷ 4
13. 2.4 ÷ 6
14. 2.4 ÷ 8
15. 2.4 ÷ 12
16. 2.4 ÷ 24

Answers

1. 24
2. 12
3. 8
4. 6
5. 4
6. 3
7. 2
8. 1
9. 2.4
10. 1.2
11. 0.8
12. 0.6
13. 0.4
14. 0.3
15. 0.2
16. 0.1

Double decimals

Learning objective
Calculate mentally with integers and decimals: U.t ± U.t, TU × U, TU ÷ U, U.t × U, U.t ÷ U.

Type of starter
Recall

Resources
None

Double:

1. 1.5
2. 3.1
3. 1.7
4. 3.3
5. 4.2
6. 2.6
7. 4.4
8. 5.9
9. 1.2
10. 0.8
11. 6.1
12. 4.6
13. 3.8
14. 9.3
15. 7.5
16. 0.7
17. 2.4
18. 1.9
19. 0.25
20. 0.18
21. 1.04
22. 2.03
23. 1.07
24. 0.58
25. 1.92
26. 0.83
27. 5.7
28. 8.4
29. 1.06
30. 4.5

Answers

1. 3
2. 6.2
3. 3.4
4. 6.6
5. 8.4
6. 5.2
7. 8.8
8. 11.8
9. 2.4
10. 1.6
11. 12.2
12. 9.2
13. 7.6
14. 18.6
15. 15
16. 1.4
17. 4.8
18. 3.8
19. 0.5
20. 0.36
21. 2.08
22. 4.06
23. 2.14
24. 1.16
25. 3.84
26. 1.66
27. 11.4
28. 16.8
29. 2.12
30. 9

7 Round up

Resources
None

Learning objective
Use decimal notation for tenths, hundredths and thousandths; round decimals with up to three places.

Type of starter
Reason

Mental strategy
Remind the children that once they have located the digit in the correct place value column, if it is 5 or larger it will be rounded up, if it is less than 5 it will stay the same.

Ask the children to round the heights of these young trees growing in the nursery to the nearest metre.

1. 3.7m
2. 4.9m
3. 5.4m
4. 1.2m
5. 4.1m
6. 9.7m
7. 8.1m
8. 4.8m
9. 2.5m
10. 3.6m
11. 2.4m
12. 7.3m

Ask the children to round these distances measured in a school long-jump event to the nearest tenth of a metre.

13. 2.34m
14. 1.78m
15. 2.16m
16. 1.83m
17. 3.21m
18. 3.19m
19. 4.02m
20. 5.71m
21. 2.98m
22. 2.75m
23. 6.50m
24. 4.48m

Answers
1. 4m
2. 5m
3. 5m
4. 1m
5. 4m
6. 10m
7. 8m
8. 5m
9. 3m
10. 4m
11. 2m
12. 7m
13. 2.3m
14. 1.8m
15. 2.2m
16. 1.8m
17. 3.2m
18. 3.2m
19. 4.0m
20. 5.7m
21. 3.0m
22. 2.8m
23. 6.5m
24. 4.5m

8 Related multiplications

Learning objective	Resources
Use knowledge of place value and multiplication facts to 10 × 10 to derive related multiplication facts involving decimals. **Type of starter** Refine	A board or flipchart; pencils and paper for each group

No set answers

Write on the board or flipchart: 2 × 7 = 14. Ask for related multiplications, such as 20 × 7, 200 × 7, 0.2 × 7, 0.02 × 7, 0.002 × 7.

Discuss the digit pattern that appears when the answers are put in order.

Divide the class into groups of three or four. Give each group a different multiplication fact and ask them to write other multiplications related to it.

1. 5 × 6
2. 9 × 3
3. 40 × 5
4. 300 × 7

After two minutes, ask each group to select a child to write their suggestions on the board in order of size. Discuss the digit patterns they see in the answers.

9 Decimal targets: addition and subtraction

Learning objective	Resources
Calculate mentally with integers and decimals: U.t ± U.t, TU × U, TU ÷ U, U.t × U, U.t ÷ U. **Type of starter** Recall	A board or flipchart; pencils and paper for each pair

Write the following numbers on the board or flipchart:

3.2 1.7 8.4 5.9

Divide the children into pairs. Tell them that they will have 30 seconds to 'hit the target', using either addition or subtraction and the numbers on the board to get as close to the target number as possible. Collect several answers and discuss the strategies used. The answer nearest to the target wins a point.

Target numbers are:

1. 10.5
2. 6.8
3. 1.9
4. 14.6
5. 2.4
6. 16.9
7. 5.1
8. 7.1

Example answers

1. 5.9 + 3.2 + 1.7 = 10.8
2. 8.4 - 1.7 = 6.7
3. 3.2 - 1.7 = 1.5
4. 8.4 + 5.9 = 14.3
5. 8.4 - 5.9 = 2.5
6. 8.4 + 5.9 + 3.2 = 17.5
7. 8.4 - 3.2 = 5.2
8. 8.4 - 1.7 = 6.7

BLOCK A

10 Doubles and halves

Resources
None

Learning objective
Calculate mentally with integers and decimals: U.t ± U.t, TU × U, TU ÷ U, U.t × U, U.t ÷ U.

Type of starter
Recall

The children stand in a line or circle. The first child doubles the start number, which is doubled again by the second child, and so on. When a child is able to say 'Over 100', he or she earns a point. The game restarts with the next child and a new start number.

1. 10
2. 3
3. 15
4. 2
5. 23
6. 17
7. 9
8. 21
9. 11
10. 13

Play again, this time halving numbers. The child whose answer is a fraction earns a point.

11. 64
12. 100
13. 80
14. 68
15. 72
16. 84
17. 60
18. 88
19. 52
20. 76

Answers

1. 20, 40, 80
2. 6, 12, 24, 48, 96
3. 30, 60
4. 4, 8, 16, 32, 64
5. 46, 92
6. 34, 68
7. 18, 36, 72
8. 42, 84
9. 22, 44, 88
10. 26, 52
11. 32, 16, 8, 4, 2, 1, ½
12. 50, 25, 12½
13. 40, 20, 10, 5, 2½
14. 34, 17, 8½
15. 36, 18, 9, 4½
16. 42, 21, 10½
17. 30, 15, 7½
18. 44, 22, 11, 5½
19. 26, 13, 6½
20. 38, 19, 9½

11 Products

Learning objective
Calculate mentally with integers and decimals: U.t ± U.t, TU × U, TU ÷ U, U.t × U, U.t ÷ U.

Type of starter
Rehearse

Mental strategy
Remind the children of the usefulness of rounding to the nearest 10 or 100 when deciding which combination of numbers to try.

Resources
A board or flipchart; paper and pencils for each pair

Write the following numbers on the board or flipchart:

6 9 3 4

Divide the children into pairs. Explain that they have to make each product by multiplying one or two of these numbers by one of the remaining numbers, eg 6 × 3, 93 × 4, 49 × 6. Discuss several of the answers given and the strategies used.

1.	36	4.	54	7.	576	10.	252
2.	204	5.	144	8.	147		
3.	372	6.	138	9.	564		

Example answers

1.	4 × 9	6.	46 × 3
2.	34 × 6	7.	64 × 9
3.	93 × 4	8.	49 × 3
4.	9 × 6	9.	94 × 6
5.	36 × 4	10.	63 × 4

12 Check time

Learning objective
Use inverse operations to check results.

Type of starter
Reason

Mental strategy
Remind children that in subtraction the largest number must come first. The number taken away and the answer must add up to the number started with.

Resources
A board or flipchart

Go through these simple examples on the board or flipchart to remind the children that addition is the inverse of subtraction and vice versa.

75 + 39 = 114, so 114 - 75 = ? and 114 - 39 = ?

145 - 67 = 78, so 78 + 67 = ? and 67 + 78 = ?

Divide the class into groups of four or five. Give each group a different calculation. Ask them to check the answer by using the inverse operation.

1.	94 + 127 = 221	4.	123 - 59 = 64
2.	254 + 309 = 563	5.	357 - 128 = 229
3.	772 + 493 = 1265	6.	502 - 296 = 206

After several minutes working, ask each group to nominate a child to write their solution on the board or flipchart.

Answers
1-6. Answers are contained in the questions

13 Circle time

Resources
A board or flipchart

Learning objective
Use decimal notation for tenths, hundredths and thousandths; partition decimals with up to three places.

Type of starter
Recall

Mental strategy
Ensure the children know that digits to the left of the decimal point are whole numbers and that digits to the right of the decimal point are parts of whole numbers (fractions).

Answers

1.	$^{2}/_{10}$	11.	$^{4}/_{10}$
2.	5	12.	100
3.	$^{7}/_{100}$	13.	$^{1}/_{100}$
4.	$^{3}/_{1000}$	14.	$^{5}/_{10}$
5.	9	15.	60
6.	$^{5}/_{100}$	16.	$^{6}/_{1000}$
7.	6	17.	4
8.	$^{2}/_{10}$	18.	$^{8}/_{10}$
9.	10	19.	1000
10.	$^{7}/_{1000}$	20.	$^{5}/_{1000}$

Write the following numbers on the board or flipchart with a circle drawn around the digit in bold.

Children identify the digit number and give its place value (eg three tenths, five thousandths). Point out that some of the answers will be whole numbers and some will be fractions.

1.	3.**2**7	6.	12.2**5**	11.	6.**4**25	16.	155.24**6**
2.	**5**.39	7.	1**6**.724	12.	**1**25.7	17.	35**4**.78
3.	10.8**7**	8.	8.**2**05	13.	76.4**1**4	18.	1654.**8**2
4.	6.24**3**	9.	**1**4.799	14.	203.**5**2	19.	**1**548.604
5.	**9**.704	10.	24.20**7**	15.	7**6**4.89	20.	3984.72**5**

Washing line

Resources
Piece of washing line or thin rope; clothes pegs; card; felt tip pens; decimal point and 1, 4 and 8 numeral cards (from photocopiable page 95)

Learning objective
Use decimal notation for tenths and hundredths; order decimals with up to three places.

Type of starter
Rehearse

Mental strategy
Remind the children that when the whole number digits are the same they must sort the numbers by using the value of the digit in the tenths column.

Answers
Decimal numbers between 1 and 10: 1.48, 1.84, 4.18, 4.81, 8.14, 8.41

Decimal numbers between 20 and 100: 14.8, 18.4, 41.8, 48.1, 81.4, 84.1

Display the numeral and decimal point cards.

Ask the children to make all the decimal numbers possible between 1 and 10 using all three numeral cards and the decimal point each time.

When the six possible numbers have been made, ask a child to write them on pieces of blank card using felt pens. Then, ask another volunteer to peg the six cards on the washing line in order of size, starting with the lowest.

Repeat the process for all decimal numbers between 20 and 100.

This activity can be extended to incorporate thousandths by including a fourth numeral card.

Over the top – decimal doubles

Learning objective
Calculate mentally with integers and decimals: U.t ± U.t, TU × U, TU ÷ U, U.t × U, U.t ÷ U.

Type of starter
Recall

Resources
A board or flipchart

Divide the class into groups of three or four.

The first group doubles the start number, which is doubled again by the second group, and so on. When a group's number would be greater than the target, they say 'Bong' instead of the number and earn a point. The group with the most points at the end wins.

Write the target number on the board each time.

Start numbers and target numbers:

	Start	Target		Start	Target
1.	1.2	8	6.	0.9	15
2.	0.4	5	7.	1.1	20
3.	1.3	12	8.	0.3	10
4.	0.7	12	9.	1.7	15
5.	1.5	30	10.	0.5	40

Answers

1. 2.4, 4.8
2. 0.8, 1.6, 3.2
3. 2.6, 5.2, 10.4
4. 1.4, 2.8, 5.6, 11.2
5. 3, 6, 12, 24
6. 1.8, 3.6, 7.2, 14.4
7. 2.2, 4.4, 8.8, 17.6
8. 0.6, 1.2, 2.4, 4.8, 9.6
9. 3.4, 6.8, 13.6
10. 1, 2, 4, 8, 16, 32

Add what?

Learning objective
Calculate mentally with integers and decimals: U.t ± U.t, TU × U, TU ÷ U, U.t × U, U.t ÷ U.

Type of starter
Refine

Resources
A board or flipchart

Write on the board or flipchart:

2.3 + ________ = 3

3.78 + ________ = 4

Ask for the missing numbers. Discuss the strategies used.

Encourage complementary addition to 10 or 100.

Ask: *How many is it up to the next whole number from...?*

1.	5.3	6.	1.6	11.	8.57	16.	6.52
2.	3.1	7.	9.4	12.	1.64	17.	9.25
3.	8.7	8.	6.8	13.	5.81	18.	4.43
4.	2.9	9.	7.5	14.	2.98	19.	5.79
5.	4.2	10.	3.83	15.	7.36	20.	3.94

Answers

1.	0.7	11.	0.43
2.	0.9	12.	0.36
3.	0.3	13.	0.19
4.	0.1	14.	0.02
5.	0.8	15.	0.64
6.	0.4	16.	0.48
7.	0.6	17.	0.75
8.	0.2	18.	0.57
9.	0.5	19.	0.21
10.	0.17	20.	0.06

BLOCK A

17 Division bingo

Resources
Paper and a pencil for each child

Learning objective
Calculate mentally with integers and decimals: U.t ± U.t, TU × U, TU ÷ U, U.t × U, U.t ÷ U.

Type of starter
Recall

Answers

Game 1		Game 2	
1.	7	1.	5
2.	3	2.	3
3.	6	3.	9
4.	10	4.	1
5.	1	5.	4
6.	5	6.	6
7.	2	7.	2
8.	9	8.	8
9.	8	9.	7
10.	4	10.	10

The children write six numbers between 1 and 10 (inclusive) on their paper. They then cross out each number that is the answer to a question. The first child to cross out all of their six numbers and calls out 'Bingo!' wins.

The same questions could be used in a different order for further games.

Game 1

1. 28 ÷ 4
2. 27 ÷ 9
3. 18 ÷ 3
4. 20 ÷ 2
5. 3 ÷ 3
6. 25 ÷ 5
7. 12 ÷ 6
8. 63 ÷ 7
9. 8 ÷ 1
10. 32 ÷ 8

Game 2

1. 10 ÷ 2
2. 21 ÷ 7
3. 72 ÷ 8
4. 4 ÷ 4
5. 24 ÷ 6
6. 54 ÷ 9
7. 6 ÷ 3
8. 40 ÷ 5
9. 42 ÷ 6
10. 30 ÷ 3

18 Match up

Resources
A board or flipchart

Learning objective
Calculate mentally with integers and decimals: U.t ± U.t, TU × U, TU ÷ U, U.t × U, U.t ÷ U.

Type of starter
Rehearse

Mental strategy
Encourage the children to think in terms of dividing whole numbers and then positioning the decimal point in the correct position in the answer. For example, 25 ÷ 5 = 5 so 2.5 ÷ 5 = 0.5.

Answers

1.	0.8	6.	0.1
2.	0.4	7.	0.9
3.	0.3	8.	0.2
4.	1.0	9.	0.6
5.	0.5	10.	0.7

Write the following decimal numbers on the board or flipchart:

0.1, 0.2, 0.3, 0.4, 0.5, 0.6, 0.7, 0.8, 0.9, 1.0

Tell the children you are going to give them some division calculations. Ask them to choose the correct answer from the list given.

1. 3.2 ÷ 4
2. 1.2 ÷ 3
3. 0.9 ÷ 3
4. 6.0 ÷ 6
5. 2.5 ÷ 5
6. 0.5 ÷ 5
7. 2.7 ÷ 3
8. 0.8 ÷ 4
9. 2.4 ÷ 4
10. 5.6 ÷ 8

BLOCK B

Unit 1

100 Mental Maths Starters				100 Maths Lessons		
Page	**Objective**	**Activity title**	**Starter type**	**Unit**	**Lesson**	**Page**
23	Use knowledge of multiplication facts to derive quickly squares of numbers to 12 × 12 and the corresponding squares of multiples of 10.	19 Master square	Refine	1	5	49
24	Use knowledge of multiplication facts to derive quickly squares of numbers to 12 × 12 and the corresponding squares of multiples of 10.	20 Square the circle: multiples of 10	Recall	1	6	50
25	Use knowledge of place value and multiplication facts to 10 × 10 to derive related multiplication and division facts involving decimals.	21 Double decimals	Rehearse	1	7	50, 51
26	Recognise that prime numbers have only two factors and identify prime numbers less than 100.	22 Prime spotting	Recall	1	8	51
27	Recognise that prime numbers have only two factors and identify prime numbers less than 100; find the prime factors of two-digit numbers.	23 Prime factors	Recall	1	9	51, 52
28	Use approximations to estimate results.	24 Season tickets	Reason	1	11	53, 54
29	Describe, identify and visualise parallel and perpendicular edges; use these properties to classify 2D shapes.	25 Recognising 2D shapes	Rehearse	1	13	54, 55
29	Describe, identify and visualise parallel and perpendicular edges or faces; use these properties to classify 3D solids.	26 Recognising 3D shapes	Reason	1	15	56

Unit 2

100 Mental Maths Starters				100 Maths Lessons		
Page	**Objective**	**Activity title**	**Starter type**	**Unit**	**Lesson**	**Page**
30	Use knowledge of multiplication facts to derive quickly squares of numbers to 12 × 12 and the corresponding squares of multiples of 10.	27 Squares?	Recall	2	7	68, 69
31	Use knowledge of multiplication facts to derive quickly squares of numbers to 12 × 12 and the corresponding squares of multiples of 10.	28 Squares more or less	Recall	2	8	69
32	Use knowledge of multiplication facts to derive quickly squares of numbers to 12 × 12 and the corresponding squares of multiples of 10.	29 More squares	Recall	2	15	73, 74

Unit 2 ...continued

100 Mental Maths Starters				100 Maths Lessons		
Page	**Objective**	**Activity title**	**Starter type**	**Unit**	**Lesson**	**Page**
33	Use knowledge of place value and multiplication facts to 10 × 10 to derive related multiplication facts involving decimals.	30 Decimal multiplication	Refine	2	9	69, 70
33	Recognise that prime numbers have only two factors and identify prime numbers less than 100; find the prime factors of two-digit numbers.	31 Prime time	Recall	2	10	70
34	Find the prime factors of two-digit numbers.	32 Factor trees	Rehearse	2	11	71
35	Use approximations, inverse operations and tests of divisibility to estimate and check results.	33 Factor wheels	Reason	2	12	71, 72
35	Describe, identify and visualise parallel and perpendicular edges; use these properties to classify 2D shapes.	34 Pegs and bands	Reason	2	14	73

Unit 3

100 Mental Maths Starters				100 Maths Lessons		
Page	**Objective**	**Activity title**	**Starter type**	**Unit**	**Lesson**	**Page**
36	Use knowledge of multiplication facts to derive quickly squares of numbers to 12 × 12 and the corresponding squares of multiples of 10.	35 Square roots	Recall	3	5	84
36	Use knowledge of multiplication facts to derive quickly squares of numbers to 12 × 12 and the corresponding squares of multiples of 10.	36 Using square numbers	Rehearse	3	6	84, 85
37	Use knowledge of place value and multiplication facts to 10 × 10 to derive related multiplication facts involving decimals.	37 Quick-fire 10	Refine	3	7	85
37	Use knowledge of place value and multiplication facts to 10 × 10 to derive related division facts involving decimals.	38 Decimal tenths	Recall	3	8	85, 86
38	Recognise that prime numbers have only two factors and identify prime numbers less than 100.	39 Prime spotting 2	Recall	3	9	86
38	Find the prime factors of two-digit numbers.	40 In the prime	Rehearse	3	10	87, 88
39	Describe, identify and visualise parallel and perpendicular edges or faces; use these properties to classify 3D solids.	41 3D nets	Reason	3	11	88
39	Make and draw shapes with increasing accuracy and apply knowledge of their properties.	42 Word shapes	Refresh	3	12	88, 89

19 Master square

Learning objective
Use knowledge of multiplication facts to derive quickly squares of numbers to 12 × 12 and the corresponding squares of multiples of 10.

Type of starter
Refine

Mental strategy
Remind children that if they already know that 3 × 3 = 9 then they should realise that 30 × 30 = 900.

Resources
'Master square' (from photocopiable page 89), one per child; plastic counters

Explain the rules of 'Master square'. You will read out numbers to be squared. The children's aim is to cover with counters four square numbers on the grid connected in a line, vertically, horizontally or diagonally. For example, if you read out *6 squared*, they should cover 36 on the grid.

Read out the numbers to be squared, from the list below, in any order. Keep going until most children have completed four in a line.

1. 9^2
2. 1^2
3. 7^2
4. 12^2
5. 50^2
6. 10^2
7. 11^2
8. 20^2
9. 4^2
10. 30^2
11. 40^2
12. 3^2
13. 2^2
14. 5^2
15. 6^2
16. 8^2

Answers
1. 81
2. 1
3. 49
4. 144
5. 2500
6. 100
7. 121
8. 400
9. 16,
10. 900
11. 1600
12. 9
13. 4
14. 25
15. 36
16. 64

20 Square the circle: multiples of 10

Resources
A board or flipchart; a pointer; a stop-watch (or similar)

Learning objective
Use knowledge of multiplication facts to derive quickly squares of numbers to 12 × 12 and the corresponding squares of multiples of 10.

Type of starter
Recall

No set answers

Draw this diagram on the board or flipchart:

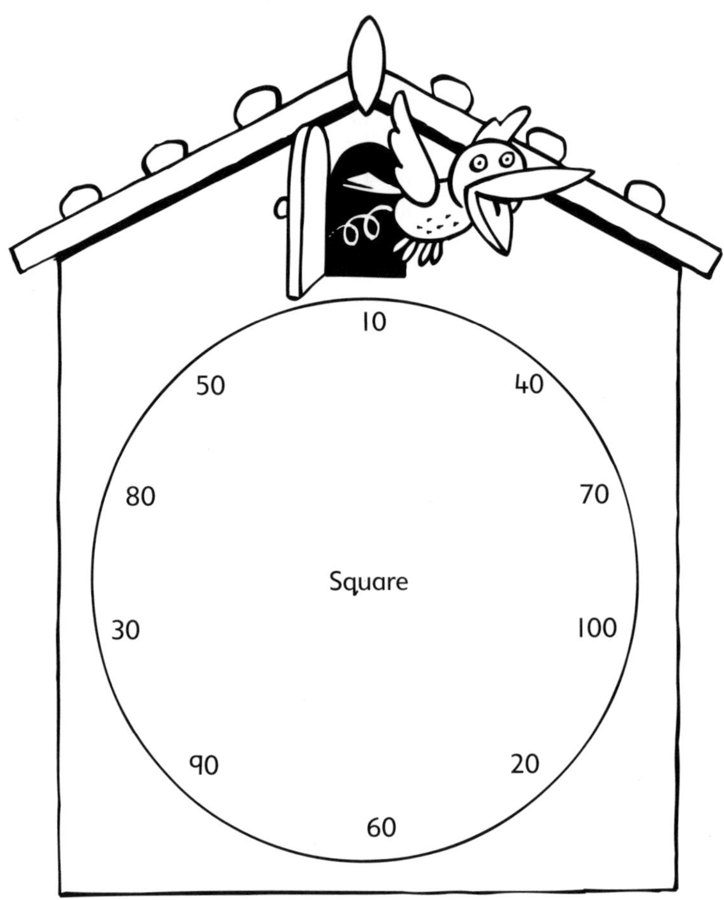

The children together say the square of each number twice as they move around the clock face (eg '40 squared is 1600'). Saying each square twice will help less confident learners, who can join in the second time. Circle the clock face twice.

Point to specific numbers, with the children together saying just the square of the number.

Individuals may volunteer to say the squares of all the numbers around the clock while being timed. The fastest wins.

21 Double decimals

Learning objective Use knowledge of place value and multiplication facts to 10 × 10 to derive related multiplication and division facts involving decimals. **Type of starter** Rehearse	**Resources** None

The children sit in a line or circle.

The first child doubles the given starting number, which is doubled again by the next child, and so on. The child who can say 'Over 10' earns a point.

The game restarts with a new start number and the next child.

The child with the most points at the end wins.

1. 1.3
2. 0.4
3. 0.7
4. 1.2
5. 2.1
6. 1.9
7. 1.1
8. 0.9
9. 2.3
10. 1.4

Answers

1. 2.6, 5.2
2. 0.8, 1.6, 3.2, 6.4
3. 1.4, 2.8, 5.6
4. 2.4, 4.8, 9.6
5. 4.2, 8.4
6. 3.8, 7.6
7. 2.2, 4.4, 8.8
8. 1.8, 3.6, 7.2
9. 4.6, 9.2
10. 2.8, 5.6

22 Prime spotting

Resources
A board or flipchart

Learning objective
Recognise that prime numbers have only two factors and identify prime numbers less than 100.

Type of starter
Recall

Mental strategy
Encourage children to use their knowledge of table facts to spot non-primes. For example, all the even numbers greater than 2 cannot be prime because they all have 2 as a factor.

Answers
1 is not usually included, so there are 15 prime numbers to identify between 1 and 50: 2, 3, 5, 7, 11, 13, 17, 19, 23, 29, 31, 37, 41, 43 and 47.

Display the numbers from 1 to 50 on the board or flipchart.

As you point to the numbers, the children have to decide if they are prime numbers or not. They call out either 'prime' or 'not a prime'.

Choose numbers at random but make sure all the prime numbers are included in the session.

Prime factors

Learning objective
Recognise that prime numbers have only two factors and identify prime numbers less than 100; find the prime factors of two-digit numbers.

Type of starter
Recall

Resources
None

Divide the class into six groups. Give each group one of the following numbers: 2, 3, 5, 7, 11 or 13.

Ask the children what they know about these numbers. (They are all prime numbers.)

Say that if their group number is a factor of the given number, they should stand up. The groups that are standing represent the prime factors of the given number.

1. 30
2. 18
3. 44
4. 56
5. 26
6. 39
7. 65
8. 77
9. 35
10. 99
11. 91
12. 55

Discuss which other 'number groups' would have stood up for 44 (4, 22). These numbers were not included because they themselves have factors, so they are not prime factors.

Answers

1. 2, 3, 5
2. 2, 3
3. 2, 11
4. 2, 7
5. 2, 13
6. 3, 13
7. 5, 13
8. 7, 11
9. 5, 7
10. 3, 11
11. 7, 13
12. 5, 11

24 Season tickets

Resources
A board or flipchart

Learning objective
Use approximations to estimate results.

Type of starter
Reason

Mental strategy
Rounding to the nearest hundred in each case will give an accurate approximate answer in these examples.

Answers
1. £1600
2. £1500
3. £1200
4. £1000
5. £1100
6. £1300
7. £1200
8. £1300
9. £1900
10. £3800

Display the following facts on the board or flipchart. Tell the children they are the prices of season tickets at various football clubs.

City £307 United £294 Rovers £411 Town £397 Rangers £509

Ask the children to estimate the cost of the following season ticket sales to the nearest hundred pounds.

1. 4 for Rovers
2. 5 for City
3. 3 for Town
4. 2 for Rangers
5. 1 for City and 2 for Rovers
6. 3 for United and 1 for Town
7. 2 each for City and United
8. 1 each for Rovers, Town and Rangers
9. 1 for each club
10. 2 for each club

25 Recognising 2D shapes

Learning objective
Describe, identify and visualise parallel and perpendicular edges; use these properties to classify 2D shapes.

Type of starter
Rehearse

Mental strategy
Make sure the children can explain the difference between 'parallel' and 'perpendicular' and use these terms in their descriptions of 2D shapes.

Resources
'2D shapes' (from photocopiable page 90), one sheet per child

Point to the 2D shapes at random. Ask children to name them. They should describe the properties of each shape identified according to its sides. For example: it has four equal sides; opposite sides are parallel. (Square.)

No set answers

26 Recognising 3D shapes

Learning objective
Describe, identify and visualise parallel and perpendicular edges or faces; use these properties to classify 3D solids.

Type of starter
Reason

Mental strategy
Ensure the children are clear about the meaning of 'face', 'edge' and 'vertex/vertices' when discussing 3D solids.

Resources
'3D shapes' (from photocopiable page 91), one sheet per child

Ask the children to name the 3D solids and to discuss their properties.

1. How many faces does it have?
2. What shape(s) are the faces?
3. How many edges does it have?
4. How many vertices does it have?
5. Which of the solids are *regular* polyhedra (ie all their faces are the same shape and size)?

Also discuss the meaning of the terms 'parallel' and 'perpendicular' when applied to faces and/or edges of a solid.

Answers

1. cube 6; cuboid 6; cylinder 3; cone 2; sphere 1; triangular prism 5.
2. cube 6 squares; cuboid 6 rectangles; cylinder 1 rectangle and 2 circles; cone 1 arc and 1 circle; sphere 0; triangular prism 3 rectangles and 2 triangles.
3. cube 12; cuboid 12; cylinder 2; cone 1; sphere 0; triangular prism 9.
4. cube 8; cuboid 8; cylinder 0; cone 1; sphere 0; triangular prism 6.
5. Cuboid.

27 Squares?

Resources
None

Learning objective
Use knowledge of multiplication facts to derive quickly squares of numbers to 12 × 12 and the corresponding squares of multiples of 10.

Type of starter
Recall

Mental strategy
Remind the children that a number multiplied by itself is said to be 'squared'. For example, 4 squared = 4 × 4 = 16.

Ask the children to say two numbers that give the target number when they are multiplied together.

Discourage the target number and 1.

If the number is a square number (eg 25), the children should say the appropriate number squared (eg '5 squared').

1. 15
2. 48
3. 36
4. 27
5. 4
6. 24
7. 80
8. 49
9. 16
10. 56
11. 28
12. 45
13. 6
14. 21
15. 9
16. 30
17. 64
18. 42
19. 8
20. 81
21. 144
22. 63
23. 32
24. 25
25. 54
26. 35
27. 121
28. 20
29. 72
30. 100

Answers
Other answers may be possible.

1. 3 × 5
2. 4 × 12 or 6 × 8
3. 6^2
4. 3 × 9
5. 2^2
6. 2 × 12, 3 × 8, or 4 × 6
7. 8 × 10
8. 7^2
9. 4^2
10. 7 × 8
11. 4 × 7
12. 5 × 9
13. 2 × 3
14. 3 × 7
15. 3^2
16. 3 × 10 or 5 × 6
17. 8^2
18. 6 × 7
19. 2 × 4
20. 9^2
21. 12^2
22. 7 × 9
23. 4 × 8
24. 5^2
25. 6 × 9
26. 5 × 7
27. 11^2
28. 2 × 10 or 4 × 5
29. 8 × 9
30. 10^2

28 Squares more or less

Learning objective
Use knowledge of multiplication facts to derive quickly squares of numbers to 12 × 12 and the corresponding squares of multiples of 10.

Type of starter
Recall

Mental strategy
Remind the children that a number multiplied by itself is said to be squared. For example, 4 squared = 4 × 4 = 16.

Resources
None

This is a rapid recall test. Children raise a hand to answer.

1. 4^2
2. 10^2
3. 5^2
4. 9^2
5. 2^2
6. 7^2
7. 11^2
8. 3^2
9. 8^2
10. 12^2
11. 6^2
12. $6^2 + 4$
13. $12^2 - 4$
14. $5^2 - 6$
15. $8^2 + 8$
16. $2^2 + 9$
17. $10^2 - 13$
18. $7^2 + 11$
19. $4^2 + 16$
20. $11^2 - 9$
21. $9^2 + 17$
22. $3^2 - 2$
23. $4^2 + 3 - 1$
24. $7^2 + 4 - 2$
25. $10^2 - 10 + 3$
26. $8^2 - 6 + 3$
27. $5^2 - 8 + 2$
28. $12^2 + 10 - 5$
29. $9^2 + 7 - 5$
30. $6^2 - 9 + 8$

Answers

1. 16
2. 100
3. 25
4. 81
5. 4
6. 49
7. 121
8. 9
9. 64
10. 144
11. 36
12. 40
13. 140
14. 19
15. 72
16. 13
17. 87
18. 60
19. 32
20. 112
21. 98
22. 7
23. 18
24. 51
25. 93
26. 61
27. 19
28. 149
29. 83
30. 35

29 More squares

Resources	Learning objective
None	**Learning objective** Use knowledge of multiplication facts to derive quickly squares of numbers to 12 × 12 and the corresponding squares of multiples of 10. **Type of starter** Recall **Mental strategy** Remind the children that a number multiplied by itself is said to be squared. For example, 4 squared = 4 × 4 = 16.

Answers

1. 25
2. 3
3. 81
4. 121
5. 33
6. 144
7. 4
8. 100
9. 78
10. 40
11. 49
12. 4900
13. 900
14. 2500
15. 1600

Children raise a hand to answer the questions as they are read out.

1. What is 5 squared?
2. What number, when squared, makes 9?
3. 9 squared equals what?
4. What is 11 squared?
5. Subtract 3 from 6 squared.
6. What is 12 squared?
7. 2 squared equals what?
8. 10 squared equals what?
9. Add 14 to 8 squared.
10. Add 24 to 4 squared.
11. What is 7 squared?
12. What is 70 squared?
13. What is 30 squared?
14. What is 50 squared?
15. What is 40 squared?

30 Decimal multiplication

Learning objective
Use knowledge of place value and multiplication facts to 10 × 10 to derive related multiplication facts involving decimals.

Type of starter
Refine

Mental strategy
Remind the children that they can work out a related whole-number multiplication, then place the decimal point in the answer. For example, if they know 7 × 3 = 21, then 0.7 × 3 = 2.1.

Resources
None

Children raise a hand to answer these questions as they are read out.

1. 0.7 × 3
2. 0.4 × 5
3. 0.8 × 3
4. 0.6 × 5
5. 0.3 × 4
6. 0.2 × 8
7. 0.1 × 9
8. 0.5 × 4
9. 0.9 × 2
10. 0.5 × 7
11. 0.8 × 4
12. 0.3 × 9
13. 0.6 × 4
14. 0.5 × 6
15. 0.4 × 7
16. 0.3 × 8
17. 1.0 × 8
18. 1.1 × 3
19. 1.2 × 4
20. 1.5 × 2

Answers

1. 2.1
2. 2.0
3. 2.4
4. 3.0
5. 1.2
6. 1.6
7. 0.9
8. 2.0
9. 1.8
10. 3.5
11. 3.2
12. 2.7
13. 2.4
14. 3.0
15. 2.8
16. 2.4
17. 8.0
18. 3.3
19. 4.8
20. 3.0

31 Prime time

Learning objective
Recognise that prime numbers have only two factors and identify prime numbers less than 100; find the prime factors of two-digit numbers.

Type of starter
Recall

Mental strategy
Remind the children that a prime number has no factors other than itself and 1.

Resources
None

Children raise a hand to answer these questions as they are read out.

1. What is the next prime number after 2?
2. Tell me the next four prime numbers after 3.
3. Which prime number is nearest to 16?
4. Is 23 a prime number?
5. What are the prime numbers between 10 and 20?

Answers

1. 3
2. 5, 7, 11, 13
3. 17
4. Yes
5. 11, 13, 17, 19

BLOCK B

32 Factor trees

Resources
A board or flipchart; individual whiteboards, marker pens and dusters

Learning objective
Find the prime factors of two-digit numbers.

Type of starter
Rehearse

Mental strategy
Numbers should be broken down until only prime numbers remain. Some revision of indices may also be necessary so children appreciate 2×2 can be written as 2^2 and $2 \times 2 \times 2$ as 2^3.

Answers

1. $16 = 2 \times 8 = 2 \times 2 \times 4 = 2 \times 2 \times 2 \times 2 = 2^4$
2. $20 = 4 \times 5 = 2 \times 10 = 2 \times 2 \times 5 = 2^2 \times 5$
3. $24 = 4 \times 6 = 3 \times 8 = 2 \times 2 \times 2 \times 3 = 2^3 \times 3$
4. $28 = 4 \times 7 = 2 \times 2 \times 7 = 2^2 \times 7$
5. $30 = 6 \times 5 = 2 \times 3 \times 5$
6. $36 = 4 \times 9 = 2 \times 2 \times 9 = 2 \times 2 \times 3 \times 3 = 2^2 \times 3^2$

Quickly revise with the children the way to express prime factors using a factor tree diagram. For example, the number 12 can be broken down in the following way:

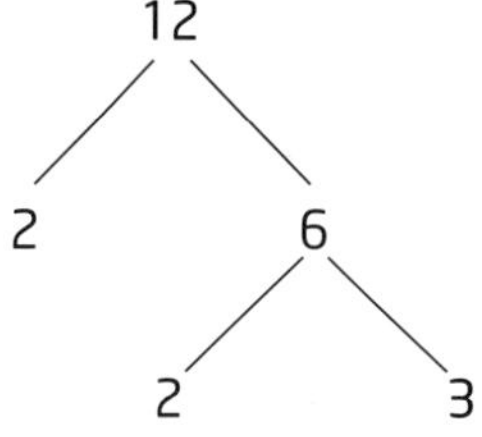

$12 = 2 \times 6 = 2 \times 2 \times 3 = 2^2 \times 3.$

Write the following numbers, one at a time, on the board or flipchart and ask the children to find the prime factors. They should write down their solutions in the form of a factor tree on their individual whiteboards.

Ask children to hold up their whiteboards to show their solutions. Discuss each one before moving on to the next.

1. 16
2. 20
3. 24
4. 28
5. 30
6. 36

33 Factor wheels

Learning objective
Use approximations, inverse operations and tests of divisibility to estimate and check results.

Type of starter
Reason

Mental strategy
Work methodically, trying consecutive numbers. Look for 'factors of factors'. For example, having identified 21 as a factor of 84, since 7 and 3 are factors of 21, they must also be factors of 84.

Resources
A board or flipchart

Write the number 84 on the board or flipchart. Invite volunteers to draw a line from 84 and write a factor of 84 at the end of the line, generating a 'factor wheel' (see diagram). Accept 84 and 1 as factors, if suggested.

Repeat the activity with these numbers:

1. 144
2. 205
3. 120

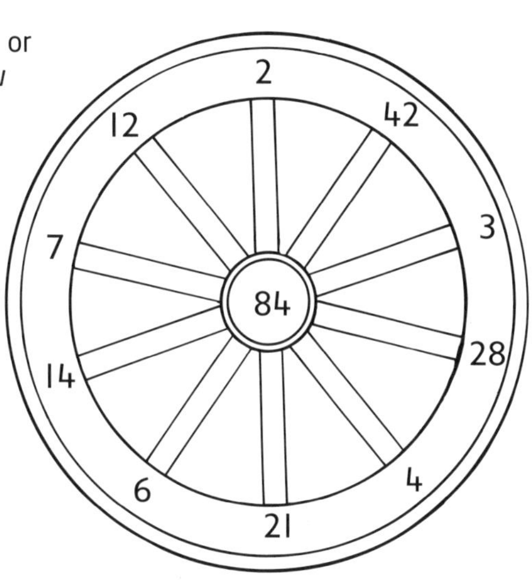

Answers
Other answers are possible.

1. 2, 72, 3, 48, 4, 36, 6, 24, 8, 18, 9, 16, 12
2. 3, 35, 5, 21, 7,15
3. 2, 60, 3, 40, 4, 30, 5, 24, 6, 20, 8, 15, 10, 12

34 Pegs and bands

Learning objective
Describe, identify and visualise parallel and perpendicular edges; use these properties to classify 2D shapes.

Type of starter
Reason

Mental strategy
Remind the children to think about the properties of the shapes as they make them. Use the following prompts: *Does your square have four equal sides? Does your trapezium have one pair of parallel sides?*

Resources
Small pegboards and elastic bands

Split the class into groups of two or three and provide each group with a pegboard and elastic bands.

Call out the names of these shapes: square; rectangle; rhombus; parallelogram; kite; trapezium.

The children, taking it in turns, construct the shapes on the pegboards with elastic bands and hold them up for you to check. Encourage them to make as many different versions of the shape as possible.

No set answers

 35 Square roots

Resources
A board or flipchart

Learning objective
Use knowledge of multiplication facts to derive quickly squares of numbers to 12 × 12 and the corresponding squares of multiples of 10.

Type of starter
Recall

Mental strategy
Remind the children that squaring a number and finding the square root of a number are inverse operations.

Answers

1.	5	9.	7
2.	3	10.	11
3.	8	11.	30
4.	4	12.	50
5.	9	13.	70
6.	6	14.	40
7.	10	15.	100
8.	12		

Write the following numbers on the board or flipchart. Ask the children to find the square roots of each number. They should raise a hand to answer. Ensure they are familiar with the square root sign before starting.

1.	$\sqrt{25}$	6.	$\sqrt{36}$	11.	$\sqrt{900}$
2.	$\sqrt{9}$	7.	$\sqrt{100}$	12.	$\sqrt{2500}$
3.	$\sqrt{64}$	8.	$\sqrt{144}$	13.	$\sqrt{4900}$
4.	$\sqrt{16}$	9.	$\sqrt{49}$	14.	$\sqrt{1600}$
5.	$\sqrt{81}$	10.	$\sqrt{121}$	15.	$\sqrt{10000}$

 36 Using square numbers

Resources
None

Learning objective
Use knowledge of multiplication facts to derive quickly squares of numbers to 12 × 12 and the corresponding squares of multiples of 10.

Type of starter
Rehearse

Mental strategy
Work from the square number that is nearest to the target number.

Answers

Other answers are possible.

1.	$3^2 + 3$	9.	$12^2 + 9$
2.	$8^2 - 2$	10.	$11^2 - 8$
3.	$10^2 - 8$	11.	$6^2 + 4$
4.	$11^2 + 4$	12.	$9^2 + 8$
5.	$4^2 + 3$	13.	$8^2 - 7$
6.	$2^2 - 1$	14.	$6^2 - 5$
7.	$8^2 + 7$	15.	$7^2 + 5$
8.	$7^2 - 6$		

The children have to reach the target number given by using a square number and either an addition or a subtraction. For example: $27 = 5^2 + 2$.

1.	12	6.	3	11.	40
2.	62	7.	71	12.	89
3.	92	8.	43	13.	57
4.	125	9.	153	14.	31
5.	19	10.	113	15.	54

Quick-fire 10

Learning objective
Use knowledge of place value and multiplication facts to 10 × 10 to derive related multiplication facts involving decimals.

Type of starter
Refine

Mental strategy
When multiplying a decimal number by 10, the digits move one place to the left.

Resources
None

Call out the decimal numbers listed. Children have to use a quick method to multiply each decimal number by 10, and raise a hand to answer.

1.	1.7	6.	10.5	11.	35.6	16.	10.70
2.	3.4	7.	12.9	12.	40.1	17.	12.65
3.	5.2	8.	14.2	13.	2.41	18.	18.68
4.	7.6	9.	18.4	14.	5.76	19.	20.17
5.	9.3	10.	20.7	15.	8.94	20.	25.49

Answers

1.	17	11.	356
2.	34	12.	401
3.	52	13.	24.1
4.	76	14.	57.6
5.	93	15.	89.4
6.	105	16.	107
7.	129	17.	126.5
8.	142	18.	186.8
9.	184	19.	201.7
10.	207	20.	254.9

38

Decimal tenths

Learning objective
Use knowledge of place value and multiplication facts to 10 × 10 to derive related division facts involving decimals.

Type of activity
Recall

Mental strategy
For whole numbers, the decimal point is positioned to the right of the digits. When dividing a decimal number by 10, the digits move one place to the right.

Resources
None

Call out the decimal numbers listed. Children have to use a quick method to divide each decimal number by 10, and raise a hand to answer.

1.	5	6.	24	11.	12.3	16.	145.8
2.	8	7.	29	12.	14.7	17.	157.6
3.	12	8.	33	13.	18.6	18.	194.5
4.	15	9.	46	14.	20.9	19.	203.4
5.	19	10.	50	15.	36.2	20.	251.1

Answers

1.	0.5	11.	1.23
2.	0.8	12.	1.47
3.	1.2	13.	1.86
4.	1.5	14.	2.09
5.	1.9	15.	3.62
6.	2.4	16.	14.58
7.	2.9	17.	15.76
8.	3.3	18.	19.45
9.	4.6	19.	20.34
10.	5.0	20.	25.11

39 Prime spotting 2

Resources
A board or flipchart

Learning objective
Recognise that prime numbers have only two factors and identify prime numbers less than 100.

Type of starter
Recall

Mental strategy
Use knowledge of table facts to spot non-primes. For example, all even numbers have 2 as a factor, all numbers ending in 0 or 5 have 5 as a factor etc.

Answers

There are 10 prime numbers to be spotted: 53, 59, 61, 67, 71, 73, 79, 83, 89 and 97.

Display the numbers from 51 to 100 on the board or flipchart. As you point to the numbers, children have to recognise whether they are prime numbers or not. They answer either 'prime' or 'not a prime'. Choose numbers at random but make sure all the prime numbers are included in the activity.

40 In the prime

Resources
A board or flipchart; individual whiteboards, marker pens and dusters

Learning objective
Find the prime factors of two-digit numbers.

Type of activity
Rehearse

Mental strategy
Remind about the use of index numbers, eg $3^2 = 3 \times 3$ and 2 to the power of 4 is the same as $2 \times 2 \times 2 \times 2$. Can they predict whether the solutions are likely to be even or odd numbers from the prime factors given?

Answers

1.	9	6.	48
2.	12	7.	60
3	28	8.	72
4	32	9.	80
5.	45	10.	96

Tell the children they are going to reverse the process carried out in the activity 'Factor trees' (page 34). This time they will be given the prime factors of a number and they will have to work out what that number is. For example, $3^3 = 27$, $2^3 \times 5 = 40$.

Write the following groups of prime factors, one at a time, on the board or flipchart. Ask the children to work out the numbers they represent. They should write their solutions on their individual whiteboards and hold them up for you to check. Discuss each one before moving on to the next.

1.	3^2	6.	$2^4 \times 3$
2.	$2^2 \times 3$	7.	$2^2 \times 3 \times 5$
3.	$2^2 \times 7$	8.	$2^3 \times 3^2$
4.	2^5	9.	$2^4 \times 5$
5.	$3^2 \times 5$	10.	$2^5 \times 3$

41 3D nets

Learning objective
Describe, identify and visualise parallel and perpendicular edges or faces; use these properties to classify 3D solids.

Type of starter
Reason

Mental strategy
Focus on the number and shape of the faces shown in each of the nets.

Resources
A board or flipchart; diagrams of nets of solids: cube, cuboid, triangular prism, tetrahedron, square-based pyramid, cylinder

Display the diagrams of the nets of 3D solids. Ask children to name them. Ask them what information they used to help them recognise the solids. Ask them to indicate the faces of the solids that will be parallel when the solids are built and the faces that will be perpendicular to each other.

No set answers

42 Word shapes

Learning objective
Make and draw shapes with increasing accuracy and apply knowledge of their properties.

Type of starter
Refresh

Mental strategy
Include as many properties as possible when describing shapes. For example, lines of symmetry, diagonals.

Resources
Individual whiteboards, marker pens and dusters

Read out these descriptions of 2D shapes. Ask the children to draw the shape on their whiteboards and hold them up for you to see. Ask: *What am I ...?*

1. I am a quadrilateral with four right angles and two pairs of equal sides.
2. I am a three-sided shape with two equal angles.
3. I am a quadrilateral with four equal sides but no right angles.
4. I am a five-sided shape with equal angles and equal sides.
5. I am a three-sided shape with three equal sides.
6. I am a quadrilateral with four lines of symmetry.
7. I am a quadrilateral with one pair of opposite sides parallel.
8. I am a quadrilateral with two pairs of adjacent sides equal.

After each shape has been drawn, ask the children to list its individual properties. Ask children for a description of any 2D shapes that are not included above.

Answers

1. rectangle
2. isosceles triangle
3. rhombus
4. regular pentagon
5. equilateral triangle
6. square
7. trapezium
8. kite

BLOCK C

Unit 1

100 Mental Maths Starters				100 Maths Lessons		
Page	**Objective**	**Activity title**	**Starter type**	**Unit**	**Lesson**	**Page**
42	Interpret pie charts.	43 Home sweet home	Read	1	2	98
43	Interpret bar charts with grouped discrete data.	44 Sponsored swim	Read	1	6	101
44	Describe and interpret results and solutions to problems using the range.	45 All sports	Rehearse	1	5	100, 101
44	Describe and interpret results and solutions to problems using the mode.	46 Shoe sale	Rehearse	1	7	102
45	Select and use standard metric units of measure and convert between units using decimals to two places.	47 Full capacity	Rehearse	1	9	103, 104
46	Select and use standard metric units of measure and convert between units using decimals to two places.	48 Weighty matters	Rehearse	1	10	104

Unit 2

100 Mental Maths Starters				100 Maths Lessons		
Page	**Objective**	**Activity title**	**Starter type**	**Unit**	**Lesson**	**Page**
47	Interpret line graphs.	49 Party election	Refresh	2	3	110, 111
47	Describe and interpret results and solutions to problems using the median.	50 Wet weather	Rehearse	2	6	113
48	Describe and interpret results and solutions to problems using the mean.	51 About average	Rehearse	2	9	115, 116
48	Describe and predict outcomes from data using the language of chance or likelihood.	52 In with a chance	Reason	2	7	114
49	Select and use standard metric units of measure.	53 Your choice	Recall	2	8	115
50	Select and use standard metric units of measure and convert between units using decimals to two places.	54 Go the distance	Rehearse	2	10	116

Unit 3

100 Mental Maths Starters				100 Maths Lessons		
Page	**Objective**	**Activity title**	**Starter type**	**Unit**	**Lesson**	**Page**
51	Solve problems by collecting, selecting, processing, presenting and interpreting data, using ICT where appropriate; draw conclusions and identify further questions to ask.	55 Famous composers	Read	3	1	121, 122
52	Describe and interpret results and solutions to problems using the median.	56 Taxi driver	Rehearse	3	5	124, 125
53	Describe and interpret results and solutions to problems using the mode, range and median.	57 Dice roll	Rehearse	3	6	125
54	Describe and predict outcomes from data using the language of chance or likelihood.	58 In a spin	Rehearse	3	7	126
55	Select and use standard metric units of measure and convert between units using decimals to two places.	59 Kilometres and miles	Rehearse	3	8	126, 127
56	Select and use standard metric units of measure and convert between units using decimals to two places.	60 Litres and pints	Rehearse	3	9	127

43 Home sweet home

Resources
'Home sweet home' (from photocopiable page 92), one copy per child

Learning objective
Interpret pie charts.

Type of starter
Read

Mental strategy
Remember the importance of the complete circle being used to show the data. Note the importance of colour coding and/or symbols, and labelling, to show what the parts of the circle represent.

Answers

1. Parts of the graph resemble pieces of a pie
2. 5
3. 3
4. 6
5. 9
6. 3
7. 3
8. 21

Explain that the pie chart on 'Home sweet home' shows the results of a survey, in which 24 people were asked about the type of home they live in.

Children should use their copy of the pie chart to answer the following questions orally.

1. Why is this type of graph called a pie chart?
2. How many different types of home are shown?
3. How many of the people surveyed live in a flat?
4. How many live in a two-bedroomed house?
5. How many live in a three-bedroomed house?
6. How many live in a bungalow?
7. How many live in a one-bedroomed house?
8. How many do not live in a flat?

44 Sponsored swim

Learning objective
Interpret bar charts with grouped discrete data.

Type of starter
Read

Mental strategy
When data are displayed in grouped intervals each interval should be the same size.

Resources
'Sponsored swim' (from photocopiable page 93), one copy per child

Explain that the bar chart on 'Sponsored swim' shows the grouped discrete data about a class' sponsored swim.

Children should use their copy of the bar chart to answer the following questions orally.

1. How many children are in the class?
2. What is the highest amount of sponsorship shown on the graph?
3. How many children collected between £5 and £9.99?
4. How many children collected between £20 and £25?
5. How many children collected less than £5?
6. Which money group had the lowest number of children?
7. Which money group had the highest number of children?
8. How much money was collected in total?

Answers

1. 30
2. £25
3. 7
4. 4
5. 4
6. £15 to £19.99
7. £10 to £14.99
8. It is not possible to know how much money was collected altogether from this type of graph, although the lowest and highest possible total that fit these data can be calculated (£280 / £404.74)

All sports

Resources
A board or flipchart

Learning objective
Describe and interpret results and solutions to problems using the range.

Type of starter
Rehearse

Mental strategy
The range of a set of data is calculated by taking the smallest amount away from the largest amount.

Answers
1. 7 - 0 = 7 goals
2. 36 - 2 = 34 runs
3. 50 - 7 = 43 points
4. 13.6 - 9.4 = 4.2 seconds
5. 11.9 - 6.7 = 5.2 metres

Write the following information on the board or flipchart. Ask the children to find the range in the following sets of data.

1. Goals scored by Ben's hockey team in the first 10 games of the season:
   3 2 0 4 5 2 7 4 1 6
2. Runs hit by players in a team in a 20-20 cricket match:
   10 5 19 12 20 2 9 36 14 3 17
3. Scores made with three darts at the Woodside Darts Championship:
   Ronnie: 38 15 20 Don: 27 34 50
   Eva: 7 18 12
4. Times recorded for the 80m sprint on sports day:
   10s 11.8s 9.4s
   10.5s 13.6s 12s
5. Distances recorded in the women's long jump event:
   6.7m 9.2m 10.3m 11.9m
   7.1m 11.8m 10.7m 8.5m

Shoe sale

Resources
A board or flipchart

Learning objective
Describe and interpret results and solutions to problems using the mode.

Type of starter
Rehearse

Mental strategy
The mode is a form of average. The mode is the data item that occurs most often in a data set.

Answers
Sunday: 7

Monday: 4

Tuesday: 3

Wednesday: 5

Thursday: 10

Friday: 5½

Saturday: 7½

Write the following data on the board or flipchart. Tell the children it shows the sizes of pairs of shoes sold in a shop during the first hour of each day. Ask them to find the mode of the shoe sizes (modal shoe size) for each day.

Sunday:	7	5	8	10	6	7	4	3	7	4				
Monday:	4	1	3	5	7	9	4	2	9	4				
Tuesday:	3	5	3	6	4	5	3	7	9	3				
Wednesday:	4	3	2	5	7	4	9	5	6	5	6	5		
Thursday:	10	9	12	11	10	8	9	11	12	10	8	10		
Friday:	4½	8	5½	5	7	7	5½	6½	4	8	5½	6		
Saturday:	3½	4	7	2	7½	9	2	3	7½	10	7½	9	7½	7

47 Full capacity

Learning objective
Select and use standard metric units of measure and convert between units using decimals to two places.

Type of starter
Rehearse

Mental strategy
Remember that there are 1000ml in a litre and 'milli' means a thousandth.

Remember that the decimal point comes between litres and parts of litres.

Resources
A board or flipchart

Ask the children to convert these capacity measurements from litres (l) to millilitres (ml).

1. 1.5 litres
2. 2.2 litres
3. 1.74 litres
4. 4.25 litres
5. 7.4 litres
6. 9.55 litres
7. 10.7 litres
8. 12.87 litres

Ask the children to convert these capacity measurements from millilitres (ml) to litres (l).

9. 600ml
10. 750ml
11. 1200ml
12. 550ml
13. 2450ml
14. 7320ml
15. 6600ml
16. 9370ml

Ask the children to say these capacity measurements in two other ways. For example, 2.7 litres is the same as 2700ml or 2 litres 700 millilitres.

17. 5 litres 300 millilitres
18. 6.80 litres
19. 4630ml
20. 9¾ litres

Answers
1. 1500ml
2. 2200ml
3. 1740ml
4. 4250ml
5. 7400ml
6. 9550ml
7. 10,700ml
8. 12,870ml
9. 0.6 litres
10. 0.75 litres
11. 1.2 litres
12. 0.55 litres
13. 2.45 litres
14. 7.32 litres
15. 6.6 litres
16. 9.37 litres
17. 5300ml and 5.3 litres
18. 6800ml and 6 litres 800 millilitres
19. 4.63 litres and 4 litres 630 millilitres
20. 9.75 litres, 9750 millilitres and 9 litres 750 millilitres

(48) Weighty matters

Resources
A board or flipchart

Learning objective
Select and use standard metric units of measure and convert between units using decimals to two places.

Type of starter
Rehearse

Mental strategy
Remember that 1000g = 1kg and that 1000kg = 1 tonne. Children should also be aware of the main fractions of 1000: ½ = 500, ¼ = 250 and ¾ = 750.

Ask the children to convert these weight measurements into kilograms or grams.

1. 440g = ________ kg
2. 2kg 300g = ________ kg
3. 3.9kg = ________ g
4. 4.5kg = ________ g
5. 6kg 840g = ________ g
6. 6100g = ________ kg
7. 5½kg = ________ g
8. 7300g = ________ kg
9. 9kg 120g = ________ kg
10. 3¾kg = ________ g

Ask the children to convert these weight measurements into kilograms or tonnes.

11. 4730kg = ________ tonne
12. 12t 400kg = ________ tonne
13. 3t 970kg = ________ kg
14. 12,420kg = ________ tonne
15. 7.37t = ________ kg
16. 4½t = ________ kg

Ask the children to give these weights in two other ways. For example, 2360g is the same as 2kg 360g or 2.36kg.

17. 4kg 650g
18. 5210g
19. 3t 400kg
20. 7.34 tonne

Answers

1. 0.44kg
2. 2.3kg
3. 3900g
4. 4500g
5. 6840g
6. 6.1kg
7. 5500g
8. 7.3kg
9. 9.12kg
10. 3750g
11. 4.73t
12. 12.4t
13. 3970kg
14. 12.42t
15. 7370kg
16. 4500kg
17. 4.65kg and 4650g
18. 5.21kg and 5kg 210g
19. 3.4t and 3400kg
20. 7340kg and 7t 340g

Party election

Learning objective
Interpret line graphs.

Type of starter
Refresh

Mental strategy
Ensure the children understand the meaning of terms, such as 'vertical axis', 'horizontal axis', 'scale'. Emphasise the part played by accurate labelling which enable graphs of this kind to be interpreted successfully.

Resources
'Party election' (from photocopiable page 94), one copy per child

Explain that the line graph on 'Party election' shows the number of votes received by the Blue Party from 1988 to 2008.

Children should use their copy of the line graph to answer the following questions orally.

1. What is this type of graph called?
2. What is shown on the vertical axis?
3. What is shown on the horizontal axis?
4. When did the Blue Party poll the lowest number of votes?
5. When did the Blue Party poll the highest number of votes?
6. How many votes did the Blue Party get in 2000?
7. How many votes did the Blue Party get in 1992?
8. How many votes in total did the Blue Party get in 2004 and 2008?
9. By how many did the Blue Party's number of votes rise between 1988 and 2008?

Answers

1. Line graph
2. Number of votes
3. Years of elections
4. 1988
5. 2008
6. 500
7. 300
8. 1350
9. 650

50 Wet weather

Learning objective
Describe and interpret results and solutions to problems using the median.

Type of starter
Rehearse

Mental strategy
The word 'median' has the same number of letters as 'middle'. The median is the middle value when a set of data is placed in order from the smallest to largest.

Resources
A board or flipchart

Write the following data on the board or flipchart. Explain that it shows the rainfall data collected in five towns during the first five months of the year. Ask the children to find the median rainfall in each of the five towns.

Templecombe:	Jan 8mm, Feb 12mm, Mar 14mm, Apr 3mm, May 13mm
Longbarrow:	Jan 13mm, Feb 20mm, Mar 7mm, Apr 9mm, May 11mm
Ravenscrag:	Jan 5mm, Feb 14mm, Mar 9mm, Apr 6mm, May 16mm
Borrowdale:	Jan 7mm, Feb 10mm, Mar 4mm, Apr 11mm, May 3mm
Usktor:	Jan 14mm, Feb 17mm, Mar 8mm, Apr 19mm, May 7mm

Answers

Templecombe: 12mm

Longbarrow: 11mm

Ravenscrag: 9mm

Borrowdale: 7mm

Usktor: 14mm

About average

Resources
A board or flipchart

Learning objective
Describe and interpret results and solutions to problems using the mean.

Type of starter
Rehearse

Mental strategy
To find the mean, add the values and divide by the number of values.

Answers

1. Usktor (13mm)
2. Borrowdale (7mm)

Use the same data as the 'Wet weather' activity (see page 47).

Discuss the importance of being able to calculate the mean when collecting weather data. Ask:

1. *Which town has the highest mean rainfall?*
2. *Which town has the lowest mean rainfall?*

In with a chance

Resources
Washing line or piece of string; clothes pegs; pieces of card labelled with the following words: 'impossible', 'very unlikely', 'unlikely', 'even chance', 'likely', 'very likely', 'certain'

Learning objective
Describe and predict outcomes from data using the language of chance or likelihood.

Type of starter
Reason

Mental strategy
Probability words can be converted into fractions, decimals or percentages. For example, 'even chance' is the same as probability of ½, 0.5 or 50%.

Answers

From left to right the cards should read: 'impossible' (0), 'very unlikely', 'unlikely', 'even chance', 'likely', 'very likely', 'certain' (1)

Stress to the children that understanding probability makes it possible to understand everything from the weather report to winning the lottery.

Tell the children that the probability of an event happening can be marked on a probability scale that runs from 0 to 1.

Ask for volunteers to come out and peg the probability word cards into the correct positions, starting with impossible representing zero on the left-hand side of the line.

Discuss the children's placements and explain the terms used.

53 Your choice

Learning objective
Select and use standard metric units of measure.

Type of starter
Recall

Mental strategy
A centilitre is equal to one hundredth of a litre (0.01 litre) or 10 millilitres (10ml).

Resources
A board or flipchart

Write the following metric measures on the board or flipchart with their abbreviations:

kilometres (km), gram (g), tonne (t), litre (l), metre (m), kilogram (kg), millilitre (ml), centimetre (cm), centilitre (cl), millimetre (mm)

The children may be less familiar with the centilitre measure. Explain that it is used for some bottled liquids. It may help to revise first the meanings of the prefixes 'kilo', 'centi' and 'milli'.

Then, provide the children with the following situations. Ask them to choose the appropriate metric unit they would use for measurement in each case.

1. Weight of a reading book.
2. Weight of a bus.
3. Weight of a child.
4. The length of a pencil.
5. The width of a postage stamp.
6. The distance between two towns.
7. The size of a small garden.
8. A dose of medicine.
9. The capacity of a swimming pool.
10. The capacity of a wine bottle.

Answers
1. gram (g)
2. tonne (t)
3. kilogram (kg)
4. centimetre (cm)
5. millimetre (mm)
6. kilometre (km)
7. metre (m)
8. millilitre (ml)
9. litre (l)
10. centilitre (cl)

54 Go the distance

Resources
A board or flipchart

Learning objective
Select and use standard metric units of measure and convert between units using decimals to two places.

Type of activity
Rehearse

Mental strategy
Remember the metric units of distance: 100cm = 1m and 1000m = 1km, and that the decimal point marks off metres from centimetres (eg 250cm = 2.5m) and kilometres from metres (eg 3400m = 3.4km).

Ask the children to convert these distance measurements

... from centimetres (cm) to metres (m):

1. 15cm
2. 39cm
3. 160cm
4. 253cm
5. 476cm

... from metres (m) to centimetres (cm):

6. 0.35m
7. 0.72m
8. 1.65m
9. 4.03m
10. 8.27m

Ask the children to convert these distance measurements

... from metres (m) into kilometres (km):

11. 500m
12. 980m
13. 1300m
14. 3572m
15. 8690m

... from kilometres (km) to metres (m):

16. 0.4km
17. 0.95km
18. 1.23km
19. 3.58km
20. 6¾km

Answers
1. 0.15m
2. 0.39m
3. 1.6m
4. 2.53m
5. 4.76m
6. 35cm
7. 72cm
8. 165cm
9. 403cm
10. 827cm
11. 0.5km
12. 0.98km
13. 1.3km
14. 3.572km
15. 8.69km
16. 400m
17. 950m
18. 1230m
19. 3580m
20. 6750m

55 Famous composers

Learning objective
Solve problems by collecting, selecting, processing, presenting and interpreting data, using ICT where appropriate; draw conclusions and identify further questions to ask.

Type of starter
Read

Mental strategy
It may help to work out the ages of each of the composers first.

Resources
A board or flipchart; individual whiteboards, marker pens and dusters, or paper and pencils

Write the following information about famous composers on the board or flipchart.

Beethoven	1770–1827
Elgar	1857–1934
Handel	1685–1759
Bach	1685–1750
Grieg	1843–1907
Mozart	1756–1791
Stravinsky	1882–1971
Dvorak	1841–1904

The children should use the information above to answer the following questions.

1. Which composers were born earliest?
2. Which composer died most recently?
3. Which composer lived to the greatest age?
4. How old was Bach when he died?
5. Which composer died at the age of 35?
6. Which composers were alive in 1700?
7. Which composers lived in the 20th century?
8. Use the birth dates to place the composers in chronological order, starting furthest away in time.

Ask the children to suggest other questions they could answer using this set of data.

Answers
1. Bach and Handel
2. Stravinsky
3. Stravinsky (89)
4. 65
5. Mozart
6. Bach and Handel
7. Elgar, Grieg, Stravinsky and Dvorak
8. Bach and Handel (1685), Mozart (1756), Beethoven (1770), Dvorak (1841), Grieg (1843), Elgar (1857), Stravinsky (1882)

 Taxi driver

Resources
A board or flipchart; individual whiteboards, marker pens and dusters, or paper and pencils

Learning objective
Describe and interpret results and solutions to problems using the median.

Type of starter
Rehearse

Mental strategy
Remember, the median is the middle item in a set of data. When there are an even number of items, the median will be found halfway between the two middle data items. For example: for the data set, 5, 9, 15, 19, 24, 28, the median is 17, the number halfway between 15 and 19.

Answers
Week 1: 9km <4, 5, 8, 10, 11, 12>

Week 2: 14½km (or 14.5km) <8, 10, 14, 15, 19, 24>

Week 3: 24 <15, 19, 24, 24, 27, 30>

Week 4: 37½ <20, 29, 37, 38, 41, 46>

Week 5: 37½ <20, 24, 37, 38, 46, 53>

Write the following information on the board or flipchart. Explain that it shows the distances a taxi driver travels each day for five working weeks.

Ask the children to put the distances in ascending order, each day, and then find the median distance travelled each week. Point out that there are an even number of days this time.

Week 1: Monday 11km, Tuesday 4km, Wednesday 12km, Thursday 5km, Friday 10km, Saturday 8km.

Week 2: Monday 24km, Tuesday 10km, Wednesday 19km, Thursday 8km, Friday 15km, Saturday 14km.

Week 3: Monday 30km, Tuesday 24km, Wednesday 15km, Thursday 27km, Friday 19km, Saturday 24km.

Week 4: Monday 41km, Tuesday 29km, Wednesday 38km, Thursday 46km, Friday 20km, Saturday 37km.

Week 5: Monday 53km, Tuesday 24km, Wednesday 38km, Thursday 46km, Friday 20km, Saturday 37km.

57 Dice roll

Learning objective
Describe and interpret results and solutions to problems using the mode, range and median.

Type of starter
Rehearse

Mental strategy
Advise the children to list all the scores in order, eg 1, 1, 1, 2, 2, 2 etc, so they can see the extent of the digits involved.

Resources
A board or flipchart; individual whiteboards, marker pens and dusters, or paper and pencils

Copy the following frequency chart onto the board or flipchart.

Working out should be done on individual whiteboards or pieces of paper that can be held up for checking.

Score	Frequency
1	3
2	3
3	4
4	5
5	2
6	3

Tell the children that Sanjay rolled a dice 20 times and obtained the results shown in the frequency chart.

Ask them to work out the following for this set of data.

1. The range.
2. The mode.
3. The mean.

Answers
1. The range is 5
2. The mode is 4
3. The mean is $3^{9}/_{20}$ or 3.45

58 In a spin

Resources
A large version of an octagonal spinner showing the numbers 1 to 8, or draw a diagram to represent a spinner on the board or flipchart

Learning objective
Describe and predict outcomes from data using the language of chance or likelihood.

Type of starter
Rehearse

Mental strategy
Probability words can be converted into fractions, decimals or percentages. For example, 'even chance' is the same as probability of ½, 0.5 or 50%.

Answers
1. $^4/_8$ or ½
2. $^4/_8$ or ½
3. $^0/_8$ (impossible)
4. $^5/_8$
5. $^4/_8$ or ½
6. $^2/_8$ or ¼
7. $^2/_8$ or ¼
8. $^4/_8$ or ½

Talk first in general terms about the likelihood of certain numbers coming up when the spinner is used.

Discuss vocabulary, such as 'impossible', 'certain' and 'even chance'.

Then, ask the children the following questions. They should give their answers as fractions.

1. What is the probability of getting an even number?
2. What is the probability of getting an odd number?
3. What is the probability of getting zero?
4. What is the probability of getting a number less than 6?
5. What is the probability of getting a number greater than 4?
6. What is the probability of getting a multiple of 3?
7. What is the probability of getting a square number?
8. What is the probability of getting a factor of 6?

Ask them to give the answers to some of the questions above in at least one other way.

59 Kilometres and miles

Learning objective
Select and use standard metric units of measure and convert between units using decimals to two places.

Type of starter
Rehearse

Mental strategy
To convert kilometres to miles multiply by 0.6. To convert miles to kilometres multiply by 1.6.

Resources
Individual whiteboards, marker pens and dusters, or paper and pencils; a calculator for each child (or pair of children)

Ensure the children are able to multiply decimal numbers using the calculator.

Tell them that they are going to use the calculator to accurately convert distances in metric units into distances in imperial units, and vice versa.

Tell them that 1 mile = 1.6km and 1km = 0.6 miles.

Ask them to work out the new distances, one at a time, then write and display their answers on their whiteboard or on a piece of paper for you to check.

Convert these distances into kilometres:

1. 10 miles
2. 15 miles
3. 45 miles
4. 60 miles
5. 150 miles
6. 180 miles

Convert these distances into miles:

7. 20km
8. 50km
9. 95km
10. 120km
11. 200km
12. 450km

Answers

1. 16km
2. 24km
3. 72km
4. 96km
5. 240km
6. 288km
7. 12 miles
8. 30 miles
9. 57 miles
10. 72 miles
11. 120 miles
12. 270 miles

(60) Litres and pints

Resources
Individual whiteboards, marker pens and dusters, or paper and pencils; a calculator for each child (or pair of children)

Learning objective
Select and use standard metric units of measure and convert between units using decimals to two places.

Type of starter
Rehearse

Mental strategy
To convert pints into litres multiply by 0.6. To convert litres into pints multiply by 1.75.

Answers
1. 2.4 litres
2. 3.6 litres
3. 4.8 litres
4. 7.2 litres
5. 12 litres
6. 21 litres
7. 12.25 pints
8. 15.75 pints
9. 26.25 pints
10. 43.75 pints
11. 78.75 pints
12. 105 pints

Ensure the children are able to multiply decimal numbers using the calculator.

Tell them that they are going to use the calculator to accurately convert capacities given in metric units into capacities in imperial units, and vice versa.

Tell them that 1 pint = 0.6 litres and 1 litre = 1.75 pints.

Ask them to work out the new amounts, one at a time, then write and display their answers on their whiteboard or on a piece of paper for you to check.

Convert these capacities into litres:

1. 4 pints
2. 6 pints
3. 8 pints
4. 12 pints
5. 20 pints
6. 35 pints

Convert these capacities into pints:

7. 7 litres
8. 9 litres
9. 15 litres
10. 25 litres
11. 45 litres
12. 60 litres

BLOCK D

Unit 1

100 Mental Maths Starters				100 Maths Lessons		
Page	**Objective**	**Activity title**	**Starter type**	**Unit**	**Lesson**	**Page**
59	Solve multi-step problems, and problems involving fractions, decimals and percentages; choose and use appropriate calculation strategies at each stage.	61 Five-second problems	Rehearse	1	3	137,138
59	Calculate mentally with integers and decimals: U.t ± U.t, TU × U, TU ÷ U, U.t × U, U.t ÷ U.	62 How much to the next 10?	Rehearse	1	2	136,137
60	Calculate mentally with integers and decimals: U.t ± U.t, TU × U, TU ÷ U, U.t × U, U.t ÷ U.	63 What's the statement?	Read	1	5	139
60	Calculate mentally with integers and decimals: U.t ± U.t, TU × U, TU ÷ U, U.t × U, U.t ÷ U.	64 Multiply by...	Recall	1	9	142,143
61	Select and use standard metric units of measure and convert between units using decimals to two places.	65 Short measure	Rehearse	1	8	141,142
61	Calculate the perimeter of rectilinear shapes.	66 All around	Rehearse	1	10	143,144

Unit 2

100 Mental Maths Starters				100 Maths Lessons		
Page	**Objective**	**Activity title**	**Starter type**	**Unit**	**Lesson**	**Page**
62	Solve multi-step problems, and problems involving fractions, decimals and percentages; choose and use appropriate calculation strategies at each stage.	67 More five-second problems	Rehearse	2	2	148
64	Calculate mentally with integers and decimals: U.t ± U.t, TU × U, TU ÷ U, U.t × U, U.t ÷ U.	68 Decimal doubles	Rehearse	2	3	148,149
63	Calculate angles in a triangle or around a point.	69 Angles on a straight line	Rehearse	2	7	152
64	Calculate angles around a point.	70 Angles around a point	Rehearse	2	9	153
65	Calculate angles in a triangle.	71 Angles in a triangle	Rehearse	2	10	153, 154
65	Use coordinates in the first quadrant to draw, locate and complete shapes.	72 Get the point	Read	2	8	152, 153

Unit 3

100 Mental Maths Starters				100 Maths Lessons		
Page	**Objective**	**Activity title**	**Starter type**	**Unit**	**Lesson**	**Page**
66	Solve multi-step problems, and problems involving fractions, decimals and percentages; choose and use appropriate calculation strategies at each stage.	(73) Ten-second problems	Rehearse	3	1	159, 160
66	Calculate mentally with integers and decimals: U.t ± U.t, TU × U, TU ÷ U, U.t × U, U.t ÷ U.	(74) Going up	Recall	3	3	160
67	Calculate mentally with integers and decimals: U.t ± U.t, TU × U, TU ÷ U, U.t × U, U.t ÷ U.	(75) Going up with money	Recall	3	4	160, 161
68	Select and use standard metric units of measure and convert between units using decimals to two places.	(76) Units change	Rehearse	3	7	163, 164
69	Calculate the perimeter and area of rectilinear shapes.	(77) Perimeters and areas	Rehearse	3	9	164, 165
69	Estimate the area of an irregular shape by counting squares.	(78) Island shapes	Reason	3	10	165

61 Five-second problems

Learning objective
Solve multi-step problems, and problems involving fractions, decimals and percentages; choose and use appropriate calculation strategies at each stage.

Type of starter
Rehearse

Resources
None

Read each question twice. Give the children five seconds to work out the answer, then ask them to raise a hand if they know it.

1. Add 150 to 60.
2. Find the difference between 170 and 90.
3. What is the remainder when 250 is divided by 4?
4. How much change will I have from £5.00 if I spend £3.75?
5. What is the cost of two books at £4.75 each?
6. How many minutes is it from 10 past 9 to 11 o'clock?
7. How many minutes is it from 14:22 to 15:00?
8. Our desks are 64cm wide. How wide are two desks put side by side?
9. I have used 1.45kg from a 3kg bag of flour. How much flour is left?
10. Multiply 26 by 3 then add 13.
11. If I save £1.60 each week, how much will I have saved in five weeks?
12. How many centimetres of wood will be left if I cut 215 centimetres from a 4-metre plank?

Answers

1. 210
2. 80
3. 2
4. £1.25
5. £9.50
6. 110 minutes
7. 38 minutes
8. 1m 28cm
9. 1.55kg
10. 91
11. £8.00
12. 185cm

62 How much to the next 10?

Learning objective
Calculate mentally with integers and decimals: U.t ± U.t, TU × U, TU ÷ U, U.t × U, U.t ÷ U.

Type of starter
Rehearse

Resources
None

Ask the children to provide the number which, when added to the given number, will take it to the next multiple of 10. For example: 6.2 + 3.8 = 10.

1.	4.7	7.	28.9	13.	7.8	19.	51.5
2.	6.1	8.	2.5	14.	29.1	20.	9.2
3.	18.5	9.	3.4	15.	32.3	21.	3.7
4.	13.2	10.	37.7	16.	24.6	22.	18.3
5.	17.3	11.	21.9	17.	25.4	23.	42.8
6.	5.4	12.	16.3	18.	30.1	24.	5.5

Answers

1.	5.3	13.	2.2
2.	3.9	14.	0.9
3.	1.5	15.	7.7
4.	6.8	16.	5.4
5.	2.7	17.	4.6
6.	4.6	18.	9.9
7.	1.1	19.	8.5
8.	7.5	20.	0.8
9.	6.6	21.	6.3
10.	2.3	22.	1.7
11.	8.1	23.	7.2
12.	3.7	24.	4.5

63 What's the statement?

Resources
Individual whiteboards, marker pens and dusters, or paper and pencils

Learning objective
Calculate mentally with integers and decimals: U.t ± U.t, TU × U, TU ÷ U, U.t × U, U.t ÷ U.

Type of starter
Read

Answers

Example for question 2:

4 × 0.5 = 2

0.5 × 4 = 2

2 ÷ 0.5 = 4

2 ÷ 4 = 0.5

Ask the children to make a multiplication statement and a division statement using the three numbers given. They should start by jotting down the three numbers.

Allow 20 seconds each time, then collect the four statements in each case.

1. 6, 18, 3
2. 0.5, 2, 4
3. 1, 5, 0.2
4. 10, 0.75, 7.5
5. 7, 21, 3
6. 1, 2, 2
7. 8, 0.5, 16
8. 0.75, 3, 4
9. 45, 9, 5
10. 3, 603, 201

64 Multiply by...

Resources
Individual whiteboards, marker pens and dusters, or paper and pencils

Learning objective
Calculate mentally with integers and decimals: U.t ± U.t, TU × U, TU ÷ U, U.t × U, U.t ÷ U.

Type of starter
Recall

Answers

1.	50	11.	34
2.	35	12.	120
3.	65	13.	76
4.	300	14.	520
5.	55	15.	118
6.	16	16.	54
7.	72	17.	5400
8.	720	18.	108
9.	120	19.	216
10.	56	20.	30

Multiply by 5:
1. 10
2. 7
3. 13
4. 60
5. 11

Multiply by 8:
6. 2
7. 9
8. 90
9. 15
10. 7

Double (x2):
11. 17
12. 60
13. 38
14. 260
15. 59

Multiply by 6:
16. 9
17. 900
18. 18
19. 36
20. 5

65 Short measure

Learning objective
Select and use standard metric units of measure and convert between units using decimals to two places.

Type of starter
Rehearse

Mental strategy
Remember, 1cm = 10mm. To convert centimetres to millimetres, multiply by 10. To convert millimetres to centimetres, divide by 10.

Resources
None

Tell the children that the focus will be converting short measurements (the kind usually found using a standard 30cm classroom ruler).

Ask them to carry out the conversions mentally and to raise a hand to answer orally.

Convert these measurements in centimetres (cm) to millimetres (mm):

1. 1cm
2. 4cm
3. 7cm
4. 9cm
5. 12cm
6. 16cm
7. 8½cm
8. 15½cm
9. 6.5cm
10. 19.5cm

Convert these measurements in millimetres (mm) to centimetres (cm):

11. 13mm
12. 20mm
13. 27mm
14. 39mm
15. 52mm
16. 74mm
17. 109mm
18. 135mm
19. 194mm
20. 256mm

Answers

1. 10mm
2. 40mm
3. 70mm
4. 90mm
5. 120mm
6. 160mm
7. 85mm
8. 155mm
9. 65mm
10. 195mm
11. 1.3cm
12. 2cm
13. 2.7cm
14. 3.9cm
15. 5.2cm
16. 7.4cm
17. 10.9cm
18. 13.5cm
19. 19.4cm
20. 25.6cm

66 All around

Learning objective
Calculate the perimeter of rectilinear shapes.

Type of starter
Rehearse

Mental strategy
Remember, perimeter is a measurement of distance. Methods of working out perimeter, depending on the type of shape, are: square perimeter = side × 4; rectangle perimeter = (length + width) × 2; equilateral triangle perimeter = side × 3; any regular shape perimeter = side × number of sides.

Resources
A board or flipchart

Ask the children to find the perimeter of the following shapes. If possible just give the dimensions orally. You may need to draw diagrams of the shapes on the board or flipchart.

1. A 4cm square.
2. A 12cm square.
3. A rectangle 5cm by 3cm.
4. A rectangle 11cm by 7cm.
5. A rectangle 15½ cm by 8½cm.
6. An equilateral triangle of side 6cm.
7. An equilateral triangle of side 14cm.
8. An isosceles triangle, two sides of 5cm and one side of 9cm.
9. A regular pentagon of side 12cm.
10. A regular octagon of side 6½cm.

Answers

1. 16cm
2. 48cm
3. 16cm
4. 36cm
5. 48cm
6. 18cm
7. 42cm
8. 19cm
9. 60cm
10. 52cm

67 More five-second problems

Resources	Learning objective
None	Solve multi-step problems, and problems involving fractions, decimals and percentages; choose and use appropriate calculation strategies at each stage. **Type of starter** Rehearse

Answers

1. 83p
2. 8.25
3. 323
4. £1.90
5. 52cm
6. 7cm
7. 70
8. 9.1
9. 3.6
10. £2.20
11. 56g
12. 900 miles
13. 24p
14. 5.35
15. £6.00

Read each question twice. Give the children five seconds to work out the answer, then ask them to raise a hand if they know it.

1. A pack of four batteries costs £3.32. How much is that for each one?
2. It takes me 20 minutes to walk to school. At what time should I leave home to be at school by a quarter to nine?
3. What is the total of 109 and 214?
4. Two articles together cost £5.20. One of them costs £3.30. How much is the other one?
5. Three pieces of wood, each 16cm long, were cut from a metre length. What length of wood was left?
6. A rectangle has a perimeter of 32cm. If the length is 9cm, what is the width?
7. What is the difference between 230 and 160?
8. Add 3.7 and 5.4.
9. Take 1.4 from 5.
10. I bought two cans of drink at 75p each and two chocolate bars at 35p each. What was the total cost?
11. What is the difference in weight between an apple weighing 168g and another at 112g?
12. A plane flew at 360 miles per hour for 2½ hours. How far did it fly?
13. I paid £1.20 for five stamps of the same value. How much would one stamp have cost?
14. The 40-minute programme finished at 6.15. At what time had it begun?
15. A driver was paid £240 for the 40 hours that he had worked. How much was that per hour?

68 Decimal doubles

Learning objective
Calculate mentally with integers and decimals: U.t ± U.t, TU × U, TU ÷ U, U.t × U, U.t ÷ U.

Type of starter
Rehearse

Resources
A board or flipchart

Divide the class into groups of three or four. The first group doubles the start number, which is doubled again by the second group, and so on. When a group's number would be greater than the target number, they say 'Bong' instead and earn a point. The group with the most points at the end wins.

Write the start and target numbers on the board or flipchart each time.

Start number	Target number	Start number	Target number
1. 1.1	20	6. 0.3	10
2. 0.2	10	7. 0.9	20
3. 1.5	80	8. 1.3	20
4. 0.7	12	9. 1.7	30
5. 0.5	180	10. 1.9	20

Answers

1. 2.2, 4.4, 8.8, 17.6
2. 0.4, 0.8, 1.6, 3.2, 6.4
3. 3, 6, 12, 24, 48
4. 1.4, 2.8, 5.6, 11.2
5. 1, 2, 4, 8, 16, 32, 64, 128
6. 0.6, 1.2, 2.4, 4.8, 9.6
7. 1.8, 3.6, 7.2, 14.4
8. 2.6, 5.2, 10.4
9. 3.4, 6.8, 13.6, 27.2
10. 3.8, 7.6, 15.2

69 Angles on a straight line

Learning objective
Calculate angles in a triangle or around a point.

Type of starter
Rehearse

Mental strategy
Remember, angles in a straight line total 180° (2 right angles).

Resources
A board or flipchart

Draw this diagram on the board or flipchart:

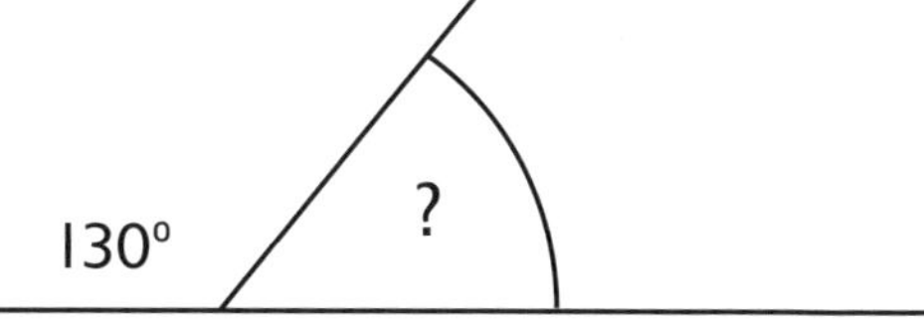

Ask the children how they can find the size of the unknown angle in the diagram (180° - 130° = 50°).

Find the other angle in a straight line if one is:

1. 120°	6. 70°	11. 84°	16. 42°
2. 100°	7. 138°	12. 117°	17. 106°
3. 40°	8. 75°	13. 60°	18. 25°
4. 95°	9. 50°	14. 153°	19. 140°
5. 145°	10. 160°	15. 125°	20. 158°

Answers

1. 60°	11. 96°
2. 80°	12. 63°
3. 140°	13. 120°
4. 85°	14. 27°
5. 35°	15. 55°
6. 110°	16. 138°
7. 42°	17. 74°
8. 105°	18. 155°
9. 130°	19. 40°
10. 20°	20. 22°

BLOCK D

(70) Angles around a point

Resources	Learning objective
A board or flipchart	Calculate angles around a point.
	Type of starter
	Rehearse

Answers

1.	120°	11.	275°
2.	60°	12.	46°
3.	190°	13.	61°
4.	145°	14.	178°
5.	252°	15.	210°
6.	160°	16.	100°
7.	300°	17.	10°
8.	303°	18.	240°
9.	227°	19.	265°
10.	260°	20.	315°

Draw this diagram on the board or flipchart:

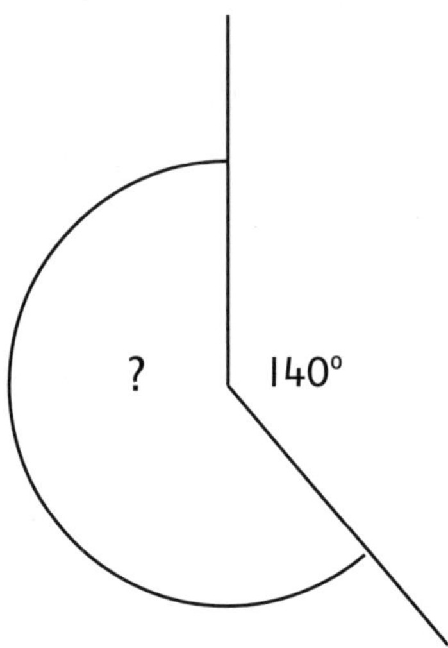

Remind the children that the sum of angles at a point is 360°.

Ask the children to find the size of the other angle in the diagram (360° - 140° = 220°).

Find the other angle at a point if one is:

1.	240°	6.	200°	11.	85°	16.	260°
2.	300°	7.	60°	12.	314°	17.	350°
3.	170°	8.	57°	13.	299°	18.	120°
4.	215°	9.	133°	14.	182°	19.	95°
5.	108°	10.	100°	15.	150°	20.	45°

Angles in a triangle

Learning objective Calculate angles in a triangle. **Type of starter** Rehearse **Mental strategy** The three angles in a triangle always total 180°. Isosceles triangles have two equal angles - so if one of these is known, it can be doubled and the total taken from 180° to give the third angle.	**Resources** None

Divide the class into mixed-ability pairs. The pairs work out the size of the third angle of a triangle from the given sum of the two known angles. After discussing the problem, they raise their hands to answer.

If this is the sum of two angles in a triangle, what is the third angle?

1.	140°	3.	95°	5.	138°	7.	112°
2.	120°	4.	115°	6.	83°	8.	146°

If this is the size of the equal angles in an isosceles triangle, what is the third angle? (One child of the pair doubles the given angle; the other calculates the third angle.)

9.	50°	11.	45°	13.	56°	15.	61°
10.	65°	12.	32°	14.	27°	16.	34°

Answers

1.	40°	9.	80°
2.	60°	10.	50°
3.	85°	11.	90°
4.	65°	12.	116°
5.	42°	13.	68°
6	97°	14.	126°
7.	68°	15.	58°
8.	34°	16.	112°

Get the point

Learning objective Use coordinates in the first quadrant to draw, locate and complete shapes. **Type of starter** Read **Mental strategy** In coordinates, across references are given before up references.	**Resources** A board or flipchart showing a 10 × 10 square grid

Make sure the grid is labelled 0 to 10 on each axis. Note: lines should be labelled, not spaces.

Name some simple 2D shapes and ask the children to give you the grid references needed to construct them on the grid. Use shapes, such as: square; rectangle; triangle; rhombus; parallelogram; kite; trapezium; hexagon.

No set answers

73 Ten-second problems

Resources
None

Learning objective
Solve multi-step problems, and problems involving fractions, decimals and percentages; choose and use appropriate calculation strategies at each stage.

Type of starter
Rehearse

Answers
1. £2.90
2. 33
3. 800g
4. 18 minutes
5. £4.00
6. 120
7. 25
8. 5.20
9. 84
10. 89
11. 19
12. 775ml

Read out each question twice. Give the children ten seconds to work out the answer, then ask them to raise a hand if they know it.

1. I buy two books. One costs £1.30 and the other £1.60. How much do they cost together?
2. I am thinking of a number that is 58 less than 91. What is my number?
3. From a 5kg bag of potatoes, 4200g are left. How many grams of potatoes have been used?
4. I left home at 1.30 to walk to my friend's house. I got there at 1.48. How long did it take me?
5. How much change would I have from £10.00 if I spent £3.50 one day and £2.50 the next day?
6. Find the difference between 410 and 290.
7. What is the sum of the odd numbers from 1 to 9 (inclusive)?
8. My favourite TV programme is on for 50 minutes. It begins at 4.30. At what time does it finish?
9. My game scores were 22, 44 and 18. What was my total score?
10. My friend's game scores were 36, 32 and 21. What was his total score?
11. Take 9 squared from 10 squared.
12. If you pour 225ml of water from a litre bottle into a glass, how much water is left in the bottle?

74 Going up

Learning objective
Calculate mentally with integers and decimals: U.t ± U.t, TU × U, TU ÷ U, U.t × U, U.t ÷ U.

Type of starter
Recall

Resources
None

How many more to 50 from...?

1. 38
2. 11
3. 27
4. 6
5. 35

How many more to 100 from...?

11. 71
12. 27
13. 64
14. 39
15. 85

How many more to 5 from...?

6. 4.2
7. 1.9
8. 0.3
9. 3.6
10. 2.4

How many more to 10 from...?

16. 8.75
17. 5.85
18. 7.64
19. 1.07
20. 6.49

Answers

1.	12	11.	29
2.	39	12.	73
3.	23	13.	36
4.	44	14.	61
5.	15	15.	15
6.	0.8	16.	1.25
7.	3.1	17.	4.15
8.	4.7	18.	2.36
9.	1.4	19.	8.93
10.	2.6	20.	3.51

75 Going up with money

Learning objective
Calculate mentally with integers and decimals: U.t ± U.t, TU × U, TU ÷ U, U.t × U, U.t ÷ U.

Type of starter
Recall

Resources
None

How much more to £1.00 from...?

1. 56p
2. 29p
3. 64p
4. 17p
5. 73p

How much more to £10.00 from...?

6. £5.50
7. £8.72
8 £2.35
9. £6.81
10. £1.49

How much more to £5.00 from...?

11. £3.80
12. £1.40
13. £4.10
14. £2.65
15. £3.15

How much more to £20.00 from...?

16. £16.50
17. £12.50
18. £15.75
19. £11.2
20. £7.50

Answers

1.	44p	11.	£1.20
2.	71p	12.	£3.60
3.	36p	13.	90p
4.	83p	14.	£2.35
5.	27p	15.	£1.85
6.	£4.50	16.	£3.50
7.	£1.28	17.	£7.50
8.	£7.65	18.	£4.25
9.	£3.19	19.	£8.75
10.	£8.51	20.	£12.50

76 Units change

Resources	Learning objective
A board or flipchart	Select and use standard metric units of measure and convert between units using decimals to two places.
	Type of starter
	Rehearse

Answers

1. 1.35km
2. 2.875kg
3. 1.055l
4. 3.682m
5. 4kg
6. 1.5l
7. 16.5cm
8. 1.65m
9. 4.392km
10. 5.75m
11. 1500g
12. 2250ml
13. 512.3cm or 5123mm
14. 10,250m
15. 34mm
16. 150cm or 1500mm
17. 1750ml
18. 2250m
19. 2485g
20. 45mm

Write these incomplete conversions on the board or flipchart:

1250m = ... km   185mm = ... cm   2250g = ... kg   3682ml = ... l

Ask for answers and an explanation of the method used. Remind the children that the zero has no place value (eg 1.25km = 1.250km).

Compare with money: £1.50 = £1 + 50p = £1.5 = £1½ .

Ask them to convert:

1. 1350m to km
2. 2875g to kg
3. 1055ml to l
4. 3682mm to m
5. 4000g to kg
6. 1500ml to l
7. 165mm to cm
8. 1650mm to m
9. 4392m to km
10. 575cm to m

Now, ask them to convert the following to a smaller unit. Remind them that the zero will now have a place value, since it is before the decimal point (eg 1.5kg = 1500g).

11. 1.5kg
12. 2.25l
13. 5.123m
14. 10.25km
15. 3.4cm
16. $1^1/_2$m
17. $1^3/_4$l
18. $2^1/_4$km
19. 2.485kg
20. $4^1/_2$cm

77 Perimeters and areas

Learning objective
Calculate the perimeter and area of rectilinear shapes.

Type of starter
Rehearse

Resources
A board or flipchart

Write on the board or flipchart:

rectangle 8cm × 4cm perimeter = ______ cm area = ______ cm^2

Ask the children to give their answers and describe the methods they used.

Now, ask them to find the following areas and perimeters. They should raise a hand to offer their answer.

1. Find the area of a square with sides 9cm.
2. Find the perimeter of a square with sides 9cm.
3. If the area of a rectangle is $24cm^2$ and the length is 8cm, what is the width?
4. What is the area of a rectangle with sides 10.5cm and 6cm?
5. What is the perimeter of a rectangle with sides 8.5cm and 4.5cm?
6. If the perimeter of a regular hexagon is 42cm, how long is each side?
7. An equilateral triangle has sides that measure 12cm. What is its perimeter?
8. What is the perimeter of a square that has an area of $64cm^2$?
9. Find the perimeter of a rectangle that has an area of $45cm^2$ and a short side that measures 5cm.
10. A regular octagon has sides that measure $5^1/_2$cm. What is its perimeter?
11. The perimeter of an isosceles triangle is 17cm. Find the length of each of the two equal sides if the third side measures 5cm.
12. A regular decagon has sides that measure 4.75cm. What is its perimeter?

Answers

1. $81cm^2$
2. 36cm
3. 3cm
4. $63cm^2$
5. 26cm
6. 7cm
7. 36cm
8. 32cm
9. 28cm
10. 44cm
11. 6cm
12. 47.5cm

78 Island shapes

Learning objective
Estimate the area of an irregular shape by counting squares.

Type of starter
Reason

Mental strategy
There are a number of possible methods that can be used but the following is the most frequently accepted. Count whole squares first. Then count squares that are a half or more than half filled. Ignore squares that are less than half filled.

Resources
A board or flipchart showing a large grid of squares

Draw a selection of small, irregular (island) shapes on the grid of squares on the board or flipchart. Ask the children to find the area of these shapes by counting squares.

In the process, discuss possible strategies that could be used. For example, dot squares as they are counted so they are not counted twice.

Stress to the children that the answers to problems of this sort will be, by their nature, approximate.

No set answers

BLOCK E

BLOCK E

Unit 1

100 Mental Maths Starters				100 Maths Lessons		
Page	Objective	Activity title	Starter type	Unit	Lesson	Page
72	Solve multi-step problems, and problems involving fractions, decimals and percentages; choose and use appropriate calculation strategies at each stage.	79 Five-second word problems	Rehearse	1	4	174
73	Solve multi-step problems, and problems involving fractions, decimals and percentages; choose and use appropriate calculation strategies at each stage.	80 Ten-second word problems	Rehearse	1	11	179
73	Use knowledge of place value and multiplication facts to 10 × 10 to derive related multiplication facts involving decimals.	81 Times tens	Refine	1	9	177
74	Use knowledge of place value and multiplication facts to 10 × 10 to derive related division facts involving decimals.	82 Divided by tens	Refine	1	10	178
74	Express a larger whole number as a fraction of a smaller one.	83 Pizza party	Rehearse	1	13	180
75	Order a set of fractions by converting them to fractions with a common denominator.	84 Happy families	Rehearse	1	14	181
75	Express a quotient as a fraction or decimal (eg $67 \div 5 = 13.4$ or $13^2/_5$).	85 Three ways	Rehearse	1	12	180
76	Solve problems involving direct proportion by scaling quantities up or down.	86 Quick-fire ratios	Reason	1	15	182

Unit 2

100 Mental Maths Starters				100 Maths Lessons		
Page	Objective	Activity title	Starter type	Unit	Lesson	Page
76	Explain reasoning and conclusions, using words, symbols or diagrams as appropriate.	87 Sequence teasers	Reason	2	5	192
77	Simplify fractions by cancelling common factors.	88 Mixed number parts	Read	2	7	194
77	Simplify fractions by cancelling common factors.	89 Cancel down	Rehearse	2	8	195
78	Simplify fractions by cancelling common factors.	90 Bits of mixed numbers	Read	2	12	198

Unit 2 ...continued

100 Mental Maths Starters				100 Maths Lessons		
Page	**Objective**	**Activity title**	**Starter type**	**Unit**	**Lesson**	**Page**
78	Express one quantity as a percentage of another; find equivalent percentages, decimals and fractions.	91 Percentage parts	Rehearse	2	11	197
79	Express one quantity as a percentage of another; find equivalent percentages, decimals and fractions.	92 Money percentages	Rehearse	2	13	198
79	Find fractions and percentages of whole-number quantities.	93 Pocket money	Rehearse	2	14	199
80	Relate fractions to multiplication and division.	94 Close relations	Refine	2	15	200

Unit 3

100 Mental Maths Starters				100 Maths Lessons		
Page	**Objective**	**Activity title**	**Starter type**	**Unit**	**Lesson**	**Page**
81	Solve multi-step problems, and problems involving fractions, decimals and percentages; choose and use appropriate calculation strategies at each stage.	95 Percentage discounts	Rehearse	3	3	207
82	Solve multi-step problems, and problems involving fractions, decimals and percentages; choose and use appropriate calculation strategies at each stage.	96 10% off	Rehearse	3	5	209
83	Use knowledge of place value and multiplication facts to 10 × 10 to derive related multiplication and division facts involving decimals (eg 0.8 × 7, 4.8 ÷ 6).	97 Tenths and hundredths	Refine	3	6	210
84	Order a set of fractions by converting them to fractions with a common denominator.	98 Bigger or smaller?	Rehearse	3	13	215
84	Find equivalent percentages, decimals and fractions.	99 Make the set	Rehearse	3	11	213
85	Find equivalent percentages, decimals and fractions.	100 Change it!	Rehearse	3	12	214
86	Relate fractions to multiplication and division; find fractions and percentages of whole-number quantities.	101 Five-second percentages	Recall	3	14	215
87	Solve problems involving direct proportion by scaling quantities up or down.	102 Biscuit tin	Rehearse	3	15	216

79 Five-second word problems

Resources	Learning objective
None	Solve multi-step problems, and problems involving fractions, decimals and percentages; choose and use appropriate calculation strategies at each stage. **Type of starter** Rehearse

Answers

1. £3.60
2. 22p
3. 14 pencils
4. 186
5. 8 tents
6. 5 hours
7. £5.00
8. £43.96
9. 18cm
10. 8.10
11. 175g
12. 7 litres
13. 15
14. 16
15. 300

Read each question twice. Give the children five seconds to work out the answer, then ask them to raise a hand if they know it.

1. One orange costs 60p. How much for six?
2. Four apples cost 88p. How much for one?
3. 112 pencil crayons were put back into eight packets after being sharpened. How many pencils are in each packet?
4. Which number that is exactly divisible by 6 is nearest to 184?
5. If each tent can sleep four children, how many tents will be needed for 30 children?
6. A worker is paid £3.80 per hour. How many hours must he work to earn £19.00?
7. How much for four ice creams if each costs £1.25?
8. I bought four CDs at £10.99 each. How much did I spend?
9. A square picture frame has a perimeter of 72cm. How long was each side?
10. My favourite TV programme lasts for 55 minutes. If it starts at 7.15, at what time does it end?
11. I used 250g of butter when I made a cake. How much was left in the 425g tub?
12. The car can travel for 40 miles on 5 litres of petrol. How many litres will be needed for 56 miles?
13. What is the quotient of 135 and 9?
14. What is the average of 22, 9 and 17?
15. Find the product of 12 and 25.

80 Ten-second word problems

Learning objective	Resources
Learning objective Solve multi-step problems, and problems involving fractions, decimals and percentages; choose and use appropriate calculation strategies at each stage. **Type of starter** Rehearse	**Resources** None

Read out each question twice. Give the children ten seconds to work out the answer, then ask them to raise a hand if they know it.

1. The time is 12.35, but the clock is showing 12.28. How many minutes slow is the clock?
2. An apple costs 18p and a banana 17p. How much are they altogether?
3. My friend had collected 37 cards. I had only 18. How many more did my friend have?
4. The difference between two numbers is 55. One of the numbers is 21. What is the other number?
5. What number must be added to 120 to give an answer of 250?
6. I spent £2.50 in one shop and £1.45 in another. How much did I have left from £5?
7. Add 4.6 to 3.9.
8. If you cut 90cm from a piece of wood that measures $2\frac{1}{2}$ metres, what length remains?
9. Take 5 squared from 6 squared.
10. Find the sum of all even numbers up to (and including) 10.
11. Find the difference between 20 and the total of 3, 5 and 7.
12. A 2-litre bottle has $1\frac{1}{4}$ litres of liquid remaining. How many millilitres have gone?

Answers

1. 7 minutes
2. 35p
3. 19 cards
4. 76
5. 130
6. £1.05
7. 8.5
8. 1m 60cm, 1.6m or 160cm
9. 11
10. 30
11. 5
12. 750ml

81 Times tens

Learning objective	Resources
Learning objective Use knowledge of place value and multiplication facts to 10 × 10 to derive related multiplication facts involving decimals. **Type of starter** Refine **Mental strategy** Remember, digits move to the left when multiplying: one place for ×10; two places for ×100; three places for ×1000.	**Resources** A board or flipchart

Write the following number statements on the board or flipchart. Ask the children to answer with the missing numbers (10, 100 or 1000).

1.	28.7 × ? = 287	7.	3.25 × ? = 325
2.	4.38 × ? = 43.8	8.	2.71 × ? = 2710
3.	1.93 × ? = 193	9.	0.8 × ? = 8
4.	0.35 × ? = 35	10.	2.79 × ? = 27.9
5.	0.83 × ? = 830	11.	43.7 × ? = 4370
6.	5.46 × ? = 5460	12.	4.57 × ? = 4570

Answers

1.	10	7.	100
2.	10	8.	1000
3.	100	9.	10
4.	100	10.	10
5.	1000	11.	100
6.	1000	12.	1000

Divided by tens

Resources
A board or flipchart

Learning objective
Use knowledge of place value and multiplication facts to 10 × 10 to derive related division facts involving decimals.

Type of starter
Refine

Mental strategy
Remember, digits will move to the right when dividing: one place for ÷10; two places for ÷100; three places for ÷1000.

Answers

1.	10	7.	100
2.	100	8.	10
3.	10	9.	1000
4.	1000	10.	10
5.	100	11.	1000
6.	10	12.	100

Write the following number statements on the board or flipchart. Ask the children to answer with the missing numbers (10, 100 or 1000).

1. 5.7 ÷ ? = 0.57
2. 1.8 ÷ ? = 0.018
3. 6 ÷ ? = 0.6
4. 39.4 ÷ ? = 0.0394
5. 472 ÷ ? = 4.72
6. 4.17 ÷ ? = 0.417
7. 31.6 ÷ ? = 0.316
8. 7.65 ÷ ? = 0.765
9. 71.5 ÷ ? = 0.0715
10. 27.6 ÷ ? = 2.76
11. 18 ÷ ? = 0.018
12. 28.6 ÷ ? = 0.286

Pizza party

Resources
None

Learning objective
Express a larger whole number as a fraction of a smaller one.

Type of starter
Rehearse

Mental strategy
Remember to divide the denominator into the numerator. The number of times it goes becomes a whole number, the remainder is left as a fraction.

Answers

1. $^{6}/_{5}$ or $1^{1}/_{5}$
2. $^{9}/_{6}$ or $1^{3}/_{6}$ (or $1^{1}/_{2}$)
3. $^{7}/_{4}$ or $1\frac{3}{4}$
4. $^{11}/_{8}$ or $1^{3}/_{8}$
5. $^{8}/_{5}$ or $1^{3}/_{5}$
6. $^{13}/_{4}$ or $3\frac{1}{4}$
7. $^{20}/_{8}$ or $2^{4}/_{8}$ (or $2^{1}/_{2}$)
8. $^{15}/_{6}$ or $2^{3}/_{6}$ (or $2^{1}/_{2}$)
9. $^{14}/_{5}$ or $2^{4}/_{5}$
10. $^{19}/_{6}$ or $3^{1}/_{6}$
11. $^{23}/_{10}$ or $2^{3}/_{10}$
12. $^{41}/_{10}$ or $4\ ^{1}/_{10}$

Ask the children to give the following amounts of pizza in two different ways. Work through several simple examples first. For example, 9 slices of a 5-slice pizza can be expressed as $^{9}/_{5}$ or $1^{4}/_{5}$ pizzas.

1. 6 slices of a 5-slice pizza.
2. 9 slices of a 6-slice pizza.
3. 7 slices of a 4-slice pizza.
4. 11 slices of an 8-slice pizza.
5. 8 slices of a 5-slice pizza.
6. 13 slices of a 4-slice pizza.
7. 20 slices of an 8-slice pizza.
8. 15 slices of a 6-slice pizza.
9. 14 slices of a 5-slice pizza.
10. 19 slices of a 6-slice pizza.
11. 23 slices of a 10-slice pizza.
12. 41 slices of 10-slice pizza.

84 Happy families

Learning objective
Order a set of fractions by converting them to fractions with a common denominator.

Type of starter
Rehearse

Mental strategy
Remember, when converting fractions, the numerator and the denominator must be multiplied by the same number.

Resources
Clothes line or piece of string; clothes pegs; set of fraction cards:
(a) $\frac{1}{2}$, $\frac{2}{3}$, $\frac{5}{8}$, $\frac{3}{4}$, $\frac{3}{8}$, $\frac{11}{12}$;
(b) $\frac{12}{24}$, $\frac{16}{24}$, $\frac{20}{24}$, $\frac{15}{24}$, $\frac{9}{24}$, $\frac{22}{24}$

Show the children the set of cards (a). Tell them that the fractions have to be pegged on the clothes line or string in order, starting with the smallest.

Discuss how to find the common denominator that can be used to convert all into the same type of fraction (24ths). Ask the children to convert these fractions into 24ths and, once this has been done, to peg fraction cards (b) on the line in the correct order.

Answers
The correct order is:
$\frac{3}{8}$ ($\frac{9}{24}$), $\frac{1}{2}$ ($\frac{12}{24}$), $\frac{3}{4}$ ($\frac{15}{24}$), $\frac{2}{3}$ ($\frac{16}{24}$), $\frac{5}{6}$ ($\frac{20}{24}$), $\frac{11}{12}$ ($\frac{22}{24}$).

85 Three ways

Learning objective
Express a quotient as a fraction or decimal (eg 67 ÷ 5 = 13.4 or $13\frac{2}{5}$).

Type of starter
Rehearse

Resources
A board or flipchart; one calculator per child, pair or small group

Explain to the children that the answer to a division problem that produces a remainder can be written in three different ways. Show them an example on the board or flipchart: 17 ÷ 4 = 4 r1, $4\frac{1}{4}$ or 4.25.

Ask the children to give the following quotients in these three different ways. Encourage them to give the decimal answer to two decimal places. They should use the calculator to check the decimal alternative.

1. 9 ÷ 2
2. 15 ÷ 2
3. 7 ÷ 3
4. 11 ÷ 4
5. 14 ÷ 5
6. 19 ÷ 3
7. 21 ÷ 5
8. 30 ÷ 4
9. 32 ÷ 3
10. 20 ÷ 6
11. 19 ÷ 7
12. 25 ÷ 6
13. 29 ÷ 8
14. 30 ÷ 7
15. 49 ÷ 8
16. 32 ÷ 9

Answers
1. 4 r1, $4\frac{1}{2}$, 4.5
2. 7 r1, $7\frac{1}{2}$, 7.5
3. 2 r1, $2\frac{1}{3}$, 2.33
4. 2 r3, $2\frac{3}{4}$, 2.75
5. 2 r4, $2\frac{4}{5}$, 2.8
6. 6 r1, $6\frac{1}{3}$, 6.33
7. 4 r1, $4\frac{1}{5}$, 4.2
8. 7 r2, $7\frac{2}{4} = 7\frac{1}{2}$, 7.5
9. 10 r2, $10\frac{2}{3}$, 10.67
10. 3 r2, $3\frac{2}{6} = 3\frac{1}{3}$, 3.33
11. 2 r5, $2\frac{5}{7}$, 2.71
12. 4 r1, $4\frac{1}{6}$, 4.17
13. 3 r5, $3\frac{5}{8}$, 3.63
14. 4 r2, $4\frac{2}{7}$, 4.29
15. 6 r1, $6\frac{1}{8}$, 6.13
16. 3 r5, $3\frac{5}{9}$, 3.56

86 Quick-fire ratios

Resources
A board or flipchart

Learning objective
Solve problems involving direct proportion by scaling quantities up or down.

Type of starter
Reason

Answers

1-5. Any numbers in the given ratio.
6. 4
7. 6
8. 6
9. 5
10. 3

Write the following on the board or flipchart: ratio of 3 to 1; 3:1.

Ask for two numbers that have the same ratio (eg 9 and 3 or 18 and 6).

Ask the children to give two numbers with the given ratio and to explain how they are calculating their answers.

1. 2:1
2. 1:4
3. 3:2
4. 5:1
5. 2:4

What is the total number of parts when the ratio is...

6. 3:1
7. 2:4
8. 1:5
9. 3:2
10. 1:2

Unit 2

87 Sequence teasers

Resources
A board or flipchart; paper and pencils for each pair

Learning objective
Explain reasoning and conclusions, using words, symbols or diagrams as appropriate.

Type of starter
Reason

No set answers

Write the following incomplete sequences on the board or flipchart:

2, 5, 4, 7, 6, 9, 8, ?, ?

100, 50, 52, 26, 28, 14, 16, ?, ?

For each sequence, ask for the next two numbers (11, 10; 8, 10) and an explanation of the sequence (+3, -1; ÷2, +2).

Divide the class into mixed-ability pairs. The children have two minutes to build a sequence ending in two unknown terms (as above).

Invite pairs of children to write their sequences on the board or flipchart for the other children to solve.

88 Mixed number parts

Learning objective Simplify fractions by cancelling common factors. **Type of starter** Read **Mental strategy** Remember, one whole is the same as four quarters, eight eighths, ten tenths, etc.	**Resources** None

Ask: *How many halves in one whole? How many fifths, thirds, sevenths?* Ask quick-fire questions. Children should raise a hand to answer. How many...?

1. halves in $1\frac{1}{2}$
2. halves in 2
3. halves in $3\frac{1}{2}$
4. quarters in 2
5. quarters in $3\frac{1}{4}$
6. quarters in $5\frac{3}{4}$
7. fifths in 1
8. fifths in 3
9. fifths in $2\frac{2}{5}$
10. tenths in 4
11. tenths in $4\frac{7}{10}$
12. eighths in $3\frac{7}{8}$
13. eighths in $1\frac{3}{4}$
14. sevenths in $2\frac{3}{7}$
15. thirds in $5\frac{1}{3}$
16. sixths in $3\frac{1}{3}$
17. sixths in $1\frac{5}{6}$
18. tenths in $3\frac{1}{10}$
19. halves in $8\frac{1}{2}$
20. sevenths in $3\frac{1}{7}$
21. twelfths in $2\frac{7}{12}$
22. quarters in $10\frac{1}{2}$
23. thirds in $2\frac{2}{3}$
24. halves in $7\frac{1}{2}$
25. thirds in $6\frac{1}{3}$
26. sixths in $2\frac{1}{2}$

Answers

1.	3	14.	17
2.	4	15.	16
3.	7	16.	20
4.	8	17.	11
5.	13	18.	31
6.	23	19.	17
7.	5	20.	22
8.	15	21.	31
9.	12	22.	42
10.	40	23.	8
11.	47	24.	15
12.	31	25.	19
13.	14	26.	15

89 Cancel down

Learning objective Simplify fractions by cancelling common factors. **Type of starter** Rehearse **Mental strategy** The factor must be common to both the denominator and the numerator, ie both parts of the fraction being considered. Look for the highest common factor each time, otherwise the fraction may need to be cancelled down several times.	**Resources** A board or flipchart

Ask the children to cancel these fractions down into their lowest terms by using the highest common factor possible each time. Ask them to state the highest common factor first when answering.

1. $\frac{5}{10}$
2. $\frac{6}{9}$
3. $\frac{2}{4}$
4. $\frac{2}{10}$
5. $\frac{4}{8}$
6. $\frac{10}{15}$
7. $\frac{16}{20}$
8. $\frac{6}{10}$
9. $\frac{7}{21}$
10. $\frac{9}{36}$
11. $\frac{8}{10}$
12. $\frac{25}{30}$

Answers

1.	(5) $\frac{1}{2}$	7.	(4) $\frac{4}{5}$
2.	(3) $\frac{2}{3}$	8.	(2) $\frac{3}{5}$
3.	(2) $\frac{1}{2}$	9.	(7) $\frac{1}{3}$
4.	(2) $\frac{1}{5}$	10.	(9) $\frac{1}{4}$
5.	(4) $\frac{1}{2}$	11.	(2) $\frac{4}{5}$
6.	(5) $\frac{2}{3}$	12.	(5) $\frac{5}{6}$

90 Bits of mixed numbers

Resources
A set of numeral cards 1–10 (from photocopiable page 95) for each pair

Learning objective
Simplify fractions by cancelling common factors.

Type of starter
Read

Answers

1. 3
2. 10
3. 13
4. 17
5. 17
6. 13
7. 8
8. 11
9. 19
10. 12
11. 37
12. 12
13. 13
14. 14
15. 18

Divide the class into mixed-ability pairs. When they agree on the answer to a question, each pair holds up the appropriate card(s).

How many...

1. halves are there in $1\frac{1}{2}$?
2. fifths are there in 2 whole ones?
3. quarters are there in $3\frac{1}{4}$?
4. eighths are there in $2\frac{1}{3}$?
5. tenths are there in $1\frac{7}{10}$?
6. halves are there in $6\frac{1}{2}$?
7. thirds are there in $2\frac{2}{3}$?
8. quarters are there in $2\frac{3}{4}$?
9. fifths are there in $3\frac{4}{5}$?
10. sevenths are there in $1\frac{5}{7}$?
11. tenths are there in $3\frac{7}{10}$?
12. eighths are there in $1\frac{1}{2}$?
13. thirds are there in $4\frac{1}{3}$?
14. sixths are there in $2\frac{1}{3}$?
15. quarters are there in $4\frac{1}{2}$?

91 Percentage parts

Resources
Individual whiteboards, marker pens and dusters, or paper and pencils, and a calculator for each child

Learning objective
Express one quantity as a percentage of another; find equivalent percentages, decimals and fractions.

Type of starter
Rehearse

Mental strategy
Follow these rules: work out the quantity as a fraction of the other (make sure you are using the same units for both items); find the equivalent fraction with the denominator 100; name the percentage.

Answers

1. 50%
2. 25%
3. 75%
4. 70%
5. 20%
6. 30%
7. 90%
8. 20%
9. 25%
10. 16%
11. 15%
12. 2%

Remind the children that 'per cent' means 'out of a hundred', so $50\% = \frac{50}{100} = \frac{1}{2}$.

Children should express the first quantity as a percentage of the second. Working out may be necessary. The last few answers may need to be checked using a calculator. Some revision of metric units may be needed.

1. 500g as a percentage of 1 kilogram
2. 250ml as a percentage of 1 litre
3. 750kg as a percentage of 1 tonne
4. 70cm as a percentage of 1 metre
5. 200m as a percentage of 1 kilometre
6. 300g as a percentage of 1 kilogram
7. 900ml as a percentage of 1 litre
8. 200kg as a percentage of 1 tonne
9. 50cm as a percentage of 2 metres
10. 800m as a percentage of 5 kilometres
11. 60cm as a percentage of 4 metres
12. 80g as a percentage of 4 kilograms

92 Money percentages

Learning objective
Express one quantity as a percentage of another; find equivalent percentages, decimals and fractions.

Type of starter
Rehearse

Mental strategy
Remember, 'per cent' means 'out of a hundred', so 50% = $\frac{50}{100} = \frac{1}{2}$.

Resources
None

Ask: *What is 25%?* ($\frac{25}{100} = \frac{1}{4}$) *What is 75%?* ($\frac{75}{100} = \frac{3}{4}$)
What is 10%? ($\frac{10}{100} = \frac{1}{10}$) *What is 20%?* ($\frac{20}{100} = \frac{2}{10} = \frac{1}{5}$)

1. 50% of £10	11. 25% of £12.00	21. 10% of £60
2 50% of £8.60	12. 25% of £22.00	22. 40% of £60
3. 50% of £3.40	13. 25% of £800	23. 10% of £3.50
4. 50% of £16.50	14. 25% of £2.80	24. 60% of £3.50
5. 50% of £11.00	15. 25% of £18.40	25. 10% of £180
6. 10% of £3.00	16. 75% of £8.00	26. 20% of £180
7. 10% of 80p	17. 75% of £24.00	27. 80% of £180
8. 10% of £9.60	18. 75% of £2.80	28. 25% of £12.80
9. 10% of £170	19. 75% of £4000	29. 50% of £400
10. 10% of £255	20. 75% of £50	30. 50% of £1.80

Answers

1. £5.00	16. £6.00
2. £4.30	17. £18.00
3. £1.70	18. £2.10
4. £8.25	19. £3000
5. £5.50	20. £37.50
6. 30p	21. £6.00
7. 8p	22. £24.00
8. 96p	23. 35p
9. £17.00	24. £2.10
10. £25.50	25. £18.00
11. £3.00	26. £36.00
12. £5.50	27. £144.00
13. £200	28. £3.20
14. 70p	29. £200.00
15. £4.60	30. 90p

93 Pocket money

Learning objective
Find fractions and percentages of whole-number quantities.

Type of starter
Rehearse

Mental strategy
When finding a fraction of an amount – divide by the denominator, then multiply by the numerator.

Resources
None

Tell the children that each of the following 12 children owes a fraction of their pocket money to their Mum. Ask them to calculate how much each child owes.

1. $\frac{1}{2}$ of £1	7. $\frac{4}{10}$ of £1.70
2. $\frac{1}{4}$ of £2	8. $\frac{5}{12}$ of £2.40
3. $\frac{3}{4}$ of £6	9. $\frac{2}{25}$ of £5
4. $\frac{2}{5}$ of £5	10. $\frac{7}{9}$ of £4.50
5. $\frac{3}{8}$ of £3.20	11. $\frac{4}{5}$ of £4
6. $\frac{2}{7}$ of £2.80	12. $\frac{9}{10}$ of £8

Answers

1. 50p	7. 68p
2. 50p	8. £1
3. £4.50	9. 40p
4. £2	10. £3.50
5. £1.20	11. £3.20
6. 80p	12. £7.20

94 Close relations

Resources
A board or flipchart

Learning objective
Relate fractions to multiplication and division.

Type of starter
Refine

Mental strategy
You need to know your tables thoroughly to carry out this type of activity.

Answers

$10 \div 2 = \frac{1}{2}$ of $10 = 10 \times \frac{1}{2}$,

$9 \div 3 = \frac{1}{3}$ of $9 = 9 \times \frac{1}{3}$,

$16 \div 4 = \frac{1}{4}$ of $16 = 16 \times \frac{1}{4}$,

$15 \div 5 = \frac{1}{5}$ of $15 = 15 \times \frac{1}{5}$,

$21 \div 7 = \frac{1}{7}$ of $21 = 21 \times \frac{1}{7}$,

$12 \div 6 = \frac{1}{6}$ of $12 = 12 \times \frac{1}{6}$,

$24 \div 8 = \frac{1}{8}$ of $24 = 24 \times \frac{1}{8}$,

$28 \div 4 = \frac{1}{4}$ of $28 = 28 \times \frac{1}{4}$

Tell the children the purpose of this activity is to show how fractions, multiplication and division are related to each other. Show them a simple example on the board or flipchart: $6 \div 3 = \frac{1}{3}$ of $6 = 6 \times \frac{1}{3}$.

Put the following three boxes of information on the board or flipchart. Ask children to choose one item from each box to make a complete related number statement, like the one given in the example.

Box A	Box B	Box C
$10 \div 2$	$\frac{1}{8}$ of 24	$21 \times \frac{1}{7}$
$24 \div 8$	$\frac{1}{2}$ of 10	$9 \times \frac{1}{3}$
$15 \div 5$	$\frac{1}{5}$ of 15	$28 \times \frac{1}{4}$
$12 \div 6$	$\frac{1}{3}$ of 9	$10 \times \frac{1}{2}$
$9 \div 3$	$\frac{1}{4}$ of 28	$24 \times \frac{1}{8}$
$21 \div 7$	$\frac{1}{4}$ of 16	$16 \times \frac{1}{4}$
$28 \div 4$	$\frac{1}{6}$ of 12	$12 \times \frac{1}{6}$
$16 \div 4$	$\frac{1}{7}$ of 21	$15 \times \frac{1}{5}$

95 Percentage discounts

Learning objective
Solve multi-step problems, and problems involving fractions, decimals and percentages; choose and use appropriate calculation strategies at each stage.

Type of starter
Rehearse

Resources
None

There is a 10% discount in a sale.

How much is saved?

1. 10% of £4.00
2. 10% of £9.00
3. 10% of £5.50
4. 10% of £18.00
5. 10% of £23.00
6. 10% of £120.00

What will be the new prices when 10% is taken off these prices?

7. £5.00
8. £12.00
9. £2.00
10. £25.00
11. £100.00
12. £80.00

What will be the new prices when 20% (10% × 2) is taken off these prices?

13. £5.00
14. £50.00
15. £15.00
16. £600.00
17. £8.00
18. £100.00
19. £10.00
20. £300.00

Answers
1. 40p
2. 90p
3. 55p
4. £1.80
5. £2.30
6. £12.00
7. £4.50
8. £10.80
9. £1.80
10. £22.50
11. £90.00
12. £72.00
13. £4.00
14. £40.00
15. £12.00
16. £480.00
17. £6.40
18. £80.00
19. £8.00
20. £240.00

96 10% off

Resources
None

Learning objective
Solve multi-step problems, and problems involving fractions, decimals and percentages; choose and use appropriate calculation strategies at each stage.

Type of starter
Rehearse

Answers

1. 20p
2. £2.00
3. 35p
4. £3.00
5. 12p
6. £1.70
7. £1.75
8. £15.00
9. £200.00
10 79p
11. £3.60
12 £36.00
13. £67.50
14. £270.00
15. £4500.00
16. £1800.00
17. £7200.00
18. £5850.00
19. £8.10
20. £9.45

There is a 10% discount in a sale.

How much is saved on an item originally priced...?

1. £2.00
2. £20.00
3. £3.50
4. £30.00
5. £1.20
6. £17.00
7. £17.50
8. £150.00
9. £2000.00
10. £7.90

What will be the new prices when 10% is taken off these prices?

11. £4.00
12. £40.00
13 £75.00
14. £300.00
15. £5000.00
16. £2000.00
17. £8000.00
18. £6500.00
19. £9.00
20. £10.50

97 Tenths and hundredths

Learning objective
Use knowledge of place value and multiplication facts to 10 × 10 to derive related multiplication and division facts involving decimals (eg 0.8 × 7, 4.8 ÷ 6).

Type of starter
Refine

Resources
A board or flipchart; calculators

Tell the children these questions are based on multiplying and dividing by one-tenth (0.1) and one-hundredth (0.01). Discuss with children multiplying and dividing decimals by 10 and 100 first, then establish rules for carrying out the same process with 0.1 and 0.01. Calculators may be needed to help with the last section.

Complete these statements.

1. 6.2 × 0.1 = ...
2. 8.4 × 0.1 = ...
3. 2.1 × 0.01 = ...
4. 54.9 × 0.01 = ...
5. 0.93 ÷ 0.01 = ...
6. 8.25 ÷ 0.1 = ...
7. 10 ÷ 0.01 = ...
8. 436 ÷ 0.1 = ...

Fill in the missing number in these statements.

9. 5.2 × ? = 0.52
10. 7.53 × ? = 0.0753
11. 4.3 × ? = 0.043
12. 123 × ? = 1.23
13. 6.8 ÷ ? = 68
14. 0.78 ÷ ? = 78
15. 15.2 ÷ ? = 152
16. 9.62 ÷ ? = 962

Say whether the following statements are True or False.

17. 0.4 ÷ 10 = 400 × 0.01
18. 1.7 × 0.1 = 0.017 ÷ 0.1
19. 174 ÷ 0.1 = 174000 × 0.01
20. 14.71 × 0.1 = 1.471 × 10

Answers

1. 0.62
2. 0.84
3. 0.021
4. 0.549
5. 93
6. 82.5
7. 1000
8. 4360
9. 0.1
10. 0.01
11. 0.01
12. 0.01
13. 0.1
14. 0.01
15. 0.1
16. 0.01
17. False
18. True
19. True
20. False

98 Bigger or smaller?

Resources
A board or flipchart

Learning objective
Order a set of fractions by converting them to fractions with a common denominator.

Type of starter
Rehearse

Mental strategy
Look for the lowest common multiple each time.

When converting fractions, make sure the denominator and the numerator are multiplied by the same number.

Answers

1. $\frac{3}{5} < \frac{2}{3}$ (15)
2. $\frac{2}{3} < \frac{3}{4}$ (12)
3. $\frac{3}{4} < \frac{4}{5}$ (20)
4. $\frac{5}{6} > \frac{7}{9}$ (18)
5. $\frac{3}{4} > \frac{5}{7}$ (28)
6. $\frac{5}{12} < \frac{3}{7}$ (84)
7. $\frac{4}{5} > \frac{7}{9}$ (45)
8. $\frac{9}{10} > \frac{4}{5}$ (10)

Tell the children they will need to sort the following pairs of fractions into order of size so they can be labelled with the 'greater than' and 'smaller than' symbols ($>$ and $<$).

Write the pairs of fractions on the board or flipchart. Ask volunteers to write in the correct symbol and name the highest common factor they have used.

1. $\frac{3}{5}$ and $\frac{2}{3}$
2. $\frac{2}{3}$ and $\frac{3}{4}$
3. $\frac{3}{4}$ and $\frac{4}{5}$
4. $\frac{5}{6}$ and $\frac{7}{9}$
5. $\frac{3}{4}$ and $\frac{5}{7}$
6. $\frac{5}{12}$ and $\frac{3}{7}$
7. $\frac{4}{5}$ and $\frac{7}{9}$
8. $\frac{9}{10}$ and $\frac{4}{5}$

99 Make the set

Resources
A board or flipchart

Learning objective
Find equivalent percentages, decimals and fractions.

Type of starter
Rehearse

Mental strategy
Remember: some decimal numbers may need to be written to two decimal places; 'per cent' means 'out of one hundred'; fractions should always be written in the lowest terms.

Answers

1. 27%
2. 0.5
3. $\frac{1}{4}$
4. 0.75
5. 60%
6. $\frac{9}{10}$
7. 0.4
8. 0.1 and $\frac{1}{10}$
9. 35% and $\frac{7}{20}$
10. 0.82 and 82%

Remind the children that equivalent amounts can be written as a decimal number, a percentage and as a fraction. Ask for volunteers to come up to the board or flipchart and complete the gaps in the following statements.

1. 0.27 = ? = $\frac{27}{100}$
2. ? = 50% = $\frac{1}{2}$
3. 0.25 = 25% = ?
4. ? = 75% = $\frac{3}{4}$
5. 0.6 = ? = $\frac{3}{5}$
6. 0.9 = 90% = ?
7. ? = 40% = $\frac{2}{5}$
8. ? = 10% = ?
9. 0.35 = ? = ?
10. ? = ? = $\frac{41}{50}$

100 Change it!

Learning objective
Find equivalent percentages, decimals and fractions.

Type of starter
Rehearse

Mental strategy
Remember: 'per cent' means 'out of one hundred'; fractions should always be written in the lowest terms.

Resources
None

Tell the children that you are going to give them a number and an instruction: 'double it', 'halve it' or 'change it to a...'.

Encourage them, when converting to fractions, to give the fraction in its lowest terms (eg $^3/_5$ rather than $^6/_{10}$).

1. $^1/_2$, decimal
2. 25%, fraction
3. 28, double it
4. 82, halve it
5. 0.1, percentage
6. 0.13, fraction
7. 20%, decimal
8. 58, halve it
9. $^1/_4$, decimal
10. 45, double it
11. 96, halve it
12. $^7/_{10}$, percentage
13. 30%, fraction
14. $^4/_5$, percentage
15. $^7/_{20}$, decimal
16. 62, double it
17. 86, double it
18. 114, halve it
19. $^{17}/_{25}$, percentage
20. $^3/_4$, decimal
21. 0.3, percentage
22. 37, double it
23. 72, halve it
24. 26, halve it
25. $^{37}/_{50}$, percentage
26. 27%, decimal
27. 0.6, fraction
28. 70, halve it
29. 59, double it
30. 28%, fraction

Answers

1. 0.5
2. ¼
3. 56
4. 41
5. 10%
6. $^{13}/_{100}$
7. 0.2
8. 29
9. 0.25
10. 90
11. 48
12. 70%
13. $^3/_{10}$
14. 80%
15. 0.35
16. 124
17. 172
18. 57
19. 68%
20. 0.75
21. 30%
22. 74
23. 36
24. 13
25. 74%
26. 0.27
27. $^3/_5$
28. 35
29. 118
30. $^7/_{25}$

(101) Five-second percentages

Resources
None

Learning objective
Relate fractions to multiplication and division; find fractions and percentages of whole-number quantities.

Type of starter
Recall

Mental strategy
Remember, 50% means 50 parts in every 100, and is equal to ½. Also that 25% = $^{25}/_{100}$ = ¼.

Answers
1. 7
2. 34
3. £2.50
4. 5
5. 40
6. 16p
7. 9
8. 60
9. 5
10. 15p
11. 80%
12. 15%
13. 40%
14. 72%
15. 70%

Ask: *What fraction is 75% equal to?* ($^3/_4$) *What fraction is 10% equal to?* ($^1/_{10}$)

Give the children five seconds to work out the answer. On a silent signal from you, they should raise a hand to answer.

1. 50% of 14
2. 50% of 68
3. 50% of £5.00
4. 25% of 20
5. 25% of 160
6. 25% of 64p
7. 75% of 12
8. 75% of 80
9. 10% of 50
10. 10% of £1.50
11. 80 out of 100. What is the percentage?
12. 15 out of 100. What is the percentage?
13. 20 out of 50. What is the percentage?
14. 36 out of 50. What is the percentage?
15. 7 out of 10. What is the percentage?

102 Biscuit tin

Learning objective
Solve problems involving direct proportion by scaling quantities up or down.

Type of starter
Rehearse

Resources
A board or flipchart

Tell the children they are going to work out how many of each different type of biscuit there is in each biscuit tin by using the ratio of one type of biscuit to another.

It may be necessary to work through an example before the children start on the questions:

16 biscuits, wafer and chocolate in the ratio 1:3.

Add the parts in the ratio 1 + 3 = 4.

Divide the total number of biscuits, 16, by this number to get one part, 16 ÷ 4 = 4.

Then multiply in the ratio: 1 × 4 = 4 wafer and 3 × 4 = 12 chocolate.

Add the amounts to make sure they equal the total, 4 + 12 = 16.

Write the following pieces of information on the board or flipchart.

1. 20 biscuits, ginger and chocolate in the ratio 3:1
2. 30 biscuits, plain and cream in the ratio 2:1
3. 25 biscuits, wafer and cream in the ratio 1:4
4. 21 biscuits, ginger and digestive in the ratio 2:5
5. 40 biscuits, ginger and jam in the ratio 2:3
6. 24 biscuits, chocolate and wafer in the ratio 5:3
7. 36 biscuits, digestive and plain in the ratio 7:5
8. 48 biscuits, plain and wafer in the ratio 1:5

Answers

1. 15 ginger and 5 chocolate
2. 20 plain and 10 cream
3. 5 wafer and 20 cream
4. 6 ginger and 15 digestive
5. 16 ginger and 24 jam
6. 15 chocolate and 9 wafer
7. 21 digestive and 15 plain
8. 8 plain and 40 wafer

Positive/negative number line

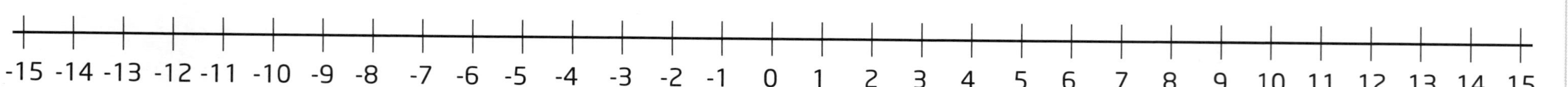

Master square

1	4	9	16
25	36	49	64
81	100	121	144
400	900	1600	2500

2D shapes

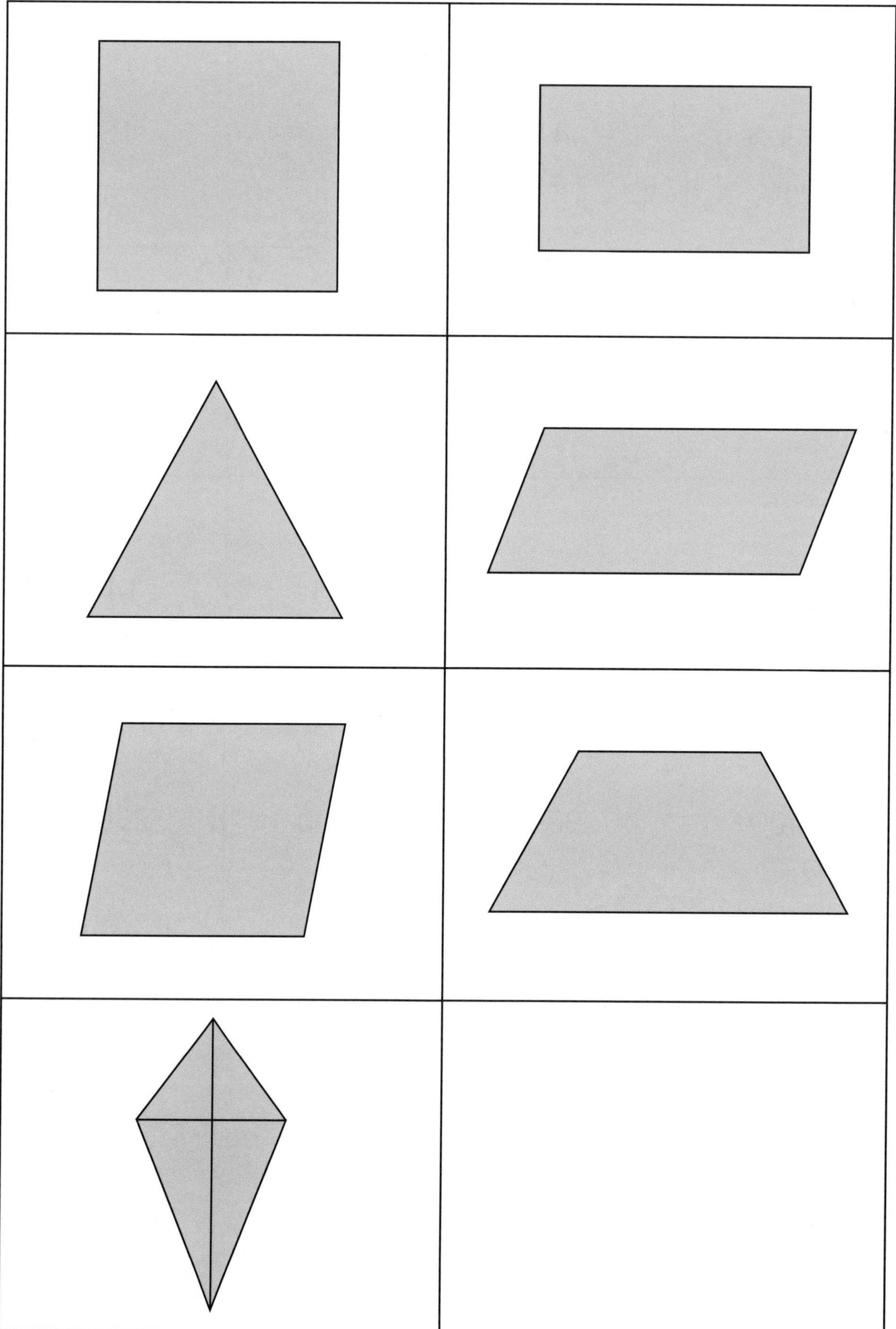

3D shapes

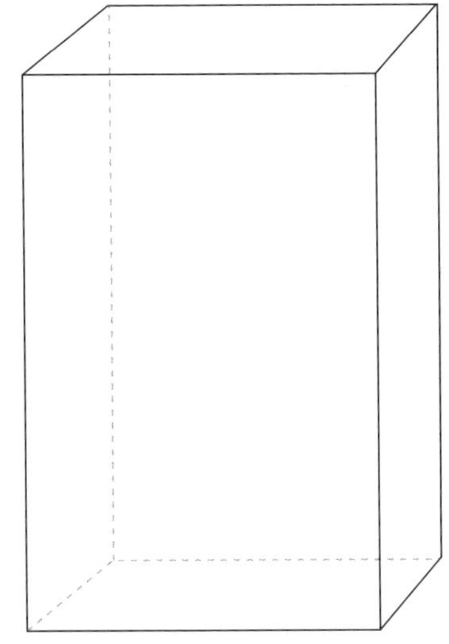

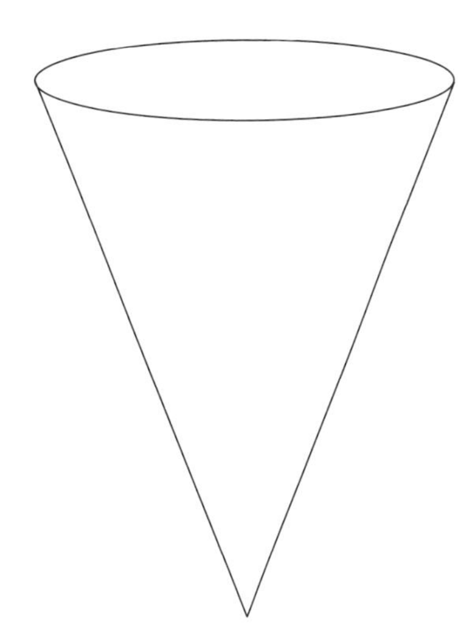

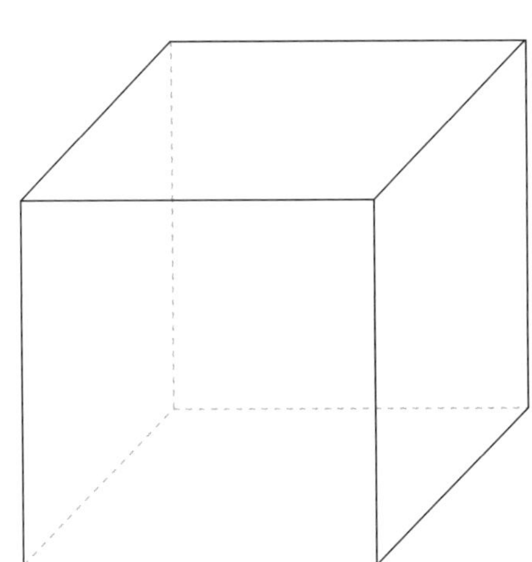

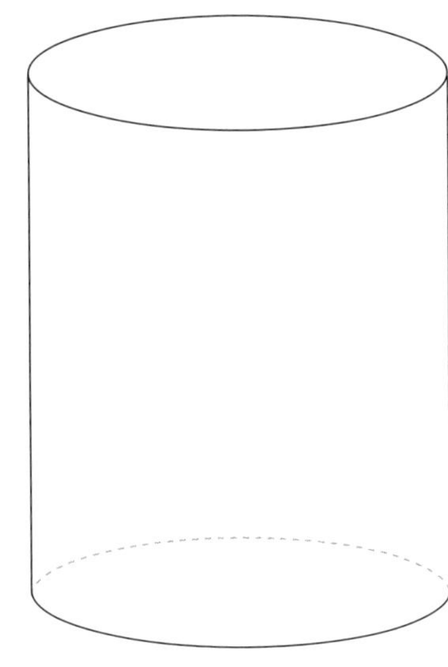

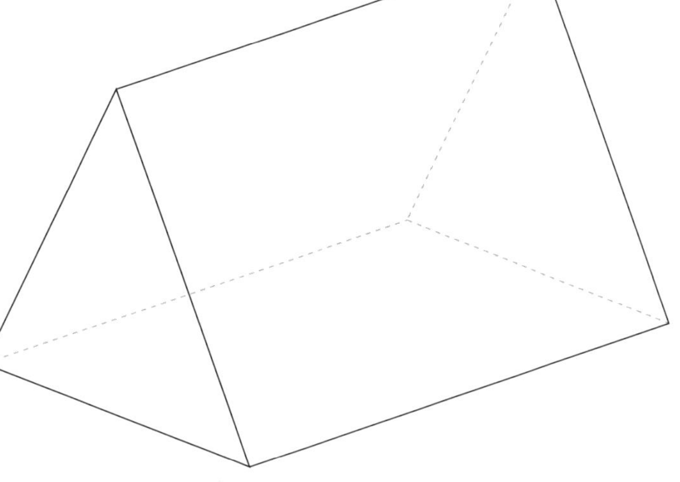

Home sweet home

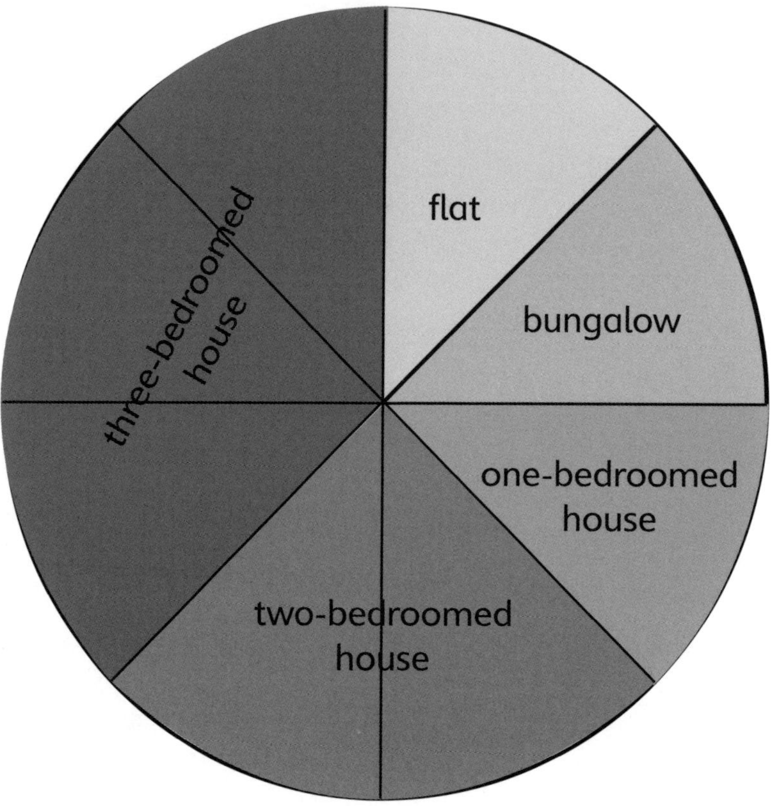

Sponsored swim

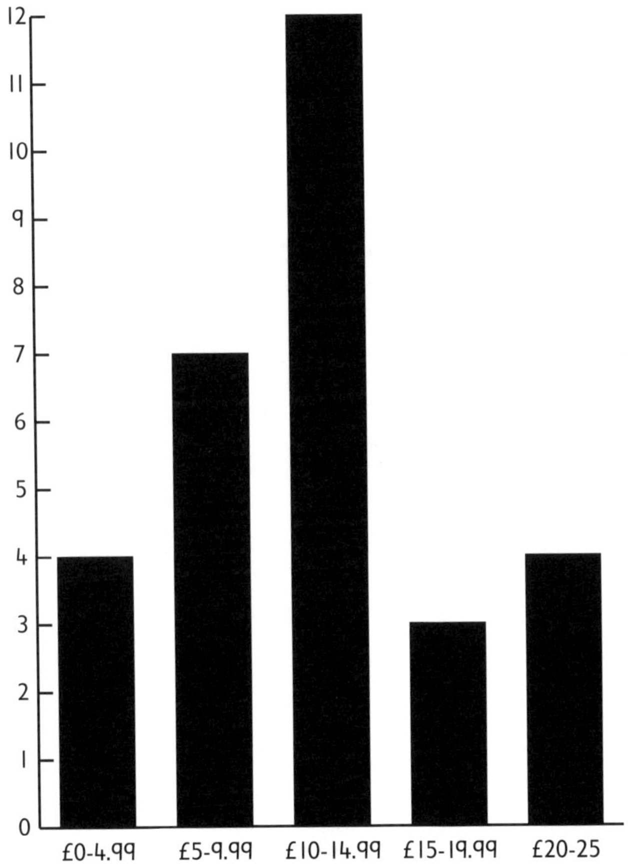

Party election

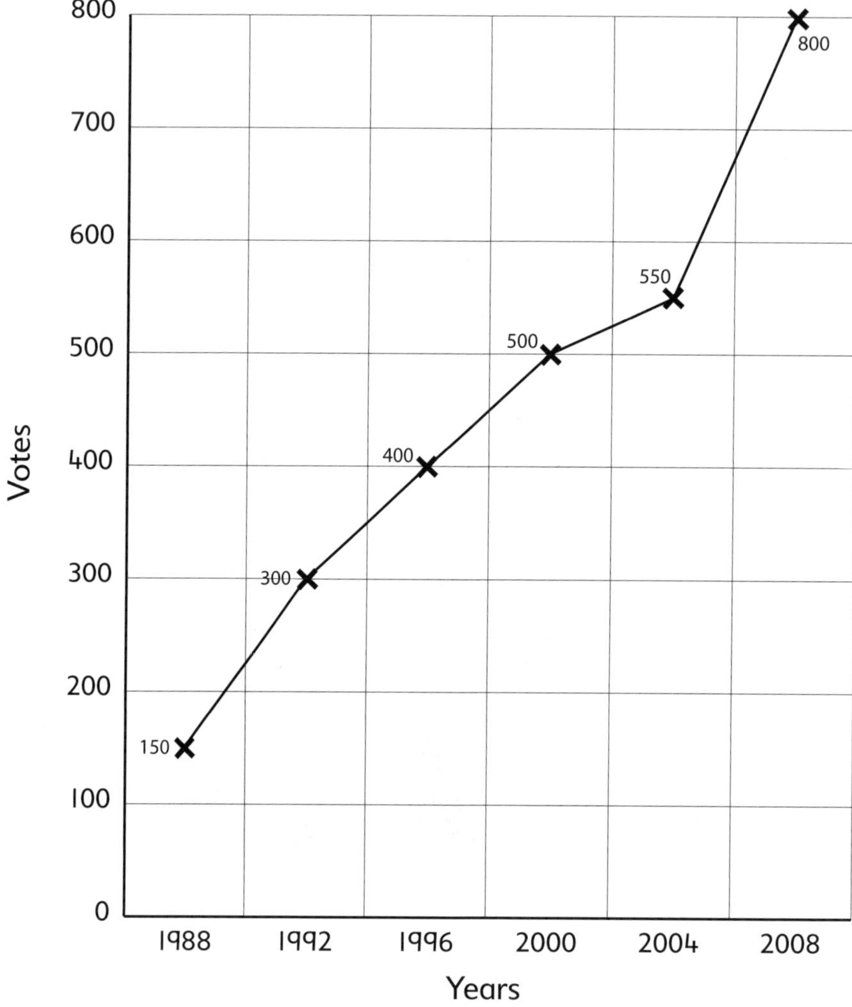

Numeral cards 0–10

0	1	2
3	4	5
6	7	8
9	10	

Level 4: Oral and mental assessments

Teachers' notes

Time: 20 minutes for each complete paper.

- Children should sit so that they cannot see each other's work.
- Do not explain questions or read numbers to the children.
- The test may be administered to groups of children or to the whole class.
- There are 20 marks available for each paper.

Delivering the tests

- Read each question to the children twice.
- Allow five seconds each for questions 1-5, ten seconds for questions 6-15 and fifteen seconds for questions 16-20.
- Answers to be recorded on the answer sheets provided.

Say to the children:

'I am going to read some questions for you to answer. I will read each question twice. You will have five seconds to answer the first five questions, then ten seconds to answer the next ten questions and finally 15 seconds for the last five questions.'

'For most of the questions you will write your answer in a box.' [Show example.]

'For some questions you may need to tick the right answer.'

'If you make a mistake, you should cross it out and write your answer again clearly.'

Levelling the children

Add up the marks.
(Possible total: 20 marks)

Below Level 4	0 - 7 marks
Low Level 4	8 - 12 marks
Secure Level 4	13 - 15 marks
High Level 4	16 - 20 marks

This assessment reflects a child's performance in mental maths. When awarding an end-of-year teacher assessment level, teachers also need to consider a child's performance on periodic and day-to-day assessments over all learning objectives.

Test 2: Mental maths assessment

Oral and mental questions (page 1 of 2)

Time: 20 minutes

- Read each question twice to the children.
- Answers to be recorded on the answer sheet on pages 99–101.
- One mark per question: 20 marks total.
- Allow five seconds for each answer for questions 1–5, ten seconds for questions 6–15, and fifteen seconds for questions 16–20.

	Question	Answer
1	What is 81 ÷ 9?	9
2	Calculate 6.2 × 10.	62
3	5000 + 400 + 67 =	5467
4	0.3 equals what fraction?	$^3/_{10}$
5	2.5 litres equals how many millilitres?	2500ml
6	I am thinking of a triangle. It has two equal angles. What is the name of this triangle?	isosceles
7	What is the square root of 64?	8
8	A book has a selling price of £2, but has been reduced by 25%. How much is it now?	£1.50
9	*(Look at the shapes.)* Tick the rhombus.	✔
10	I start a journey at 6.20 and finish it at 7:05. How long was my journey?	45 minutes

Test 2: Mental maths assessment

Oral and mental questions (page 2 of 2)

	Question	Answer
11	Fill in the blank spaces to complete the table.	see table below
12	*(Look at the jug.)* This jug holds 500 millilitres. I pour out 50 millilitres. How much is left?	325ml
13	*(Look at the numbers.)* Tick the smallest number.	4.26
14	I have 60 marbles. Two-fifths are blue and the rest are red. How many are red?	36
15	*(Look at the angles.)* Tick the angle that is about 45°.	✔
16	*(Look at the pictogram.)* The pictogram shows how much money Jack spends each week. He earns £150. How much will he have left?	£90
17	Six bags of crisps weigh 54g. What would be the mass of 20 bags?	180g
18	Add together 340 and 90 and then subtract 35.	395
19	Subtract 0.4 from 2.3.	1.9
20	The temperature inside a plane is 25° but outside it is -32°. What is the difference in temperature?	57°

Answer to question 11:

3D shape	vertices	edges	faces
cube	8	**12**	6
square-based pyramid	5	8	**5**
cone	**1**	1	2

End of test

Name Date

Test 2: Mental maths assessment

Oral and mental assessment answer sheet (1 of 2)

Time: 5 seconds per question

	Answer	Mark
1		
2		
3		
4		
5		

Time: 10 seconds per question

	Answer	Mark
6		
7		
8		
9	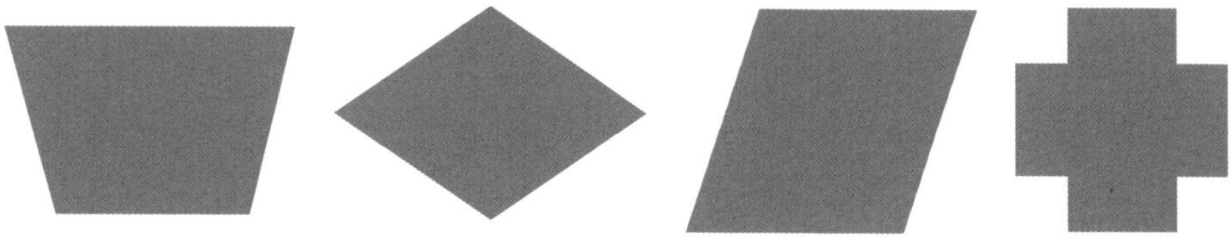	
10		
11		

3D shape	vertices	edges	faces
cube	8		6
square-based pyramid	5	8	
cone		1	2

Name Date

Test 2: Mental maths assessment

Oral and mental assessment answer sheet (2 of 2)

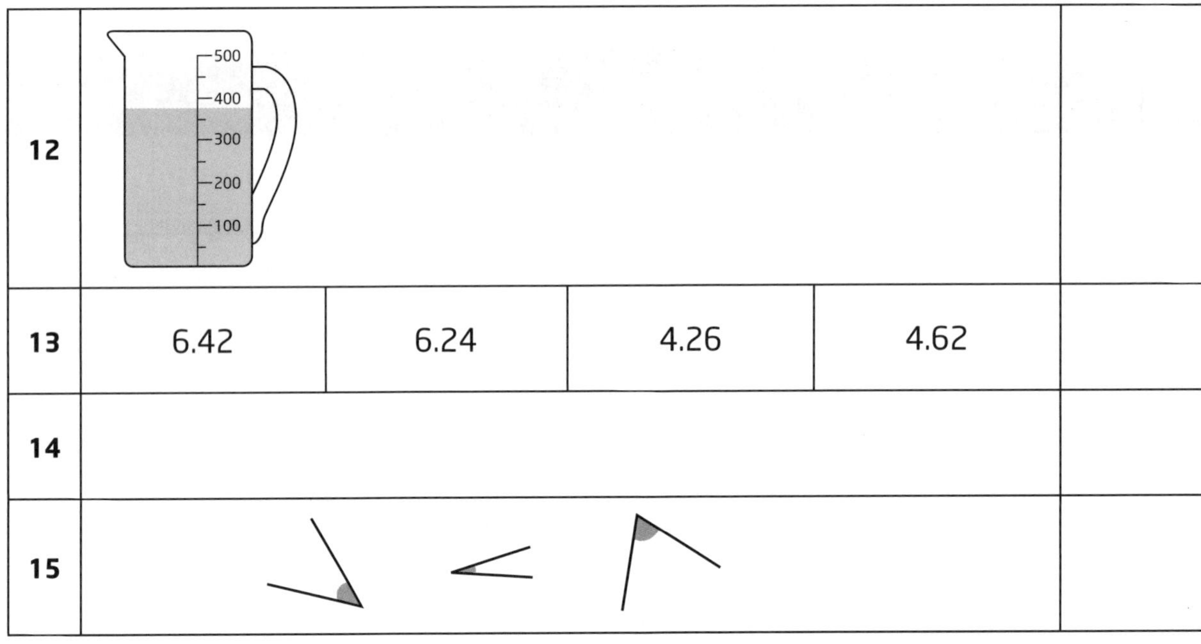

12					
13	6.42	6.24	4.26	4.62	
14					
15					

Time: 15 seconds per question

	Answer	Mark
16	clothes: £5 food: £5 £5 £5 petrol: £5 £5 £5 £5 gas: £5 £5 telephone: £5 £5	
17		
18		
19		
20		
End of test	**Total**	

Level 5: Oral and mental assessments

Teachers' notes

Time: 20 minutes for each complete paper.

- Children should sit so that they cannot see each other's work.
- Do not explain questions or read numbers to the children.
- The test may be administered to groups of children or to the whole class.
- There are 20 marks available for each paper.

Delivering the tests

- Read each question to the children twice.
- Allow five seconds each for questions 1-5, ten seconds for questions 6–15 and fifteen seconds for questions 16–20.
- Answers to be recorded on the answer sheets provided.

Say to the children:

'I am going to read some questions for you to answer. I will read each question twice. You will have five seconds to answer the first five questions, then ten seconds to answer the next ten questions and finally 15 seconds for the last five questions.'

'For most of the questions you will write your answer in a box.' [Show example.]

'For some questions you may need to tick the right answer.'

'If you make a mistake, you should cross it out and write your answer again clearly.'

Levelling the children

Add up the marks.

(Possible total: 20 marks)

Below Level 5	0 - 7 marks
Low Level 5	8 - 12 marks
Secure Level 5	13 - 15 marks
High Level 5	16 - 20 marks

This assessment reflects a child's performance in mental maths. When awarding an end-of-year teacher assessment level, teachers also need to consider a child's performance on periodic and day-to-day assessments over all learning objectives.

Test 1: Mental maths assessment

Oral and mental questions (page 1 of 2)

Time: 20 minutes

- Read each question twice to the children.
- Answers to be recorded on the answer sheet on pages 104-105.
- One mark per question: 20 marks total.
- Allow five seconds for each answer for questions 1-5, ten seconds for questions 6-15, and fifteen seconds for questions 16-20.

	Question	Answer
1	What is 0.7 as a percentage?	70%
2	Calculate 6.3 ÷ 100.	0.063
3	What is the square root of 81?	9
4	How many do I add to 457 to make 1000?	543
5	What is the product of 40 and 60?	2400
6	A right-angled triangle has a second angle of 30°. How much does the third angle measure?	60°
7	*(Look at the number sequence.)* What is the next number in this sequence? Write it in the empty box.	3(.0)
8	*(Look at the decimals.)* Tick the decimal that is equal to two-fifths.	0.4
9	How many 20p coins are there in £3.40?	17
10	Write two factors of 56 that have a difference of 10.	14, 4

Test 1: Mental maths assessment

Oral and mental questions (page 2 of 2)

	Question	Answer
11	I use two eggs to make 12 buns. How many eggs will I use to make 54 buns?	9
12	How many eights are there in 720?	90
13	Add 6.4 to 4.7.	11.1
14	The radius of a rug is 525 centimetres. What is its diameter?	1050cm or 10.5m
15	Imagine a pentagonal-based pyramid. How many faces does it have?	6
16	I leave Manchester at 10:20am and arrive in Dallas 14 hours later. Dallas is 6 hours behind GMT. What time is it in Dallas when I arrive?	18:20 or 6:20pm
17	Garden furniture was on sale for £620.00. It has been reduced by 20%. How much is it now?	£496
18	Katie is 63 centimetres tall. Daniel is one-third taller than that. How tall is Daniel?	84cm
19	*(Look at the fractions.)* Tick the smallest fraction.	$^{3}/_{19}$
20	*(Look at the number line.)* The difference between A and B is 280. What are the values of A and B?	A = -120 B = 160

End of test

Name Date

Test 1: Mental maths assessment

Oral and mental assessment answer sheet (1 of 2)

Time: 5 seconds per question

	Answer	Mark
1		
2		
3		
4		
5		

Time: 10 seconds per question

	Answer					Mark
6						
7	4.2	3.8	3.4			
8	0.2	0.3	0.4	0.5	0.6	
9						
10						

Name Date

Test 1: Mental maths assessment

Oral and mental assessment answer sheet (2 of 2)

Time: 10 seconds per question

	Answer	Mark
11		
12		
13		
14		
15		

Time: 15 seconds per question

	Answer				Mark
16					
17					
18					
19	$\frac{2}{5}$	$\frac{17}{18}$	$\frac{3}{19}$	$\frac{11}{17}$	
20	A	O	B		
	A =		B =		

End of test

Total	

Test 2: Mental maths assessment

Oral and mental questions (page 1 of 2)

Time: 20 minutes

- Read each question twice to the children.
- Answers to be recorded on the answer sheet on pages 108-110.
- One mark per question: 20 marks total.
- Allow five seconds for each answer for questions 1-5, ten seconds for questions 6-15, and fifteen seconds for questions 16-20.

	Question	Answer
1	What is 7 squared?	49
2	Calculate one-hundredth of 8.5.	0.085
3	How many do I add to 6050 to make 10,000?	3950
4	What is three-tenths as a percentage?	30%
5	Write a quarter of a million in figures.	250,000
6	Which solid shape has a square base and four triangular faces?	square-based pyramid
7	What is 16.758 to two decimal places?	16.76
8	Calculate $^1/_3$ of (2 × 80) + 200	120
9	*(Look at the Venn diagram.)* Tick the shape that is in the wrong place.	✔
10	What is $^{19}/_6$ as a mixed number?	$3^1/_6$

Test 2: Mental maths assessment

Oral and mental questions (page 2 of 2)

	Question	Answer
11	*(Look at the diagram.)* What is the value of angle x?	135°
12	*(Look at the scale.)* What mass is the arrow pointing to?	140g
13	I need 350g of flour for my recipe. I have already weighed out 80 grams. How much more flour do I need to add to the scale?	270g
14	Divide 0.3 by 100.	0.003
15	What number is halfway between 6.2 and 6.3?	6.25
16	An isosceles triangle has one side of 6cm and a perimeter of 15cm. What are the possible measurements of the other two sides?	6cm and 3cm (or 4.5cm and 4.5cm)
17	I am thinking of a number. I square it and then divide it by 3. My answer is 27. What was my number?	9
18	*(Look at the grid.)* What fraction is shaded? Write your answer in the lowest denominator.	$^2/_7$
19	450g mince will make a lasagne for six people. How much mince do I need to make lasagnes for 20 people?	1500g or 1.5kg
20	30,000 people go to a pop concert and each pay £40 for a ticket. What are the total takings for the concert?	£1,200,000

End of test

Name Date

Test 2: Mental maths assessment

Oral and mental assessment answer sheet (1 of 3)

Time: 5 seconds per question

	Answer	Mark
1		
2		
3		
4		
5		

Time: 10 seconds per question

	Answer	Mark
6		
7		
8		
9	parallel lines perpendicular lines	
10		

Name Date

Test 2: Mental maths assessment

Oral and mental assessment answer sheet (2 of 3)

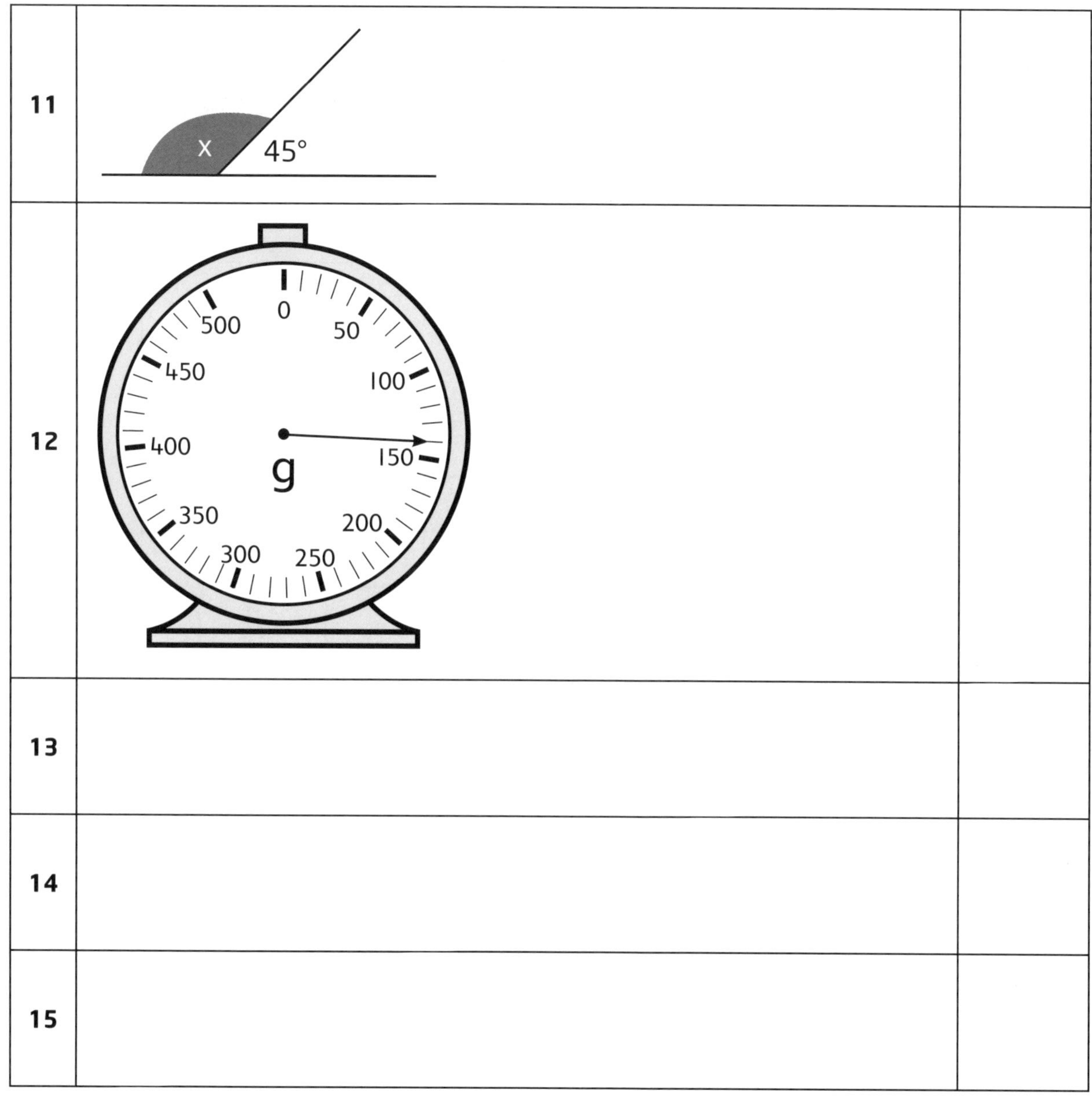

11		
12		
13		
14		
15		

Name Date

Test 2: Mental maths assessment

Oral and mental assessment answer sheet (3 of 3)

Time: 15 seconds per question

	Answer	Mark
16		
17		
18		
19		
20		
	Total	

End of test

Mental maths teacher record sheet

Teacher's name: ____________________

Name of starter	PNS objectives covered	Block/unit	Date activity was used

SCHOLASTIC

Also available in this series:

100 MATHS ASSESSMENT LESSONS Y1
ISBN 978-1407-10183-5

100 MATHS ASSESSMENT LESSONS Y2
ISBN 978-1407-10184-2

100 MATHS ASSESSMENT LESSONS Y3
ISBN 978-1407-10185-9

100 MATHS ASSESSMENT LESSONS Y4
ISBN 978-1407-10192-7

100 MATHS ASSESSMENT LESSONS Y5
ISBN 978-1407-10193-4

100 MATHS ASSESSMENT LESSONS Y6
ISBN 978-1407-10194-1

100 MATHS FRAMEWORK LESSONS Y1
ISBN 978-0439-94546-2

100 MATHS FRAMEWORK LESSONS Y2
ISBN 978-0439-94547-9

100 MATHS FRAMEWORK LESSONS Y3
ISBN 978-0439-94548-6

100 MATHS FRAMEWORK LESSONS Y4
ISBN 978-0439-94549-3

100 MATHS FRAMEWORK LESSONS Y5
ISBN 978-0439-94550-9

100 MATHS FRAMEWORK LESSONS Y6
ISBN 978-0439-94551-6

100 MATHS HOMEWORK ACTIVITIES Y1
ISBN 978-1407-10216-0

100 MATHS HOMEWORK ACTIVITIES Y2
ISBN 978-1407-10217-7

100 MATHS HOMEWORK ACTIVITIES Y3
ISBN 978-1407-10218-4

100 MATHS HOMEWORK ACTIVITIES Y4
ISBN 978-1407-10219-1

100 MATHS HOMEWORK ACTIVITIES Y5
ISBN 978-1407-10220-7

100 MATHS HOMEWORK ACTIVITIES Y6
ISBN 978-1407-10221-4

100 MENTAL MATHS ACTIVITIES Y1
ISBN 9781407114156

100 MENTAL MATHS ACTIVITIES Y2
ISBN 9781407114163

100 MENTAL MATHS ACTIVITIES Y3
ISBN 9781407114170

100 MENTAL MATHS ACTIVITIES Y4
ISBN 9781407114187

100 MENTAL MATHS ACTIVITIES Y5
ISBN 9781407114194

100 MENTAL MATHS ACTIVITIES Y6
ISBN 9781407114200

For further information, visit www.scholastic.co.uk/classpet

The Leghs and

Haydock Coal

A study of early coal mining in Haydock between 1700-1833

by Geoff Simm

First Published 2001 by
Geoff Simm, 19 Park Road North
Newton-le-Willows WA12 9TF
Tel: (01925) 224088

ISBN 0 9524787 3 0

Design by Geoff Simm

Printed by Willow Printing
75/79 Back Cross Lane,
Newton-le-Willows,
Merseyside WA12 9YE
Tel: (01925) 222449

Acknowledgments

I would like to thank the following people and institutions for their help in the production of this book: St.Helens Local History and Archives Library, St.Helens Metropolitan Borough Council, John Rylands University Library, The Greater Manchester Record Office, The National Trust, Kate Atkinson and Dave Knowles.

Permission to use the Legh family letters in this publication has been kindly given by Lord Newton.

Front: - Chairman's chain of office of the former Haydock Urban District Council. The Urban District was set up by the Local Government Act 1894. Jack Case, a local businessman, presented the Chain in April 1953.

Back: - Top - Hand & Banner badge from the ceiling of Lyme Park.

Bottom - Haydock Collieries in the twentieth century.

Errata

Page 15 should read: The geological map, on page 14, ...

Page 59 should read: The 1820 sale notice on page 60, ...

Introduction.

Coal has probably been mined in Haydock in some fashion for over 400 years. The township we know today was built from the production of coal. Coal attracted people, produced work and created a close knit mining community. However before and during most of the 17th century coal mining in Haydock was of little consequence. It was the link with the Cheshire salt trade that caused a massive increase in production and attracted the attention of local landowners.

At the end of the 17th century there were two rival factions in the Cheshire salt fields, the brine men and the rock salt men. In the 1670s rock salt had been discovered near Great Budworth. Twenty years later mining started and rock salt was transported to refineries on the Mersey and, more importantly, to Liverpool. The resulting product was of high quality and could easily be exported. In the saltfields the traditional method of boiling brine was still being used with great success. Both processes required large amounts of coal but, because of the shorter distance involved, the rock salt men paid less in transportation charges.

In the 1720s the River Weaver was made navigable and this enabled salt production to double in 10 years. All the coal used was transported by packhorse to the Mersey, a difficult and costly journey. There was a clear danger of the salt trade being restricted through lack of fuel. At Liverpool the road from Prescot and St. Helens was turnpiked to improve its condition. This created a monopoly because some coal owners were using their position to hold the market and keep up prices. Powerful Liverpool merchants required another source of fuel to further their interest in the salt trade. In 1754 the Sankey Brook was surveyed to see if it could be made navigable. Henry Berry, the Liverpool dock engineer, took on the task of making the Sankey navigable. But instead he produced a complete cut the full length of the proposed section of the Sankey Brook. This opened up the rest of the south west section of the Lancashire coalfield to the salt fields and Liverpool. Haydock coal producers were quick to take advantage and became one of the major users of this new form of transport.

Throughout this time of industrial activity and expansion the people who were involved in mining in the Haydock area were the Leghs of Lyme. They were local landowners who had owned Haydock since the beginning of the fifteenth century. The Legh family was instrumental in developing the Haydock coal mines from their early days at the beginning of the eighteenth century up to the 1830s. It was the Leghs of Lyme who changed Haydock from a series of fields into a mining village. But who were the Leghs and how did they come to be coal mining in Haydock?

Lyme Hall, Cheshire

The Leghs of Lyme.

The Leghs of Lyme were originally a Cheshire family but became major landowners in both Lancashire and Cheshire. Their line sprang initially from the Leghs of Adlington in the 14th century. Over the next 300 years good fortune and fortuitous marriages resulted in the Leghs of Lyme rising rapidly in the Lancashire and Cheshire gentry. Their initial stroke of luck was the marriage of Piers I to Margaret, the descendant of Sir Thomas Danyers of Bradley near Grappenhall in Cheshire. Sir Thomas Danyers had been pledged land in Lyme Hanley by King Edward III for his services in the battle before the gates of Caen. It is reputed that during the battle of Crecy Sir Thomas rescued the standard of the Black Prince from a French knight. A gorier version of the story states that he brought the standard back with the arm still attached. The Leghs have always been fiercely proud of their connection to the event and the emblem of the Hand and Banner appears everywhere at Lyme. After his marriage to Margaret Danyers Piers I applied for the land at Lyme Hanley and it was granted to his family in 1398. In the previous year Richard II had granted the family their coat of arms, incorporating the Rams Head, an emblem that has become famous in the districts surrounding many of the Legh estates. Because of his loyalty to Richard II Piers I was executed at Chester by Henry Bolinbroke in 1399. His son, Peter II, married in 1403 Joan, the daughter and heiress of Sir Gilbert de Haydock. This marriage brought a large number of Lancashire and Cheshire estates into the family. The de Haydocks were the ancient owners of Haydock and Bradley, their family home being Bradley House near Burtonwood. It seems ironic that Sir Peter Legh and Joan, after their marriage, moved from Bradley, Cheshire, the home of Sir Peter's grandparents, to Bradley, Lancashire. Bradley House, near the village of Burtonwood, became the home of the Legh Family for many generations. Little did they realise that with the acquisition of the land in Haydock the wealth of the Leghs was assured albeit 300 years in the future.

Between the fifteenth and seventeenth centuries the Leghs increased their power and influence in Cheshire and Lancashire. Some of the Lords of Lyme were knighted, some became Sheriffs of Chester and others became involved in various wars in Europe. In 1660 Richard Legh, the then Lord of Lyme, consolidated his lands in Lancashire by purchasing the Barony of Newton together with the manor house, land and hereditaments. This purchase enabled him to gain control of the election of two members of parliament, a very important acquisition indeed. It was at the time of Richard Legh (1634-87) that coal mining was first mentioned in the Legh family papers. He was elected MP for Newton in 1661 and gave his own crest as the arms for the borough. Richard married, in 1661, Elizabeth, daughter of Sir Thomas Chicheley and during their happy marriage they had thirteen children. Richard Legh was greatly involved at court, being a conscientious MP and a great supporter of Charles II. He died at the relatively young age of 53 and was buried in the Legh chapel at Winwick church.

The Legh estates were settled on Richard's eldest son, Peter Legh, who later became known as the Elder. In 1687 he married his cousin Frances Legh, the daughter of Piers Legh of Bruche. During Peter's reign coal production from the Haydock coalfield increased and was regularly mentioned in the family correspondence. In the 1690s Peter Legh the Elder became involved in the 'Lancashire Plot' - a Jacobite conspiracy. He was arrested, thrown in Chester Castle and accused of conspiring against William III. Peter was then removed to the Tower of London and charged with high treason, but was later discharged. His complete disgust at the authorities caused him never again to apply for public office. In the later part of his life, because he had no children of his own, Peter Legh the Elder formerly settled all his estates on his brother Thomas' four sons, Fleetwood, Peter, Piers and Ashburnham. The eldest son, Fleetwood Legh, was destined to become Lord of Lyme on his uncle's death, but in 1726 he suffered a violent pleurisy attack and died at the age of 25.

Peter Legh the Elder died in 1744 and was buried at Winwick. His nephew Peter Legh, who became known as the Younger, succeeded him. Peter Legh the Younger had married, in 1737, Martha the only daughter of Thomas Benet of Salthrop, Wiltshire. At the beginning of their marriage they were a loving couple becoming involved in the hectic social life of eighteenth century England. Later in their life they became embittered and a separation occurred. Members of the family said this was probably because their two sons died very young and they had no heir. Peter was Lord of Lyme during the great expansion of their coal industry. He mined in Haydock and Norbury and also became one of the major shippers of coal on the newly opened Sankey Navigation. Peter was also interested in local politics and stood as MP for Newton no less than 5 times between 1747-68. Because of his lack of an heir Peter began to sponsor his brother's eldest son, Thomas Peter Legh, supporting him and helping in his education.

Richard Legh
1634-1687

Peter Legh the Elder
1669-1744

Thomas Peter Legh
1754-1797

Thomas Legh
1792-1857

In 1792 Thomas Peter Legh, the son of Ashburnham Legh of Golborne Park, succeeded Peter Legh the Younger. He had spent most of his childhood at Golborne Park, an attractive estate situated off Rob Lane on the border with Newton. The buildings were extended and developed in the nineteenth century and in the twentieth century it became Haydock Golf Club. Thomas Peter Legh succeeded to the title at the late age of 38. During his life he had raised a regiment of horse called the Third Lancashire Light Dragoons, becoming Colonel in the process. He rebuilt Haydock Lodge in the 1790s producing the impressive building that is still remembered today. After his death it became the home of Thomas Claughton, the mining and salt proprietor, who is referred to later in this work. In the 1850s it was converted into a select lunatic asylum. This is how many local people remember it. It is with Thomas Peter that the Legh family had a problem with the succession. He died quite young and unmarried leaving a number of illegitimate children. His will stated that he bequeathed his estates to Richard Cross and George Heron until his natural son, Thomas Legh, had reached the age of 21. This was to enable them to raise money for the purpose of educating and raising his children.

Thomas Legh gained control of his estates in 1813 and soon began to show his mettle. He was elected MP for Newton in 1816 and served in that capacity until 1832. He improved his lands in Newton, Haydock and Warrington and attempted to attract business people to the area. Thomas Legh modernised his mining concern in Haydock, installing up to date equipment at all of the collieries. One thing he passionately enjoyed was travelling in the Middle East. He visited the Aegean Islands, sailed up the Nile as far as the capital of Nubia, was shot at by an Albanian soldier, and travelled to Palestine, on the way becoming involved in an archaeological dig at Petra. The large portrait of him at Lyme shows a dramatic, flamboyant figure, dressed in an Arabian outfit. Thomas Legh's first marriage was very much an intriguing one. Four unscrupulous people: Edward Gibbon Wakefield, William Wakefield, Edward Thevenot and Frances Wakefield abducted Ellen Turner, the daughter of William Turner of Shrigley Hall, a close neighbour of his at Lyme. She was tricked into going to Gretna Green where she was married to Edward Gibbon Wakefield under false pretences. They had told Ellen that her father was in debt and the only way she could save him was to marry Wakefield. They were eventually found in France at Calais from where Ellen was rescued by her two uncles. Two of the Wakefields were arrested when they returned to this country and they were committed to Lancaster Castle. At that time the nearest magistrate to Shrigley was Thomas Legh, who could have been involved in the case. It is possible that during the proceedings Thomas was attracted to Ellen, whom he eventually married. They did not have a long marriage however, because after the birth of a daughter, Ellen died suddenly in 1831. Thomas's second marriage was to Maud, the daughter of George Lowther.

Thomas Legh was the last of the coal mining Leghs because in the 1830s he sold all the Haydock coal mines to Richard Evans and William Turner, collecting coal rents instead of mining himself. At the end of his life he suffered greatly from gout, which at that time was attributed to his extensive exposure to foreign climates. After his death in 1857 his nephew, William John Legh, succeeded to the Legh estates. In 1892 he was awarded the title 1st Lord Newton for political services. He married Emily Jane, daughter of the Rev. C.N. Wodehouse and was succeeded by his son Thomas Wodehouse Legh, 2nd Lord Newton, who had a distinguished war record. Thomas Wodehouse Legh was succeeded by his son, Richard William Davenport Legh, 3rd Lord Newton. It was the 3rd Lord Newton who gave Lyme Hall to the National Trust in 1946, leaving many family treasures on loan. The present holder of the title is Richard Thomas Legh, 5th Lord Newton.

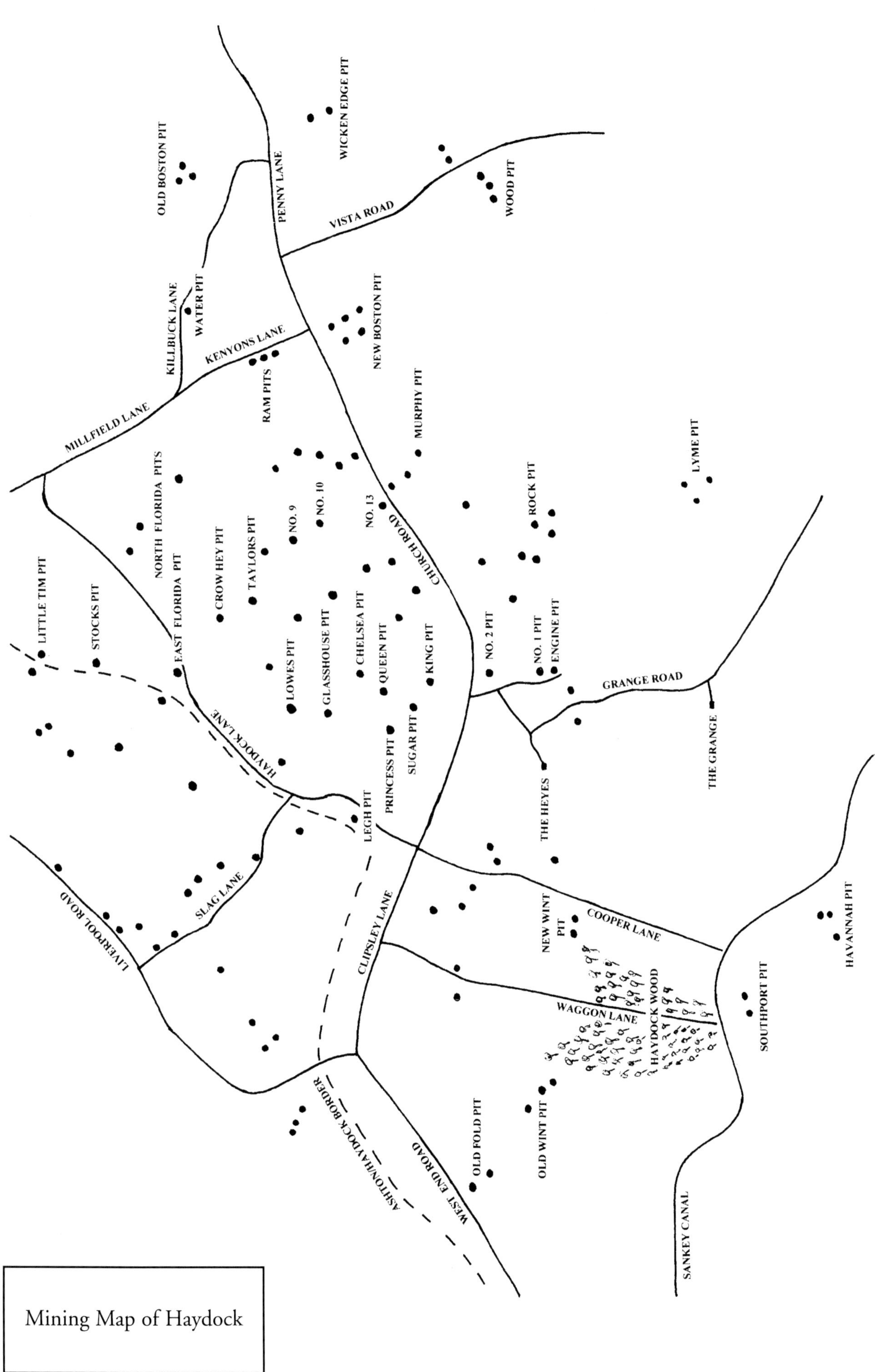

Mining Map of Haydock

The Mine Adventures

At the beginning of the 18th century the Lord of Lyme was Peter Legh the Elder, who had succeeded his father, Richard Legh, in 1687. Knowing that there was coal under his lands in Haydock and being in contact with other landed gentry adjacent to him, he must have decided to take advantage of the increasing trade to the salt fields. The various references to coal mining on the Legh estates before that were of little consequence. One reference can be found in a letter written to Thomas Legh in 1630 by a Mr. Brotherton, who was examining the Haydock estates: -

'Accordinge to your desire Ja: Wosencrofte and I went through hedockwood and found that my maister hath beene evelly delt withall boath by the tenantes Swyne lyinge in the wood and by excessive gatheringe therof hath beene sould a warrington bushell in one place and the like gatheringe did I never hereof you knowe Tho: Risley excused himself that hee had not time (though hee went to the colepitt once a weeke) to vewe the weast, but he hath tyme for his one occacions, as will appeare in time, you knowe in tyme, and my maister to his loose find in tyme. As we came backe from the wood and colepit through Ja: Lowes ground wee found good fast newe styles and newe fence, and him repering his house,'

Plainly this is clear evidence that coal was being mined in Haydock in the 17th century. Haydock Wood stretched from the Sankey Brook towards the centre of the township and sections of it are still in existence today. Throughout the 17th century there was little or no reference to coal production in the Legh correspondence. It must have been thought of as a low priority product from the estates. It was only at the beginning of the 18th century that they began to concentrate on commercial coal mining. The first inkling in the family correspondence was in a letter written by John Ward, a lawyer, to Peter Legh the Elder in 1704: -

'I have seen great variety of the oar at the mine adventures. And my Lord Barnard who has great mines in Durham will furnish me with instructions for you.'

What a wonderful term, *the mine adventures!* It conjures up ideas of a glorious enterprise into the unknown, an idea soon to be tainted with the hard work, uncertainty and unpleasantness of working in the depths of a coal mine. It is obvious from the letter that Peter Legh had little knowledge of coal mining. John Ward was an eminent lawyer at the Inner Temple, London, a personal friend of Peter Legh the Elder and served on many cases for him. He later complained to Peter Legh that his *'coals prove only some broken pieces in a bank which I knew of long ago they lie open to the road and your man says they were brought by Noah's flood.'* Not finding commercial coal on his land must have been a big disappointment to Mr. Ward, who could see that there were large profits to be made in coal mining.

A few years later Peter Legh was employing experts in the mining field so his mine adventures must have started to pick up around that time. The majority of these men did not have any academic qualifications but would have gained their knowledge practically, by trial and error. Peter Legh put an agent in charge who employed labourers to do the hard work and brought in men of experience when problems were encountered. An example of this was in the letter written by William Brock to Peter Legh the Elder in August 1707: -

'My distemper confines mee to keep hom, I desire you wold send Mr. Richardson to mee Friday or tomorrow; And I will give him draughts how to carry on your work for the more I think of a Rayy wheele upon the shaft and better I like it, soo that I cannot possibly comply with Frank Rigbys ways thogh cannot at present persuade him to my way, my desire is to doo your worthy the best service I can in the matter here.'

Obviously William Brock was giving instructions on a piece of mining equipment. His term *Rayy wheele* must certainly refer to a spoked wheel or pulley for winding purposes mounted at the pit top. William Brock and Frank Rigby could have been brought in as advisers from any of the surrounding mining districts. The Mr. Richardson mentioned was John Richardson, the agent, who wrote in 1708 to Peter Legh regarding mining in

Haydock. The next letter, the best of the early coal letters, showed that they finally preferred Frank Rigby's opinion to that of Mr. Brock: -

'Francis Rigby was here on Monday last, and does approve of your Coale Worke very well he has sett out another Pitt which will be both for drawing water and winding up coale, the spring being soe very easy will be drawn by one horse with a small engine which will be made att an easy charge he has looged out foure trees for making it; if the water should proove more than can be maniged by this Engine you have a fall of ground that it may be taken of by a sough Francis Rigby will then waite of you att Lime, I will be preparing timber ready for the new Pitt to sink whilst the days are something long that it may be gott down before the deep of winter, the Pitt will not be much deeper than the last which is 22yds.'

What a marvellous letter! It fairly bristles with information. Even after 280 years the excitement in the agent's words can still be felt. The fall of ground mentioned indicates that the pit was at the top of Haydock, probably situated close to the border with the Gerard Estates. The border between the two estates ran behind the road from Blackbrook to Ashton, along Clipsley Brook to Haydock Lane, then northwards towards Ashton. The Gerard family of Garswood had been mining north of Clipsley Brook for a number of years. The geological map shows that most of the seams outcrop in that section of Haydock. They must have been working very close to the outcrop because the pit was only 22yds deep.

The engine referred to would be a type of whimsey or horse gin using a hoppet for lifting water. John Richardson also mentioned the use of a Sough or drainage tunnel, which was driven into the rising ground until it encountered the waterlogged workings to drain off the water.

The letter also relates that Peter Legh had started mining at Norbury, a township south of Manchester, close to Lyme Park.

During that decade Peter Legh the Elder was in contact with the Byroms of Parr Hall, who had worked a colliery in Parr between 1704 and 1707. They later sold their estates to the Clayton family. The Clayton family, of which Sarah Clayton was a prominent member, became a major force in coal mining in the Parr area. In a letter written by a friend in 1707, Peter Legh was informed that: -

'Mr.Byrom will tell you how the matter stands with your own borers, where they are now and how Mr. Worseley would have them proceed.'

He was probably referring to a piece of land in Laffak, which Samuel Byrom was surveying at that time. In his report Samuel Byrom said that the land was of some value with much coal. In a later letter he advised Peter Legh to invest in the estate. Later that century the Leghs did mine extensively at Laffak so possibly Peter Legh took the advice.

In 1714 an important report was made to Peter Legh by John Mottram, probably a mining expert, who was ordered to answer a series of questions about the coal works: -

'John Mottram's Answer to Mr. Legh's Orders.

1st and 2nd—-The Mapp.
3rd—-The Banksman is charged with the Coales hee makes into Coaks, and pays the burner thereof his wages: Tis thought the Banksman is something a gainer by them but 'tis no disadvantage to the Master for he takes the smaller coals for that purpose; and the larger ones please the country better.
4th—-It may bee proper to order the workmen to give John Orford's son (or who else may be thought proper) an amount each weeks end, or oftener, if he shall think fitt to require it, which may bee compared with the amount which the Banksman gives in.
5th—-Drifts are very wide, and the coales gotten (generally speaking) clean which causes something more timber to bee used than ordinary for Propps; and Mr. Legh pays the carpenters charge for cleaving and cutting into lengths the said Propps, but I take that to bee repaid double by the quantities of coales gotten out of these places supported by Propps where wee use to leave Pillars. The cleaner the Coales are gotten and the more benefitt for the Master being there is no danger of ever hurting the Lands by any Falls that can bee there; by reason of the thickness of the Stone and Marle above the Coale.
6th—-They say 'tis a custom in the Country that the Workmen send Coales for to pay the Smith for Sharpening their

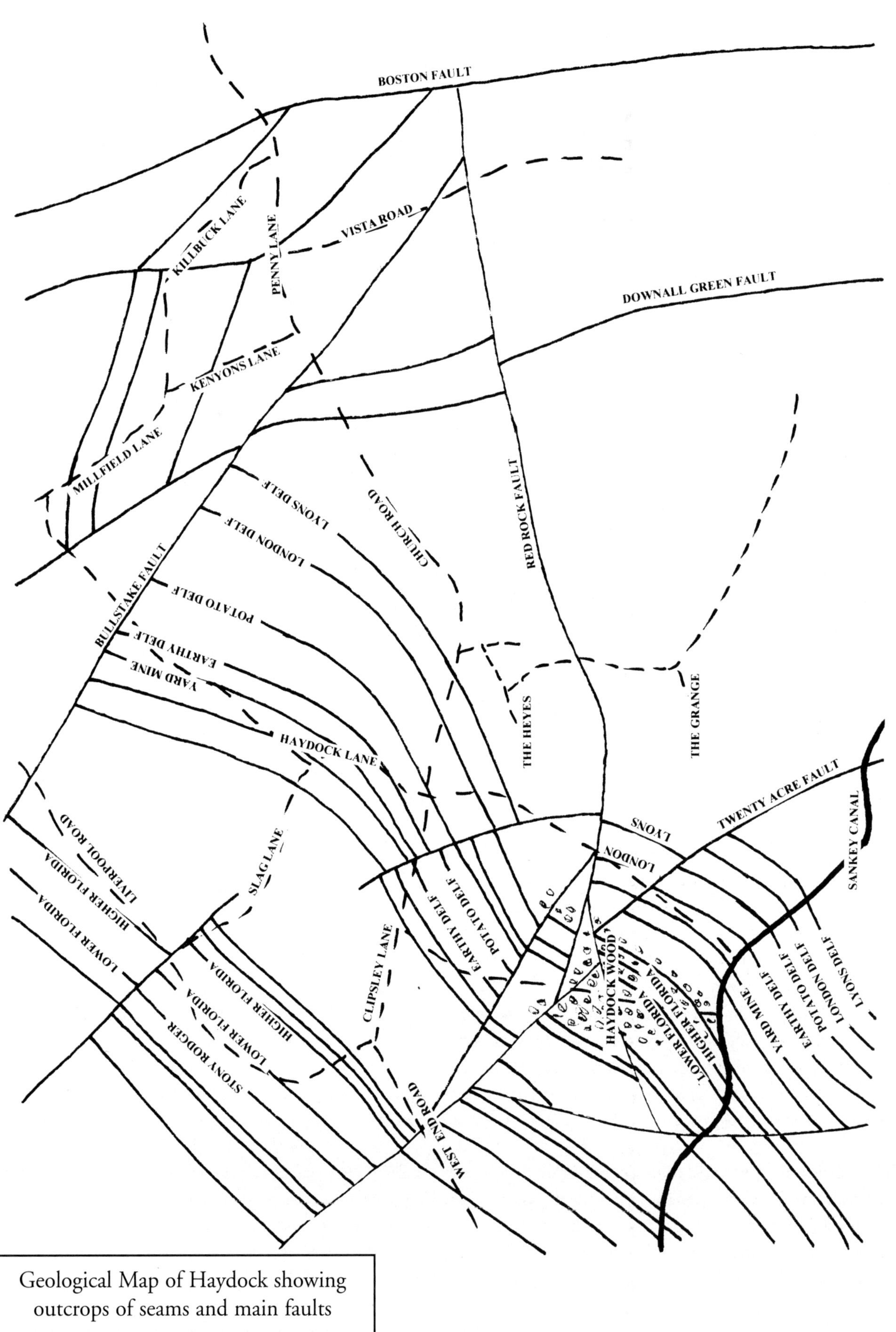

Geological Map of Haydock showing outcrops of seams and main faults

Picks, Wedges etc. Viz. each getter 2 baskets a weake: I take the Smiths wages to bee fully as reasonable as the Smiths in Chesh: and Derbysh: considering the number of points and wedges which they say the generally have. Note the Master is not any Charge of the getting, drawing or winding the said Coales.
7th—I am of opinion that a horse engine might bee proper att Norbury if the Mine prove hopefull and likely to continue.
Note—The letter "a" below the letter "E" in the Mapp betokens the place where the Levell is designed to run 35yds below the letter "E"; for which 35yds they are now Sinking in the bottom of "E": And according as the Fault is found in the said Levell: the Pitts proposed to sunk upon the Levells of "b" and "c" (and marked with this "I" mark) may bee altered att pleasure.
The Levell of "b" takes about the Middle of William Gaskells Leather Hey and the levellof "c" runs through the Highest Corner of Haydock Wood.
I take all the Coales above the levell of "D" to bee gotten (Except where some Levell is lost betwixt "C" and "D": and those may very easily bee gotten) but the Falls were so great that wee could not goe into those works.'

John Mottram's report, being very early in date, is of great importance because of the amount of information it contains. It was originally attached to a map, but that has not survived. The last section, which refers to the map, is still detailed enough to give clear indications as to where they were actually mining. William Gaskell's Leather Hey was at the top of Haydock, near to the border with Ashton. The mention of Haydock Wood in the report is very interesting. The geological map, on page 13, shows that there was a small triangular panel of strata, centred on Haydock Wood, where Lower and Higher Florida seams outcropped. He also mentioned unstable roof conditions, which would be likely in that highly faulted area of Haydock.

A family named Orford was farming that area of Haydock from Sankey Brook to Clipsley Lane in the early 1700s. They must have been of some importance because of the reference to one of its members being trustworthy enough to hold money for Peter Legh.

The report also shows the rising importance of the Banksman. Basically his job was to unload the baskets at the surface or pit bank, but in most cases he was in virtual control of the colliery. He organised the running of the surface, checked the amounts of coal being raised and even took on men on his own authority. At some collieries in south Lancashire he was looked on as a type of surface manager. Part 3 of John Mottram's report shows a side line or 'perk' that the Banksman had with regard to the coke production and sale. Coke was used locally for industrial processes that required a fuel with less fumes and impurities.

Part 5 gives an indication of working methods that they were using and the state of the strata. John Mottram certainly sounded pleased with the quality of the coal under Haydock. The Florida seams, which we shall hear more of later, were of the highest quality and coal from them was coveted by customers. His reference to Props to support the roof, a method he was not used to, shows he was an outsider.

In part 6, he refers to the Blacksmith's perk of being paid for sharpening picks and wedges. This custom, though open to corruption, was used for many years in the Legh coal pits.

Overall the report is well detailed in regard to working practices, coal production and surveying of seams - a surviving tribute to the expertise of John Mottram.

At the beginning of the 18th century coal production in Haydock was approaching a time of great expansion. Coal and its side products, such as coke, were becoming required in ever increasing amounts for industry. The accompanying increase in population in the local towns and cities also raised the demand for coal for domestic use. As the century progressed various groups and some individuals like John Mackay began to assert their importance in the coalfield. The Cases, the Claytons and John Mackay readied themselves for their endeavours in the coal trade in the years to come. Little did they know that most of them would fall by the wayside.

Haydock had quite a unique position within the Legh estates because it was so far removed from Lyme Hall. This necessitated the continual written reports by the Haydock based agents on the goings on in the township. The wealth of information that this correspondence provided has been to our great advantage in the present day. Besides coal mining the agent had to inform his master about a multitude of jobs, crops, husbandry and security, to name a few. Sometimes if the agent was an outsider it caused conflict with the locals, as we can see in the next letter: -

'I must entreate you to send a letter to mee with positive orders to goe to some of your tenants livinge near the

rough parke in Haddocke, and tell them neither to destroye the fowle nor the Rapitts, the tenant John Pierpoint the Miller and his son who are both very bold and keep not only Gunn, but greyhound or mongrell also, a severe letter from you to mee to that effect I think might be very useful especially att this season, and I beg of you to name Pierpoint and Naylor.'

Thomas Stirrup the writer of the letter seemed to be having a slight problem with the locals. It can only be imagined what the bold John Pierpoint said to him!

In the 1720s there was little reference to the Haydock coal pits. One small mention appears in a contract for the letting of Bradley Farm in 1725: -

'It is agreed this 16th day of October 1725 between John Worthington (for and on the behalf of Peter Legh of Lyme Esquire) and Henry Holbrooke of Bradley Hall within Burtonwood, that the said John Worthington hath sett and lett to farm onto the said Henry Holbrooke the Capital Messuage and demesne lands of Braddley aforesaid (which now is in his possesion) for the term of 7 years commencing at Candlemas now next att and under the clear yearly rent of £85 payable at Candlemas yearly at our entire payment without any deductions or abatements to be made for or in respect of any taxes or repairs of the said Capital Messuages or buildings or of the road or bridges leading from Braddley Hall to Newton Common which is to be kept open and repaired at and during the pleasure of the said Peter Legh for the benifit of his Coalery at Haydock.'

In the late 1720s Peter Legh the Elder required large amounts of money to pay for his alterations to Lyme Hall. He referred to this in a letter dated June 1730 from Haydock Lodge: -

'I have been in these parts 10 days. I propose to stay another week and then return to my Masons. I am raising money in these parts for them and endeavouring to amend your Coal pit road.'

It was 1735 before any further information appeared about the Haydock coal works. In that year a serious dispute occurred between the Legh and Gerard estates in connection with coal pit water being discharged into Clipsley Brook. The dispute commenced with the following letter written by John Stafford, a lawyer, to Peter Legh the Elder in December 1735: -

'On Saturday morning I went with Mr.Steel, accompanied with Mathew Houghton, John Orford and John Hurst (your tenants) to view the Sough from Sir Wm Gerard's Cole pitts and after we had taken all proper observations upon it and examined into the affair I find it appears to be somewhat different from what I at first imagined. For I don't find that any of 'em could remember when the Sough was first made, but they all concurred that there had been for all the time of their knowledge a Sough or drain from the Pitts, which ran down the Brook in a Drumble (which is the division or boundary of the townships of Ashton and Haydock). But that a good many years ago Sir Wm Gerard (grandfather of the present Baronet) finding that the part of the brook where the Sough from his Cole pitts first came into it was not deep enough to convey the Cole pitt water down, and that sinking the Brook would be a considerable expence to him. He therefore agreed with Hurst (a tenant of yours) to cut a new Channell in the Drumble and turn both the Brook and the Cole pitt water down this new Channell, for which he paid Hurst a satisfaction and the same hath run ever since down this new Channell.'

The argument between the two families was that the cutting of the new channel had caused the border between the two estates to move and that the movement was to the advantage of the Gerard estate. John Stafford carried on in the letter: -

'After we had learned all we could Mr.Steel and I went to Garswood and because I then apprehended that the Sough had been a very ancient one and nobody could tell when it was first made I only told Mr.Sanderson (the Steward), that I was come from you with directions to acquaint him that you found your self agrieved by the Sough running down the New Channell and that therefore you intended to stop it from running down there any longer, but would not proceed in doing anything of that kind without first giving notice to some of Lady Gerards agents that they might have an oppertunity of turning the water into its old course without any more ado.'

Another point then became involved in the argument. The road down to Peter Legh's pits was in poor repair. The letter goes on: -

'Mr.Sanderson seemed a little surprised, and showed a good deal of concern to think that there should be any dispute betwixt you and the family he is concerned for and pressing pretty much to know your reasons, I thought it proper to acquaint him that you had no prejudice against his Lady or him, but that you had met with some unkindness from a Gentleman (naming no name) who took upon him to act for your family and in particular with relation to the repair of the Highways in Haydock leading to your cole pits.'

The mysterious gentleman must have wanted to cause a rift between the families. Mr. Sanderson asked John Stafford to wait until he had informed Lady Gerard of the problem and he would then get back to him. He also mentioned that the sough had been in existence for 50 years, showing how long the Gerards had been mining in that area. John Stafford concluded in the letter: -

'But there's no question but that you may stop the new channell when you please. But as Mr.Sanderson talked "Such Fair" terms I thought it was better to waive doing it immediately, till you were fully apprized of the affair.'

The dispute carried on and eventually went to court. All the arguments were settled amicably by what John Stafford termed, *'the Great Wisdom of Mr. Justice Blackburn.'*

The two adjoining families had been on friendly terms for many years intermarrying several times. Throughout the 18th century their friendship continued and they combined many times against other coal proprietors.

During the 1730s and early 1740s there is a lack of information on coal mining in the correspondence. This was probably due to the ill health of Peter Legh the Elder. A general running down of the pits occurred. It was to be left to his nephew to expand the Legh coal pits into a viable concern.

Early Type of Colliery

Peter Legh the Younger.

After the death of Peter Legh the Elder in 1744 the estates passed to his nephew, Peter Legh the Younger. It must have taken a certain amount of time before he acquainted himself with the intricacies of estate business, but inevitably he became immersed in the technicalities and problems of coal mining. From other sources we hear that he was a weak ineffectual character, but when it came to coal mining he approached the work with vigour. Peter Legh the Younger must have realised that there was profit to be made from coal and profit inevitably leads to an increase in social standing. He had inherited two small coalfields in Haydock and Norbury and there was some evidence that the coal works were in a poor state of repair. This point was confirmed in two letters written to Peter Legh the Younger in 1746 and 1747 from his brother Peers Legh: -

'I doubt not but we shall do very well with the Colliery our custom increasing, the men being more diligent.'

'My Brother Collier and I have had a settling, which turned out better than I expected, considering the bad news we had when began, and the condition of the works.'

On the whole Peers Legh was a capable young man. In the 1740s he had assisted his Uncle Peter in the running of the estates and was also in charge of the shipping trade to the Caribbean in which the Leghs had become involved.

In the mid 1740s the agent in charge of coal mining was John Tomlinson who in 1747 had come in for some criticism from Peers Legh: -

'Mr Tomlinson is under a good deal of concern for fear of being discharged, hope his behaviour for the future will be more satisfactory to you.'

John Tomlinson had been reporting to Peter Legh for some time of the goings on at the coalpits. In December 1746 he informed his master that: -

'John Hartly came here on Saturday from Norbury they have found the coal mine again at 55 yds deep. I desired to bore again on that side of the lane towards Middlewood, and when they have found it there, will send you a plan of the ground and how they lie; the mine is a very good one at all the 4 places they have bored to it, it appears to be 5 ft 11 inches thick.'

And again later that month: -

'I have concluded (if you approve of it) to put down a pump to carry of the water at Disley Coal Pitt, which will be at a small expence, by this means we shall be able to get coal at this pitt for near a year without sinking another pitt,'

Water problems were obviously limiting the extent of the underground tunnels. The pump referred to would have been a primitive gin engine driven by horsepower. The John Hartley referred to in the letters was a mining expert. He was looked upon with a certain amount of respect by Peter Legh. Although he was a competent man John Hartley's great failing was the demon drink. Robert Dodge, one of the estate stewards, referred to it in 1757: -

'Ralph Leigh tells me J. Hartley has been very diligent and sober since he was conformed.'

The period of temperance was short lived as this 1760 letter shows: -

'Mr Downs was in great spirits about getting the great mine in Worth and sent for Hartley, upon the seme hee was there 9 or 10 days and by report was drunk 7 or 8 of them'

In 1747 Peter Legh must have become dissatisfied with John Tomlinson, because he replaced him with a John Worthington who became a well-trusted and liked servant of the Legh Family. Peter Legh, in all his correspondence, always referred to him as Mr Worthington, a title not even given to Richard Orford, the most powerful of the Legh stewards. At that time Peter Legh was an active Member of Parliament and was away from Lyme for long periods of time. His four children were left in the care of John Worthington, who reported in all his letters about their progress. Peter Legh continually requested information about his children or, as he called them, *'His dear little Jewels.'*

By the late 1740s Norbury coal works had encountered the great problem of early coal mining - water. In March 1749, Peter Legh was becoming concerned over the time and money being spent on winding water: -

'As Norbury Coal works are so expensive in drawing water consult with Hartley to looke out for an engineer and let him give in an estimate of the expense of a Fire Engine for I apprehend they're very expensive to make and when done consume a Fourth part of the coal.'

The Legh coal works were now entering a new era - The Steam Age. *The Fire Engine* under consideration would have been a condensing beam engine of the Newcomen type. Thomas Newcomen had invented this type of pumping engine in 1712. It was mounted at the pit top and connected to a pumping range in the shaft. Condensing steam engines of the Newcomen type worked on low pressure steam and were not very efficient. They consumed such vast amounts of coal that they were only ever a practical proposition in coalfields. In August 1750 Peter Legh congratulated John Worthington for his efforts over the fire engine: -

'You've done well in the consultation about the Fire Engine. And I very much incline towards it, and tho' its expensive I'l assuredly undertake it provided the quantity of coal to be got is likely to answer.'

Over eighteen months were to pass by before the engine was working; it was the first fire engine used on the Legh estates. In April 1752 Peter Legh sounded very pleased: -

'You give me great comfort in the very good account of the Norbury Engine and the coal works especially. I hear they are reached the four foot mine and it prooves so good.'

And again in May 1752: -

'I can readily believe the dilegence of the engineer and the hands you've put under him and am glad to find the four foot mine so well approved which I hope will keepe us in play till our Engine is so far perfected as to be usefull to us in sinking a fresh Pitt to the Lower Delph.'

This is a clear indication that the fire engine had been successful and had enabled the miners to reach otherwise inaccessible seams. At that time in Haydock such machines were not yet required because they were working at the top of the township. Here the water was drawn off by simpler methods, such as soughs and whimseys. The man in charge at Haydock at that time was Gerard Ashton, a Haydock man who had lived for some years at Leathers Farm. In 1752 word must have got round that he was sick, because in March of that year Peter Legh enquired about his health: -

'Do you hear any more how Gerard Ashton at Haydock goes on, if you find him passt business Mr Houghton of the Common (my tennant) has long been conversant in the Prescott Coal works and bears a very good character.'

In a later letter Peter Legh acknowledged John Worthington's information that Gerard Ashton had recovered. It is possible that the speedy recovery was prompted by the knowledge that another man was waiting in the wings.

The next letter is typical of Peter Legh. It is shown in its entirety to give an indication of his personality. He referred twice to his children and it was written from London where Peter Legh was possibly on parliamentary business. He also mentioned that he and his wife were on the way to Bath, where they would partake of the spa waters.

'Mr. Worthington.

I had your letter this day and am made happy by your good accounts of our dear little Jewels. I'm glad to hear Gerard Ashton is recov'd, and in case of any decide at then I do believe that Mr. Houghton of Prescot wou'd do our business well. You are assuredly right in getting Mr Faulkner to Lyme, for as its impossible to see each handycraft does his duty, Frank will want no following. Tho' slow, I rejoice to hear Haydock and Norbury works go on so sure. I can't yet fix a time for setting out to Bath but it shall be as soon as possible. We are all quite well and send our best affections to our little ones.

I am Yr very Att. Master.

P. Legh.'

The Legh correspondence of the late 1740s shows a very easy attitude towards coal mining. There was a distinct lack of urgency in the mining proceedings. The only large trade was with the salt proprietors of Northwich, a trade that was beset by transport problems. But in the 1750s things were to enter an entirely new phase. Peter Legh and his advisors must have realised by that time that there were large amounts of coal under Haydock, reasonably accessible, with only transport to the various markets limiting production - a limiting factor that was soon to be eradicated.

For some time great pressure had been applied by the Liverpool salt manufacturers to make the Sankey Brook navigable because they were having difficulties with their coal supplies. The Prescot coal proprietors had held a virtual monopoly upon the Liverpool salt manufacturers for a number of years. At that time the roads being used to transport the coal were in a poor condition, bad in summer and virtually impassable in winter. If repairs were required to the road's surface they were funded by an increase in tolls. Earlier that century the rivers Weaver and Douglas had been made navigable with some success. The difference with the Sankey Navigation was that during its implementation a cut or canal was produced along its complete length. This in itself did not contravene the Act of Parliament, passed in 1754, which stated that various cuts could be made to ease the problems of the navigators. This must have occurred to Henry Berry, the engineer in charge, before the canal's construction possibly during the surveying of the Brook.

Work on the Sankey Navigation began in June 1755 and the entire canal was in use by 1757. It was the first industrial canal in the country. A large section of it ran through the Legh Estates and Peter Legh, though irritated initially, eventually realised that it was a godsend.

In the following years adverts appeared many times in the Liverpool newspapers, proclaiming the great success of the Sankey Navigation. This is the report in the William's Liverpool Advertiser for April 21st 1758: -

'There is a Flat constantly bringing down Coals from Peter Leigh's Esquires Collieries in Haddock, adjoining to the Sankey Navigation; and Coals will be delivered to such vessels at Liverpool as the Flats can lie along side to discharge into, after the Rate of 7s-4d for thirty sealed Bushels, weighing about a Ton, and to all Housekeepers or Places in Liverpool after the Rate of 8s for the same Quantity, to be delivered at their respective Houses, etc. These Coals are allowed to be the best Coal that comes down the Navigation by Two Shillings a Ton.'

The Sankey Canal served Haydock Colliery for many years, the trade only declining during the railway age.

James Gatley and Ralph Leigh.

In the beginning of 1755 a man named James Gatley was in charge of coal mining at Haydock, but the overall steward was a Mr. F. Worthington, possibly the son of the previous steward. James Gatley's first report to Peter Legh was in February 1755. The first part of the letter shows that he is having trouble with money, a problem that dogged him throughout his short career with the Legh Estates: -

'I have sent our settling of the last years account. When Worthington was over at Haydock he examined my books over. And it appears that I am indebted to you for the last year, one hundred and four pounds fifteen shillings and three half pence. I have sent you a bill for one hundred pound payable one month after date. If you remember, you allowed Gerard Ashton five pound a year for John Gaskile writing for him. And you promissed to allow it me for the last year towards my expense and horse hire in getting my outstanding debts and other expense about business. If you please to allow me the odd money, which is four pound fifteen shillings and three half pence would help my wages. I have been at a deal of charge which could not charge to you.'

Further on in the same letter, James Gatley indicated that he was mining near to the border with the Gerard Estates, at the top end of Haydock.

'We have the deep pitt quite down at the Ginn for coleing. Which we shall have in order in a few days, and now we shall have Seven Pitts going. Which will lay us by a large quantity of coles before the sale comes in which will be about the latter end of May. We have had a sale for all the coles that we have gotten since Christmas.'

'Mr Worthington promised to send John Hartly down here in a week or 10 days time, and we will take a look down towards the Bottom of Haydock if the Navigation goes on. I suppose you will be looking for coles that way.'

It is worth noting that John Hartly was to start working at the bottom of Haydock. Peter Legh must have decided that it was advantageous to have a pit in close proximity to the Navigation. In May, later that year, F. Worthington paid a visit to Haydock and reported some good news: -

'I have the pleasure of informing you of two agreeable things at Haydock. One that the borers have found the coal again at nine score yards to the right rather of the Ginn pitt in the new works, which proves there's a vast breadth of coal with a fault there. —- The sinkers were in the field next to the great Millfield trying there afresh. When I came away were got about 15 yards deep and in very likely mettle, and expect at that place to meet with the Lower Delph. They bored this 15 yards in 3 days and when they proved this place they'l try ours again for another mine. I saw Thomas Gaskell who says 'He's heard no more of the Navigators issue he wrote to you' they have not yet made any beginning, nor could I hear for any certainty when they would. And now people seem to doubt how it will be, and question whether the cut will be carried into execution or not, be this as it will, it allows time to prove the land about the present new work. And as soon as the undertakers set about the navigation but do not doubt that you'l be ready there before they come.'

Good news indeed! The fact that they were working next to the great Millfield shows that they were close to Millfield Lane. The boring referred to was done by hand with an auger, a very difficult and time-consuming job. James Gatley wrote another informative letter in June 1755: -

'I received yours last Sunday — and had a desire to see how these borers from Norbury would proceed before I acquainted you they are going home today and I suppose John Heartly will come hear on Monday next and bring the same men with him or some others for the same work. Wee have proceeded in the boreing only one hole in a field belonging to Thomas Boardman and next to the Millfields where wee find the same delf that wee found in boreing at the bottom of our Crop pitt in this boreing wee find a cole Three foot thick sixteen yards from and Ten yards lower wee find a cole half a yard thick and next are gotten four yards lower and find a strong flagg and what we call a burrstone which wee are not gotten through which is very hard in state now under this all our old workmen are of opinion that there is

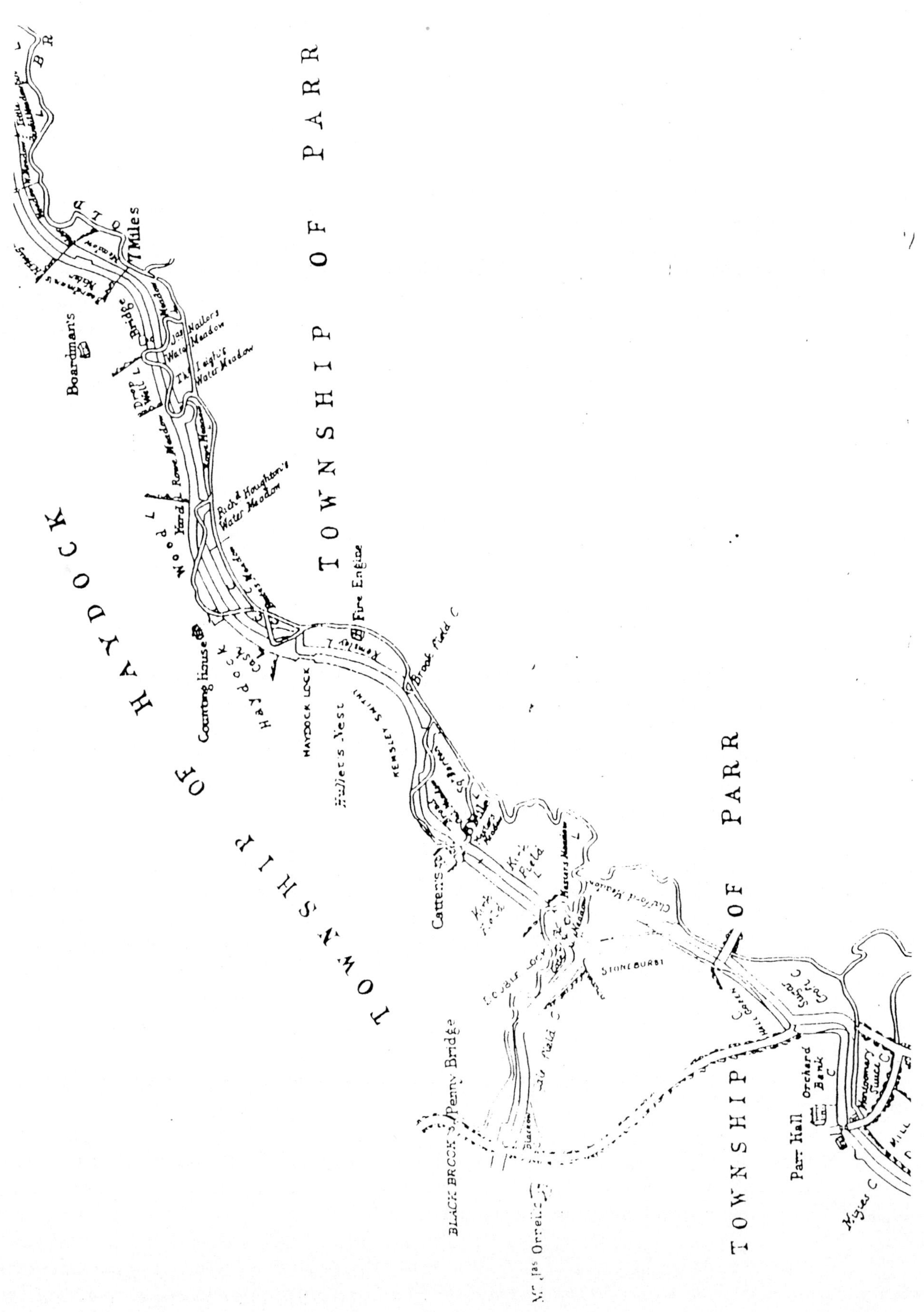

MAP of the SANKEY CANAL in PARR and HAYDOCK
showing the position of Peter Legh's Fire Engine near to Haydock lock

SANKEY-BROOK NAVIGATION

Is now opened for the PASSAGE of FLATS to the HAYDOCK and PARR COLLIERIES.

AND there is a very conſiderable Quantity of COAL laid near the ſaid NAVIGATION, ready for Sale, and Three Collieries already opened, which will be capable to ſupply any other Quantity of COAL which is likely to be wanted this preſent Seaſon.

Advertisement from the Liverpool Chronicle, November 1757

A modern coal tipper on a British Canal

a delf under but are not certain that we can reach it in this hole if wee cannot wee must go higher upon the crop. I expect after wee have proved this you will order them to try at the bottom of Haydock by boreing to find how the coal will lye there for the Navigation. I hear they are begun to cutt and sett out the ground where they propose to go on they say there will not be much done this year about it.'

And further on in the same letter: -

'Wee had a misfortune the other day with one of our getters as he was working a stone fell out of the roof and broke his legg that the bone came out, he has three or four little children.'

It's obvious that James Gatley and his men were having good success in Haydock and their thoughts were turning to proving the coal near to the Navigation. In 1756 there was another report from Mr Worthington, in which he sends an account of six weeks work to Peter Legh: -

'Haydock Coal works from the 1st January to the 14th February stand thus: -

Profits —— £215 19s 21/2d
Disbursements —— £40 18s 10d
Clear profits —— £175 0s 41/2d'

The account showed a tidy profit of £175 for six weeks work. If this amount remained constant for twelve months the profit would have been over £1000. The same letter shows Mr Worthington had become dissatisfied with James Gatley and his lack of information. He gave him strict orders of procedure: -

'I have ordered Mr Gatley to give you a just account how matters go on every week or ten days without fail.'

James Gatley acknowledged those orders in his next report on 24th Feb. 1756, when it's clear that all was not well: -

'Mr Worthington left Haydock on Sunday last he told me would give of all account to you from John Heartly of our proceeding about boreing at the Bottom of Haydock Wood wee have had but bad success since the Pitt was sunk. I am afraid it will be longer before wee come to any resolutions here the Engine Pitt must be (more) then what wee at first expected haveing so many disapointments by the quicksands which will be very tedious boreing through and likewise for sinking through.'

He goes on: -

'I am afraid I cannot pay you the balance of last year's account before the summer there is so much charges sinking here.'

They had started sinking an engine pit in the proximity of the Navigation. Its purpose was to drain the strata above the Navigation to enable further pits to be sunk in the area. Besides sinking the engine pit, James Gatley decided in March 1756 to try somewhere else: -

'Wee have left of boreing this day and purpose to begin to sink a pitt on Monday at top of Twenty acre which wee expect will be about twenty eight yards deep to the higher delf as we have the higher and lower delf at Bottom of Haydock Wood and likewise at this end of the town it must certainly be in the middle.'

The Twenty Acre field was directly north of Haydock Wood. The problems with the water in the engine pit continued throughout the summer of 1756, the amount far exceeded anything that they had met with before. It seems that James Gatley's money problems must have come to a head for in the latter half of that year Peter Legh asked Ralph Leigh of Lowton, who had worked for the Legh estates for some time, to look into the goings on at Haydock. That examination resulted in a marvellously detailed report from him in January 1757: -

'According to your order. I've received from James Gatley an account of the outstanding debts, coles on the brows, and discharges since the settlement with Mr Dodge which amounts to £742 : 19 : 0. Which is considerably more than his arrears, given in which way seems a little odd, though its not to be wondered at, (if I am rightly informed) but he may have more money oweing to him, than what he calls yours. For this reason I am told, he receives from every getter (who are 32 in number) weekly eight baskets of coles. Which they say belongs to him for paying for sharpening the colliers picks, and finding them what they call Way Candles. Now eight baskets from 32 getters amounts to 256 baskets weekly which at 2d per basket comes to £110 : 18 : 8 per year. The outgoings I am told are, six shillings a week to the smith for sharpening the picks which makes £15 : 12 : 0 per year and they say every getter has one pound of what they call way candles weekly to draw by in the pitt. Which I compute upon an average to be worth 6d a pound. Now 32 pound per week makes £41 : 12 : 0 added to the sharpening makes the outgoings to be £57 : 4 : 0 which taken from (the value of the coal) £110 : 18 : 0 leaves if I am right £53 : 14 : 8 clear cash in pocket besides his weekly wages, Slack and I apprehend some other priviledges that I am not yet acquainted with. Now if these priviledges (to your knowledge) are allowed by you, all is well, but if not they ought you'l say to be sett right.'

The letter showed that James Gatley had fiddled the books and had finally met his match. Ralph Leigh completely exposed him for what he was - a rogue. After that Ralph Leigh took over even though he had little knowledge of coal mining. Another man to go was Mr Worthington, who had already been replaced by Robert Dodge.

Ralph Leigh was well thought of in the district. He must have been an upright religious man with a strict sense of duty. His letters were always full of interesting details about local mining and local people. Members of the Legh family sometimes referred to him as 'Honest Ralph.' When he required information on coal mining Ralph Leigh drew on the expertise of his mining engineers, John Hartly and John Serjeant. In August 1757 he sounded very worried about the water in the engine pit: -

'According to the account I gave you the men went down in your Engine pit to sink but to no purpose the water was so strong (viz springs they say) since then they have kept it drained and yesterday went down again but still to no purpose your water is so excesive strong in short notwithstanding what J. Hartley says I am afraid he does not know what to think of it nor from where your water prove of, it was said it would drain Mrs Claytons 50 acres of coals dry and that it had drained a ginn pit near Bartons Bank and sunk it 5 or 7 yards. Upon which I sent privately, last Sunday, a man who knows all these old pits and a man I can trust, to prove the trouble of that, who went amongst them and prove nothing but false storys and not one word of trouble. We have 4 pits at the coal and 2 others very near it, but cannot get forward with the Engine pit. I could wish you'd find J. Sargent and lett him stay a day or two to see if he can find out the fault. One fault is as well as the strongness of the water I think the men are jaded. If this wether holds we shall have a good quantity of coal down at the Wood very soon, I apprehend we get down 150 tons in a day somedays.'

The water problems in the engine pit near the Navigation were always evident throughout its short life. Peter Legh later abandoned it and concentrated on more accessible coal in the north part of Haydock. It was only in the Victorian era that they returned to this area near the Sankey Navigation to try coal mining when the Parr Collieries were sunk.

The Mrs Clayton mentioned was of course Sarah Clayton, who became famous for coal mining in the Parr area. Later on in the letter Ralph Leigh also referred to Stocks Pit, where he was trying shallow mining. The area was close to the border with Ashton, at the most northerly point of Haydock. The only other mention of the term Stock in Haydock is Stock Terrace, which is close to the Rams Head Hotel.

The Steward, Robert Dodge, paid a visit to Haydock in January 1758: -

'I was at the Bottom of Haydock on Friday where things begin to have a better face. They are begun to get coal. The Engine Shaft 44 yds deep, and they are got thro the second mine sooner than they expected, and Hartley saies he expects to be at the lowest in 6 weeks time. So that if they will push forward they may have a large quantity of coals on the Bank by the time the Salt Proprietors stocks are grown lowe.'

This was better news at the pits for Peter Legh. Production at the engine pit could not have been that consistent but it was essential that enough coal was being shipped on the canal, otherwise the flats would go elsewhere. In the next relevant report, in March 1759, Ralph Leigh was shrewdly arranging a deal: -

'I've allready agreed with 8 or 9 of your tenants to cart down from the Stocks to the Navigation 540 works of the crop coal at 2/- per work which they grumble hard at tho' they know it's as good as they can gett elsewhere. If I had called 'em together I cou'd not have done it for I find they wo'd have combined but I take 'em as I can one by one and I doubt not getting any quantity down at the price for in short the people have nothing to do with their teams so that this small employ amonst your tenants seems to keep up their spirits as I tell 'em no man shall cart a coal but 'emselves if they'l do it otherways I must seek elsewhere.'

So although Ralph Leigh was basically honest, he was not above a bit of wheeler-dealing with the farm tenants. The coal was being moved to keep the flats going on the canal. A work was an amount of coal roughly equivalent to 3 tons. In July of the same year he reported that some of the carters had cheated the Turnpike Tolls:-

'I am glad to here your for Lancashire so soon where I hope you'l find matters to your liking. Except the sale at Haydock Stocks which is very slender, all the cheshire sale and part of Warrington go wholey to Ms Claytons works. Viz they go through Holme Turnpike empty and through Sankey Back, and mostly draw the load with one horse through the Turnpike and hook the other off and when they come off the Turnpike and hook on again and so pay nothing at all, others draw through with two horses and pay only 2d (this is what I am credibly informed).'

Alongside the coal reports Ralph Leigh kept Peter Legh informed of the day to day running of the Haydock estates. As well as mining at Stocks and Haydock Wood Peter Legh was also producing coal from Laffak. This is from February 1760: -

'We have a deal of coal up at Laffack. But they go so fast at the Engine that I am fearfull we shall want men and we pick up all we can meet with but if we can do no better — wo'd it not be as well to stop at Laffack a little while and see how those coals offer to go and lay on those men at the Engine — we can spare them from Haydock Stocks as we are in expectation of very great sale we are makeing preparation accordingly by sinking new pitts laying by coal etc for that purpose.'

Ralph Leigh sounded happy enough with the coal mining position. The next letter written later the same month gives an indication of Ralph Leigh's standing with his Master. He had contravened one of Peter Legh's orders, although he quickly gave a good reason why: -

'We expect a very extra-ordinary sale the next summer from all parts — against which time we are providing — by sinking new pits — which I think is much better to have a number of fresh pits and workmen than to have too many laid by — for then the country will have fresh coal — which they like — the coal at the engine tomorrow will be sold at 2d per basket — which I have let all our customers know — at St. Hellens they are sold at 2d — now this is contrary to your orders — which I hartily beg pardon for which I hope you'l grant — the reason of my not falling lower than St. Hellens is — there is not a customer we have that desires 'em lower but earn at the price — because your works are so much nearer the market than the rest, if they'l can have 'em on the same terms they'l not go past us — and to drop a farthing further and that before we have occasion will make a great dificiency — but if you are determined to do so — after now I've aquainted you with the nature of the matter — I certainly will — if they at St. Hellens fall again I'll follow 'em until you've entirely Knokt 'em up — for that will certainly be the case and soon — at Laffack we are now got fairly Gate'd — we can now get forty works a week or more if occasion — but they prove soft and do not yeeld much to round coal — they are exceeding good fire and the men at Carr furness are in high spirits that they will answer tho' they have not fetched any from the new pits but will very soon — notwithstanding they are small they doubt not but they will Sowder — we shall have a deal of coal there up by May next — then we shall see how the sale offers so soon as we can cart 'em to the navigation I doubt not but we can afford to sell 'em so, and that they'l be of such a quality that we can sell 'em to Mr. Ashton and Mr. Blackburn for their Salt Works — and also to the Copper House — as Richard Sharrat thinks they'l be shaleable for 'em — as they say the engine coal is not — we shall have a sort of the engine via the upper most Delf that we expect will be right for both Glass House, Copper House and Mr. Blackburn and Mr. Ashtons works — which your engine men say is best for that purpose if so we expect they will answer the above purposes — Mrs. Claytons works has very little to do, it's said she will not gate another worke only get those few she has by the engine — she has a great quantity of coal upon the Brows — which I imagine they expect a summer sale for — but perhaps she'l meet with a disappointment for expect a part of that kind of sale at Laffack, with her, and another part at Haydock Stocks — in short it's got to Live that can live amongst us — we do all we can to be uppermost (which we are by much)

our sale is good.'

The last letter is of great interest because of the amount of information about the St Helens coal industry. It is full of intriguing characters and a feeling of exciting competition. It's obvious that Peter Legh was very lucky to have the first coal works reached by the flats on their way up the canal. The Mr. Ashton and Mr. Blackburn referred to were powerful Liverpool salt works proprietors. Also quality as well as quantity was becoming a significant factor in the sale of coal. The tone of the letter shows what a tough character Ralph Leigh was and how he was committed to making a profit for his master.

Early Coal Mining using baskets

Richard Orford takes Charge.

The year 1760 saw the arrival of one of the major characters in the story of Haydock coal. It was during that year that references to Richard Orford dealing with accounts for the Lyme Hall estate began to appear. He was the son of John Orford of Bradley in Burtonwood where the family had farmed extensively during the early part of the century. They also leased Lions Farm in Haydock, a large tenement that stretched from Sankey Brook to Clipsley Lane. It later became known as Heyes Green and will be remembered by many Haydock people today. Richard Orford gained the position of Steward at the age of 28 and ran the Legh estates for over 30 years becoming a very powerful and wealthy man. At the peak of his career all aspects of estate business passed through his hands. His power stretched from Lyme Hall to St.Helens where he became involved in the infighting that went on in the 1770s over coal production and price fixing.

In 1767 he married Nancy Gaskell of Prestbury and over the next 15 years they had 6 children. They lived for many years in a large house in High Lane, a village very near to the Lyme Park.

Richard Orford was well educated and possessed a good strong handwriting style. There is evidence that he was a large man, one of his friends commented *'you are very heavy and ought to be very careful what you ride.'* Over the years he became a friend of most members of the Legh family. Peter Legh's daughter Elizabeth Keck referred to him as *'Orford'* but signed her letters *'your obliged friend EK.'* She continually asked him for all the gossip about the staff at Lyme. He was also on good terms with Peter Legh's brother Ashburnham who at that time was living at Golborne Park. In a letter in 1770 he teased Richard Orford about the non-delivery of his socks:-

'My Dear friend Richard has forgot to send my six pair of stockings from thy Disley Merchant, I fancy your living in Sunshine while my poor North Britons are starved in Snow and Frost, your sending them by ye bearer and giving me a line on G.B. affair turns out you will oblige.'

Ashburnham Legh was the father of the future Lord of Lyme, Thomas Peter Legh. Although he was a powerful man Richard was noted for his good nature and was prepared to put himself out to a great extent for friend and stranger alike. George Oliver made reference to that point in 1790: -

'Am happy to hear yourself as well as Miss Orford is much better, and sincerely hope you both will soon be restored to your former state in good health thank god this leaves our family well, I am sorry my sister was not successfull at Lyme, I have reason to think she had to overcome a person that has too much influence with Mrs. A. Legh. I am extremly obliged to you Sir, for your kindness to her, she writes to mee acknowledging it with sensations of gratitude and respect and be pleased to accept my best thanks for your civilities.'

He was also on good terms with other members of the household. In 1778 W. Newhouse, a retired butler, invited him for an interesting day out: -

'If the Dignity of the Lord of Lyme's Steward, and the Gravity of Mr.Orford can so far descend, Old Newhouse will be happy to see you on Wensday next the 21st Inst at the Top of Handley where you may expect to see some few Relations and Friends. Men, that you respect, and may laugh one hour with, at the Oddity of the Country and the F—-y of the Host who has Hunted so many Sons of Bacchus together to hold a Feast at the Building of a Temple Dedicated to the Goddess Cloacina or in more humble Strains to Celebrate the Festival of the Sh—thouse Rearing. I have taken the liberty which I hope you will second to write to John Wood to Meet us with a Greyhound, as Benny you know is fond of a Course and Kettleshulme side of Handley is out of sight at Lyme.'

This was obviously a secret meeting of old friends out of sight of prying eyes. Richard Orford was well known for his boasting about the quality of his ale. As a friend, Samuel Daniel, jokingly remarked on the subject: -

'I have agreeable to your request sent Mrs.Orford very good Hops. But you are a tantalizing Chap to tell one of your good ale and would make a show of blaming me for not tasting it often. But you are not come of in that manner

for tho' you make an offer of your good liquor, yet you are never at home for me or any one else, so that I can hear of no body but yourself that praises Mr. Orford's ale.'

In his capable hands the Legh Estates improved greatly in efficiency and production. As time went on Peter Legh put more and more trust and power into Richard Orford's hands and he became indispensable to the running of the estates.

Strata photograph of Haydock, showing coal seam in relation to the surface

The Rise and Fall of John Serjeant.

It was during January 1757 that the first references to John Serjeant, the engineer, began to appear. A letter by Ralph Leigh referred to him working at Haydock: -

'J.Serjeant is working hard at the Engain, and Hartley says he expects to gett cole to fitt the Engain with in a few days.'

It is possible that John Serjeant was the engineer who worked on the Norbury engine and, due to his success there, it was decided to use him at Haydock. In his early days at the Legh estates he was looked upon as the great mining expert having the ability to solve all the problems that they encountered. Another report in February 1757 by Robert Dodge, the Steward, gave an indication of his powers: -

'I returned hither the morning after and spent the remainder of that Day at the Fire Engine which is a very neat peice of work. Serjeant has been very indefatigable and works almost night and day to finish it, which is now done and was set to work late last night, and by the account I hear tonight it is like to answer very well. They are got down to the coal at the pit lately sunk on the rise so that there will be a supply of coal.'

The engine referred to was the first fire engine erected on the Haydock estate. It was situated opposite Haydock Wood near the Sankey Navigation. Over the next few years John Serjeant was called upon many times to give his opinion about coal mining in Haydock, Norbury and Laffack. He also began making his own reports to Peter Legh, although we can see by the spelling that he was not well educated. The first that appeared was in May 1760: -

'Last Munday and Tusday and Wednesday I was at Hadock and Lafak I examand into every afour consarning Lafak works there is 50 work picked out of the very best of the coale and lede by for the furnis I beleve there is pritey near 300 work mor work all redey pild upon the banks I think theirs to maney beforhand for the ere very soft and will not abid the wedder and without the go of very soone I dout ther will be a great deal of loss in them the reason of them being so soft is the ere gott intirley upon the out brook there is one pitt is but about 12 yds deep so that your worship may redely judge this must be soft piking the best of the coale out for the furnis has don the other part of the coale a deale of harm and sertinly will be a disadvantig for the will not be sould for above 9s works.'

The furnace he refers to would be the one previously mentioned at Carr or Carr Mill. Most of his letters contain complaints about other men's work. In the next letter, written in Nov. 1762, he continued: -

'I received yours and will promise you every time I come to haydock will go downe into the Bothom And I humble thanck you for your kind thoughts and expressions in the behalf of me before Mr Peers and Madam Ann Legh and whenever I am in all my buseyness and slavery that shall be in my thoughts, I will asure you that ever since Ralph Leigh and these other men have been concerned I've done all that ever lay in my power to direct them to carry the works forward to your Honours advantage you are sencable the was all strong in that buseyness when the undertoke it; however the have been so bigoted in there one opinions that the have moov'd matters that as been fix't betwixt them and I when my back as been turnd, which I know as been to your disadvantage'

So John Serjeant had come in for some criticism from Peter Legh. Overall the first section of the letter had an unpleasant ingratiating tone about it. He carried on: -

'And at first when we begun at Laffack I had fixt the very place where the water pit shud a been and as soon as I had turnd my back the remov'd 30 or 40 yds from that place and just throde themselves upon the fault, ——— I did hurry them about it two or three times but the add allways Ralph Leigh at there backs so that what I say'd did not stand for much;'

Mr Peter Seaman & Co. Dr for Coal

1763			£	s	d
		Brought from Page 290		8	8
April 9	13	Jno Twist		4	4½
	30	Ackers		6	3
11	30	Do		6	3
	24	Jno Twist		5	–
12	24	Do		5	
13	25	Do		5	2½
	24	Ackers		5	–
	20	Spencer		4	2
14	30	Ackers		6	3
15	31	Do		6	5½
	24	Twist		5	–
16	21	Wm Burrows		4	4½
	24	J. Twist		5	0
	30	Ackers		6	3
	23	H. Fireshaw		4	9½
19	54	J. Houghton		11	3
20	30	Do		6	3
	21	J. Twist		4	4½
	48	H. Fireshaw		10	–
	26	Rt Houghton Senr		5	5
	24	Thos Gorce		5	–
21	30	Naylor		6	3
	42	H. Fireshaw		8	9
23	20	J. Twist		4	2
	26	Rt Houghton Senr		5	5
	24	Jas Houghton		5	–
16	24	Ackers Omitted		5	–
25	26	Rt Houghn Senr		5	5
25.26	100	Naylor	1	–	10
25	24	Jno Twist		5	–
		Carrd Forward	£17	17	6

29 To De Warrington Cr

1763			£	s	d
11th		Brought Over Peter Seaman & Co Dr	17	17	6
Apl 26	25	J. Twist		5	2½
	26	Rt Houghn Senr		5	5
	25	Do		5	2½
27	27	Do		5	7½
	26	J. Houghton		5	5
	20	Naylor		4	2
	23	J. Twist		4	9½
	30	Ackers		6	3
	22	Thos Gorce		4	7
28	21	Do		4	4½
	23	J. Twist		4	9½
	20	Naylor		4	2
	26	Rt Houghn Senr		5	5
	20	Twist		4	2
	30	Naylor		6	3
	20	Wm Burrows		4	2
29	28	Rt Houn Senr		5	10
	24	Ackers		5	–
30	24	J. Twist		5	–
	24	Ackers		5	–
	20	Thos Naylor		4	2
2d May	24	J. Twist		5	–
4	24	Do		5	–
6	42	Do		8	9
7	44	Do		9	2
9	43	Do		8	11½
	21	Fireshaw		4	4½
10	45	John Twist		9	4½
	22	Spencer		4	7
11	22	Do		4	7
	20	Wm Burrows		4	2
11.12.13	133	John Twist	1	7	8½
13.20.25.26	130	Do	1	7	1
18	20	Burrows		4	2
		Carrd to Page 304	£29	5	5

A page from the 1763 account book showing deliveries to Peter Seaman & Co. of Warrington by various carters

A page from the 1764 account book for William Cundley's Pit:-
Top section shows the deliveries to customers with number of baskets and price.
Bottom section shows the men working at the pit with amounts produced and wages for a fortnight's work.
The men were paid 7½d per load for getting and 1d per load for drawing.
The above page was signed by Harry Richardson and Richard Orford.

Relations with Ralph Leigh were reaching low ebb. One problem that John Serjeant had was that Ralph Leigh was well thought of at Lyme and it's obvious from the letter that the men were ganging up on him. He also complained about the methods they were using in a new pit just sunk at the bottom of Haydock: -

'the last time I was downe the drove under the pit and when the came under it the opened the drift very wide evry way and so let it fall downe and that certenly was the only method of throwing it in I emagen there thoughts to be just geting what few Coles the cold easly and then throwing it up but I told them very off that fault must be tried if posable or else we cold not give our master satisfaction, I dar say after we have prov'd this fault and find the mine to continue the next pit we sink I will undertake my selfe,'

It seems that the men had taken too much coal close to the pit shaft thereby causing it to fall in. In the postscript he suggested that a Bailiff would be useful at Haydock and typical of him he has a dig at John Shaw for not doing his job: -

'Sir I make bould to mention one thing further which I thinck will be something in your faviour it will be laying a fresh charge upon the worcks that is to fix what I call a Baileff to be allways the day over upon the ground at Laffach and sometimes to walk downe to the Bothom of haydock when Shaw is out of the way as there is very often the care to take care of shiping of coles and all other odd matters as Shaw pretends he as a deal of buseyness among carpenters and timber and I'me sure somebody ought to be upon the ground continualy If this be pleasing to your honour Henry Richardson as a son which is very likely for that Buseyness if he chueses,'

The Henry Richardson mentioned was in charge at Norbury. His son Harry did get the Bailiff's job at Haydock and was later put in charge of mining there. John Serjeant's next letter was a very sad one. He had lost one of his workmen in an accident in a shaft and his first thoughts are to providing money for the widow: -

'I make bold to aquint you with a mis fortune wee have had at Norbury on Munday last while I was at Haydock we have a man kill'd After he add done his worck and was going into the basket something fell out of the shaft and kill'd him that expire in a few minuets after; which as put all our workmen in a very great confugion and there as been very little worck done this week but I hope to get them all settled into buseyness by Thursday next, Humble beg that your Honour will allow the poor widdow 20s to'rds the funerall expense as she has seven chilldren but are all of them got up but two which are very small on's he as been an Old worckman and I your Honour will not thinck amiss of me for asking this faviour,'

In the postscript to this letter is a very interesting point:-

'In my next letter I will explain and lay before you evry reason I have to thinck that a Masheen upon that raild rode will be benefecial,'

The machine he referred to would have been a weighing machine to check on the amount of coal transported. The raild rode or rail road probably ran from the collieries down to the canal making transport easier in winter or wet conditions.

John Serjeant continued working for Peter Legh during the early 1760s. It is a number of years, however, before anything is heard of him again. It is possible that some of the correspondence was lost concerning that period. The next significant letter was written in December 1766 reporting progress at Norbury: -

'I make Bould to lay before you our goings on at Norbury, and how fair we have sunk and driven in each place we have sunk the Ingen pitt 37 yds and have not mett with cole nor Black I expected to a mett with the Black at 33 yds, but it ar not prov'd so luckey, as soon as I perceiv'd the coal was flung down deeper I begun a tunniling and have driven 12 yds plum upon the rise and have mett with the Black which is very strong and good, it is a very great token of the coal being good, we are now the thickness of the Black from the coal and how thick that will be I cannot justly say, wheather 5 yds or 7 yds because it as never been prov'd so far upon the deep,'

They were having problems with finding coal at Norbury. The term Black that he refers to was black bass, a hard stone usually found above coal. He carried on: -

'I do believe we shall need no more sinking this 2 years, so in that time I am not afread but I can make your Honour amends for all this dead expence. I had rather bring a 100 pounds to your hand then take 1 pound from it (upon this occation) I hope your honour will not be discourag'd for I am not afraid but you will have satisfaction from your works hear in a short time.'

But all was not well in his relationships with the workmen and it's obvious from some of the letters that he had in some way crossed Peter Legh. After 1760 he had to deal with Richard Orford, the new Steward, who would certainly not brook any disobedience. Problems with Norbury coal works carried on and John Serjeant was eventually dismissed, but kept returning to the coal mines and upsetting the men. Everything came to a head when they set one of the young men on him. Peter Legh mentioned it in a letter:-

'Young Hyde has drubed Serjeant till he cried enough, accordingly he has had Hyde before a justice and has swore heartily to a lie, by ye post I've wrote to Hen. Richardson with assurances.'

Things from this stage went from bad to worse. Peter Legh wrote to Richard Orford, in May 1768: -

'That rascail Serjeant won't be satisfied till he's thrown into prison and if it's practicable I'l willingly subscribe to it,'

Later that month John Serjeant wrote to Peter Legh begging, in the most abject terms, for his job, or any job: -

I am informed that your coal winders at Norbury are ill natur'd seys the will not wind your coale under 4d per quarter and iff it be agreable to you I will undertake to winde them at 3d per quarter for seven together I will also do the smiths work at 3d per week I will take care of your Ingen upon the same terms that I did it for before otherways I will finde leather solther candles oil and workmanship for the Ingen and dow your underlooking and take care of all your works at eight and thirty shillings per week for seven years together.

Dear Master I humble beg that you will be so kind as to forgive me for what is past and take me into your service again as I never have been easye since I left it if it be posible that I can double my dilligence you may depend upon it I will,'

However this grovelling to his Master was to no avail. Peter Legh had hardened his heart against him and later stated: -

'I enclose you a villainous letter from Serjeant, for the openess of my heart I hope will never permitt me to secret a letter so vilely levell'd at ye inocent, shew it to H. Richardson and let him use him with the contempt it deserves. I see plainly ye rascails starving and may it be so for me.'

This must have been a sad end for the indefatigable John Serjeant, who disappeared completely from the correspondence. But his name lived on. At the end of the eighteenth century when the Norbury pits were leased out, some of them were still called Serjeant's Pits.

The Richardsons.

After John Serjeant's demise Henry and Harry Richardson, a father and son team, carried out the running of the collieries. Harry probably used that name to differentiate himself from his father. Henry Richardson was in control at Norbury but it was Young Harry, as he was sometimes called, who took on the difficult job of the Haydock coalfield. The coal industry in Britain was developing rapidly. Ventilation was better understood and was being used to combat the various gases that miners encountered. In Haydock the main problem was water but pumping engines and soughs were controlling this.

Harry Richardson's correspondence began in January 1767 with a report to Richard Orford. Young Harry's first problem was with water: -

'Last Monday morning we began to Boar the water out of Thos. Lowes pit but had the bad fortune to miss the pit. Old Ned set them to Boaring in another place which found it's way into the pit on Wednesday evening. It was Thursday morning before we could go down to do anything, we had everything ready upon the Brow as was thought needfull, I got Ra. Hunt to go down to assist them in seting brick but all to no purpose. We had no sooner put in the Plug but in about 2 or 3 minutes time it whent through all parts of the wall which was 3 Brick thick set in Leigh Lime as well as possable could be. I do asure you it's out of the power of Man to stop it, as what I thought it was, However the men as done as much as ever lay in their power to do it, We had 20 down in the pit besides a number upon the Brow which whent down last Thursday morning early and never was out of the pit but at hard labour day and night till yesterday about one o'clock.'

He also reported to Peter Legh on the same date with more information: -

'I have taken particular notice of the pitts in the Redmans Earth where the work first began, that the water has had a continual waste in them. The work as we are opening below the Redmans Earth we are sinking and pushing it forward as fast as possable.'

Poor Harry seemed beset with insurmountable problems but he soldiered on through the early months of 1767. The Lowes pit he mentioned was north of the present Church Road, very near to Haydock Lane. Redmans Earth was the soft red sandstone that predominates in that part of Haydock. By the 11th Jan. he had made further progress with stopping the water: -

'I got one Lyon of Parr who is acquainted with Leigh Lime and knows the nature of tempering it, and at the same time is really a good hand in Bricksetting, after this I had some discourse along with young Greenall of Parr who was the stoppage of the grievance there. We concluded to begin of it last Monday evening which was the time I saw them, accordingly we made a foundation for our wall which was about 32ft 9ins long 9ft deep and 6ft 9ins thick at the bottom, but as we kept raising our wall we diminished it in thickness. Friday evening we plugg'd it up, the wall not being properly simmer'd together, it issued out of a great many joints in the wall by the violence of the water and air in the cavity, last night it burst out the plug but was stopp'd immediately, today we have been down, and have corked it well with Ocum and Wedges where it issued the most, that I dare say it does not make above 2 buckets in a hour; When the Morter is grow'd hard, I do not doubt but we can stop the whole by corking, if it does not break out elsewhere,'

By February things were looking up: -

'This morning going down to the Colliery's I found things more promising then I mentioned in my last. The pit behind Old Neds was last night set upon the hard, so it will stand with little Boarding. Today the metal is harder and floors better, I expect we are about 8 or 9 yds from the Coal and shall be down at them soon. We are casting clay here in order to make Brick. The pit in Killbuck Lane where Jos. Twist burns Charcoal is done. I don't understand this way of going on, surely the pit is runing together, there has but very few Coals come out of it. Old Ned says the Smothering Damp is in it. Yesterday he set them out another pit to sink near to it.'

A happier picture began to unfold. The term setting upon the hard meant getting through the drift, which consisted of boulder clay and shale. Killbuck Lane ran from the modern Kenyons Lane towards Old Boston. *Smothering Damp* was a term for Blackdamp or Carbon Dioxide, a type of gas that suffocated miners.

For the next few years Peter Legh concentrated on two main colliery groups, Florida Colliery and Stocks or Stocks End Colliery. Florida Colliery was north of the present Church Road close to the border with the Gerard's land. It supplied mostly the Navigation trade and consisted of various shafts sunk at different times during the 1760s and 1770s. The majority of the coal it produced was from the famous Florida Seam named after the farm where it outcropped. It ran southwards under Legh estate land from Florida Farm towards Newton at an incline of 1 in 12. Florida coal was one of the best quality coals in the country, which allowed Peter Legh to sell it at a higher price in Liverpool.

Later in 1767, Harry Richardson decided to try sinking a pit in another part of Haydock. He reported to Richard Orford in September: -

'As today turns out so very wet we are not able to do anything at the sinking near Finger Post. We should a set the pit upon hard today and get up the Eye Coal tomorrow had the weather been good.'

Later that month he had trouble extracting boring rods: -

'Yesterday morning we got the rods and punch out the hole as we had last at the Guide post. I imagined by the rods being so fast that some pieces of iron stone had fallen out of the side, but it proved to the contrary. It being the punch unscrew'd from the rods and puting the rods below it could not raise them being jam'd by the shoulders of the punch and rods. We had two screw jacks fix'd to the rods and the rope from the Ginn and not stir them upwards at all, but by us working downwards and upwards we work'd the punch so small that we had room to draw the rods by the punch so got them all. We are about 17 yds below the first Coal and the ground is partly the same metal as what we have had. I have sent for Sharret to come over in the morning to see what he thinks of it, as we have not had the Coal before now.'

Their endeavours at the Finger or Guide Post Colliery did not come to much, they only gained a small amount of coal. There was a Guide or Finger Post at what became known as the Huntsman corner, so that is the most likely place for the colliery. Harry Richardson gave a vivid account of an explosion at one of the pits: -

'Last Wednesday morning we had 2 men burn'd in Davies pit, the pit I mention'd to you when you was over last time, it being set to fire. The Damp and fire together is so strong that no man living can bear in it. We attempted to drive it by the steel mill, but no person could stay in it (the Damp being so striking) and we have as good air in it as possable can be. As the Coal bleeds so very fast in every vein and likely to be at some distance from the Grand fault. I have set out another pit above the level of this, for to have it air'd from it.'

The *Damp* was firedamp or methane and the steel mill was a very dangerous method of removing it, by actually firing the gas. Normally a steel mill, invented by Spedding in 1760, was used for illumination in gaseous conditions. The Grand fault would be the Bullstake Fault that ran north to south through the centre of Haydock.

In 1768 there occurred a series of meetings between the coal proprietors on the Sankey Navigation. Certain members of this group, Peter Legh among them, had decided that there should be an increase in the price of coal. Of course it was realised that it could only be done en bloc. Peter Legh wrote the first letter on this point to Richard Orford in April 1768: -

'I had your letter yesterday and highly approve the Coal meeting you've already had and tho' unsuccessful at first make no doubt of Makeys coming in when he has duely weighed matters.'

The Makey referred to was John Mackay who mined at Parr and Ravenhead. He was one of the most powerful of the St Helens coal magnates and his policy was to keep prices down and increase production. About that time Peter Legh received a letter from John Mackay, which he immediately passed on to Richard Orford with a wry comment: -

'The enclosed letter from Mr Mackay I received ys morning which is so long and so full of invective I had neither patience to read it nor sufficient knowledge to understand it to ye effect I have replied. The coals are now sold on Sankey

has been sufficiently tried to convince every coal proprietors they must want to ye bad, and to prevent that its highly necessary we should come into an agreement to make ye country pay a fair price, but whether its to be done by each of us being stinted to quantity or otherwise is quite immaterial to me if ye owners agree to raise their Coal properly. If Mackey persists in obstructing our desire we must find ways to squeeze him into terms'

So Peter Legh passed a hot potato onto Richard Orford who had increasingly taken on the burden of the estates. It's obvious that Peter Legh wanted to raise coal prices at all costs and he was prepared to take on John Mackay to do it. Later that month he again referred to Mr Mackay: -

'if we can but bring Mackey to consent to raise ye price all would do well again, he's a whimsical man and not a little positive, but when he finds the rest of proprietors determined perhaps he may listen to reason.'

In the same letter he also said that things were looking up in the coalfields: -

'I had your letter ys day and am glad to hear you confirm ye good prospect we have at Norbury and which Hen. Richardson wrote me to ye same effect. And Young Harry from Haydock writes me word they have coal two yards thick on ye other side ye fault and better in its kind than he expected, so that in time I hope we may renew onst more a land trade;'

By May 1768 they had nearly reached a settlement over the price of coal, only John Mackay was sticking out. In addition Richard Orford was insisting on a binding agreement: -

'I had yours of the 29th this day and am perfectly satisfied of the necesity of having a solid agreement entered into writing to be binding as to quantity to all the proprietors, And why Mr Mackay shu'd make ye least difficulty as he is allowed so much a greater share is a mistery to me, but I fancy the utter hatred he has to Mrs Clayton is one reason of his objecting,'

From the short comment in the letter we can see that John Mackay was the major shipper on the Sankey Canal and that he was not on the best of terms with Sarah Clayton. During April and May 1768, letters passed thick and fast between Peter Legh and Richard Orford. Some of the letters and replies were only days apart. Peter Legh's next letter, on 7th May, was written in his usual melancholy manner: -

'I had your letter ys morning and am glad to hear you spieke with spirit of our Norbury work, which to be sure has been very expensive but I must I'm hearty enough to see myself repaid but as the Irish say a single misfortune never comes alone for ye greatest is ever attended with a greater, Haydock works for that.'

And again five days later: -

'your anxiety and labours for ye Haydock works I must ever with gratitude remember and I think I can depend on Mr Mackay to do nought unresonable when I'm concerned and whatever agreements you make on my account I shall most readily assent to.'

Richard Orford had worked very hard on the Haydock coal negotiations and Peter Legh was prepared to give him complete support. A week later Peter Legh was in a sorrowful mood: -

'I had your letter ys day and not a little pleased to see ye spirit its wrote in, disappointments have been so natural to me all my life that in truth I am satisfied as to expect nothing more, however it's happy for me that I can bear whatever my lot is. I'm well pleased to hear you are come to an agreement relating to ye price of coals, I was inclined to think Mr Mackay would operate with us when he duly considered ye affair.'

Peter Legh had had many problems throughout his life including the loss of his two sons and the separation from his wife. But his disappointments in the coalfields were soon alleviated because a fortnight later he wrote to Richard Orford congratulating him: -

I had yours of the 22 this morning and am well pleased to see you write with so much spirit on our Colliery affairs at Haydock, glad to see ye attempts you have already made towards the rise of coals which undoubtedly is absolutely necessary. As to ye work Mackay would erect it will require circumspection before I will give an answer, at ye same time I would not do him harme (if it would not hurt my own interest).'

Peter Legh was obviously on friendly terms with John Mackay but the friendship did not stretch to giving money away. The coal agreement was duly made between the coal proprietors, all be it with reluctance on the part of John Mackay: -

'I had yours ys day and am well pleased to hear you are come to a present conclusive agreement on our navigation coal work as to ye price, nor was I surprised at Mackays standing off at first, he loves his own conjectures and by ye time its high time he shu'd be convinced of sticking too long to his own concerns,'

The agreement lasted at least until 1771 but there is evidence that certain members of the group began to drop their coal prices after that date. The next letter of interest was from Harry Richardson to Peter Legh in July 1768. It gives a graphic account of a near flooding due to heavy rains at John Mackay's colliery: -

'At Mr Mackay's colliery they had a fair chance of their Colliery being filled with water, but as fortune would have it, they cut the navigation bank thro' and let the Brook into the Navigation, or else the work had been totally filled with water. By them cuting the bank thro' has filled the navigation fully more with sand then what the Floods did last Winter when there was so much damage done. That there will not be passage for the Flatts for some time. We go very well at the Guide Post Colliery and are now sinking down a New Ginn and two other pits on the other side the fault. Whilst the navigation is in cleansing we have a fine oppertunity of paving our raild road. The Colliery at Haydock Stocks as we are opening, turns out as well as any persons in the world could wish. We have sunk a water pit and have two others down at Coal, besides one that we are sinking, and everything lies according to our expectation, that there is not the least danger but we shall have a good run, after so long search of getting hold of the right end.'

Harry Richardson had excellent news and was even having some success at the Guide Post Colliery. The railroad to the canal would have been well established, the coal being transported by tubs drawn by horses or even being allowed to run down by gravity. At the canal side there was a tipping frame for loading the coal into the flatts. The base for such a frame still exists on the canal basin behind the Ship Inn at Haydock. It was used for many years by the Gerard Family at the end of their gravity railroad from their Pewfall Pits.

Later in the year Harry reported that: *'The Navigation is open and we have begun of puting a board.' and that: 'we shall be in good Bread for the winter season at both Collierys.'*

Twelve months go by before another of Harry Richardson's reports when he informed Peter Legh of great news at Florida: -

'We have had great demand for Coal at Florida, no less then 6 or 7 Flatts waiting for loading every day. The last fortnight we put a board 681 tons of Coal, And got at 4 pitts 165 tons, we have near 250 tons beforehand, that it will be near a month before we have the Brows clear, They would all be gone by tomorrow night if we could Wagon them fast enough down the rail'd road, whatever quantity we can get at Florida there is not the least danger of them being sold, for they will oversell any other coal 6d per ton at Liverpoole,'

Proof of the good quality of Florida coal. In August 1770 he again has good news: -

'At Haydock Stocks our sale begins to encrease very much now as Hay time is over, it's likely to continue till corn cutting comes, We have that in our favour the coal being of so good a quality they'l not stay long on the brows, Claytons have raised their coal to 4d a Basket, which as thrown Burtonwood, Bold, Sankey etc sale into our hands here. At Florida we have some few beforehand and not many, The new pitts we have got air'd, and in fine order to raise a large quantity, What ever quantity we can get here, are sure to go they'l not stick upon our hands.'

After his early disappointments Harry Richardson seems to have hit on a good run, producing excellent outputs at both his main collieries. In the early 1770s things went on in much the same vein. It seems he had a few money problems in 1772 because one month he had to wait for Richard Orford to send him cash. He complained in a letter of paying out £125 in a day and that: *'If I have shillings more than teeth I have ten thousand Pounds.'* He also reported: -

'Last week we shipp'd a many coal at Florida and have the Brows clear, I do not doubt but ours will go at the old price if we but keep up our measure to make it some what equal to the price. Tarbuck, Speakman and Sharrets come to the counting House last Saturday in order to consider if there was any probability of keeping up the price of coal, Tarbuck said they should reduce them to 4/9 and 4/6 money same as was before time,'

Alexander Tarbuck, Thomas Speakman and Richard Sherrat were all agents of the main coal proprietors. The next interesting report from Harry Richardson was in October 1772 when he was having trouble with water at Florida: -

'I am afraid matters at Florida are not going on well, we but get few at three pitts and have no less than 12 hands in sinking at a great expense, doubtful if we get down to the lower delf upon the Crop for water it's so very strong.'

In December 1772 he reported on his decision to use a sough or drainage tunnel to run from the Florida pits to Clipsley Brook: -

'The suff at Florida no doubt will answer the intended effect when compleated, but an Engine must be the Doctor on the Deep, as the suff was only intended to carry off the Brook water, Crop water, and Sir Thomas Gerard's water, was these waters to come to the deep part of the work all the Engines round about us could not draw it, our Brows keep clear from coal at this place, Haydock Stocks we have had a great sale since the Frost began but a deal beforehand remains.'

The fire engine, which he termed *The Doctor on the Deep* was installed in the following years and proved successful. Later that year John Mackay and Sarah Clayton began a price war on the navigation: -

'I am in afraid Mr Mackay and Mrs Clayton are selling underhand at Parr, by reason of them shipping so much of their old coal, which is of bad quality, and ours at Florida of as good quality, and quantity in measure as any upon the river, with quick dispatch, so that I cannot help but think they are underselling us, as ours does not go off as fast as I could wish,'

In 1774 Richard Orford was having money problems at the pits. There must have been suspicious circumstances about the case because Richard was forced to explain to Peter Legh in the most abject terms: -

'It is with no little concern to me I read your expression, that the Coal works turning out as they have, hurt you not only circumstantially but no little in mind, I can truly and honestly answer that I do believe there as been no misapplied money that ever was given in by the Brow men, and on the first of hints I got to the bottom of it, and hope and believe everything is honest now, The letters I have rec'd from your Honour of late has been no little uneasyness to me, for they are not on such terms as they used to be, and sorry you think if any fault is in me but if you do shall be happy an enquiry might be made into my conduct and honesty, for I have been unhappy in your letters as they did not seem to me to be on the usual terms and am at a loss to think which way I have disobliged you, as I am certain within my own breast I ever made it my constant study to serve you to the best of my Knowledge and power for your interest and quiet.'

This can only be described as a placating letter, Richard Orford must have thought that his own job was on the line, but he was still there later on in the year, so Peter Legh must have reassured him. It was then that Harry Richardson reported about a flooding at Newton: -

'Last Monday but one we had the highest flood ever known in these parts, At Newton Mill the Tenders could not take it but burst over betwixt the Mill and Newton Hall, took down the Cart house etc, had it burst a few yards nearer the Mill mankind could not have saved it.'

In the same letter he wrote about his attempts to extract money from the coal dealers: -

'Last Friday and Saturday I was over at Liverpoole amongst the Coal Dealers and never met with so bad success. Enclosed you have the greatest part I received but have fair promises they will come over in a few days time. I do assure you we must take some other method for to sell our Coal or stop.'

He also complained that his coals are too dear and everybody seems to be underselling him: -

'In the first place Sir Thos. Gerard has reduced his coal to 3/6 per ton money and 3/8 credit. The Leeds Canal now sells at 9/- per ton laid down in any part of the town. The inhabitants of Liverpoole find that by mixing the Sankey Coal and Leeds Coal together makes good firing. Mr Geldard of liverpoole effects very much by his landsale, and as we are now working our measure rather better, and the coal greatly larger out of the pits, I do believe would answer by reducing them to 4/6 ready money and 4/9 credit.'

Harry got his wish later when his coal prices were reduced: -

'We have had plenty of sale since the coal was lowered and doubt not but it will continue,'

The last coal letter we have from Harry Richardson was in March 1775 when he gave an account of the new engine that was being installed: -

'I have paid Mr Rathbone One Hundred Pounds on Account of the Engine, Bellasses 50 guineas and Ashton the Plummer 20 which they say you promised them after I had been at Lerple. I do not see but what the coal trade is worst then ever, I mean the old coal dealers to collect fro.'

Harry sounded disconsolate in this letter. Perhaps he called it a day and moved on to pastures new because this was his last surviving letter. For eight years he had run Haydock coal works with a great amount of effort and style. The next man to run the collieries was already waiting in the wings. Samuel Rigby came from Warrington but made Haydock his home.

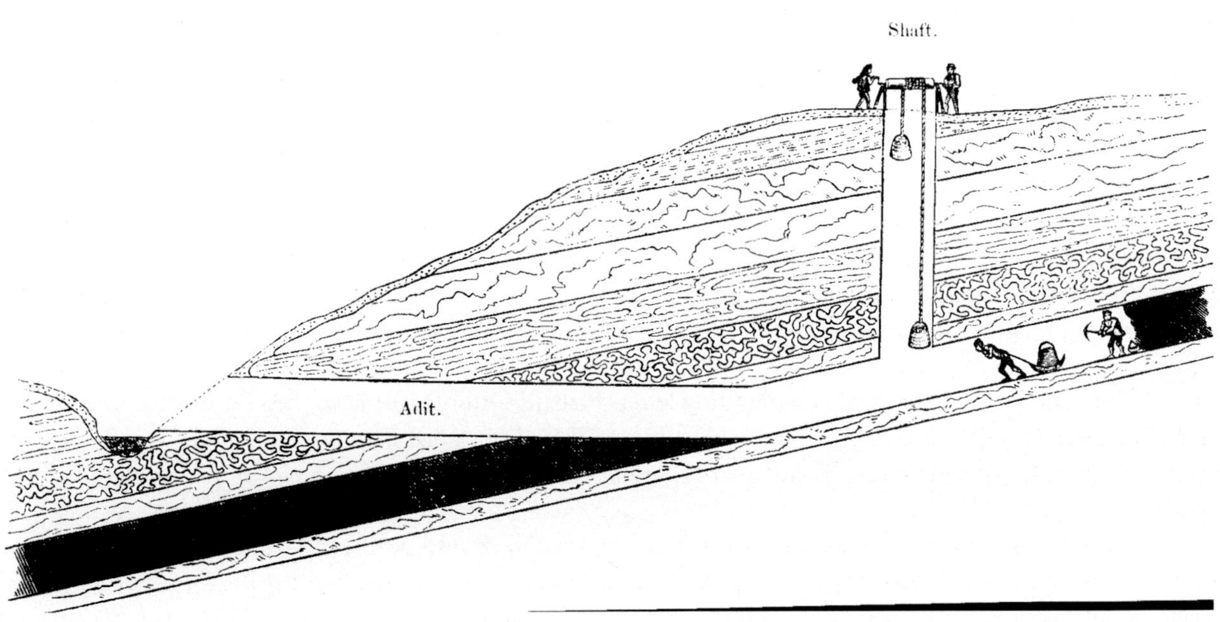

Early Coal Mining

Samuel Rigby and the Stone Parlour.

Samuel Rigby became involved with Legh estates in the early 1770s. His request for a job was included in a letter written to Richard Orford in December 1773: -

'Sir I desire to see you before you leave Haydock that things may be settled won way or other for me father wants to know whether he must Lett the house or no where he lives, which I cannot resolve him till I know whether I stay or go home, If you will give me £40 a year and the house you menshon'd and keep me low it would do, and I dont think Mr Legh would wish to pinch me so that I could not live decantly which we could not of less, the house would want some little alteration to make it conveniant which I hope you will not be against, pray let me have a line from you as soon as posable from yr Humble Servant.'

Richard Orford duly took him on but it was a number of years before anything is heard from him. His early career with Legh estates must have been taken at Lyme under the close tutorship of the Steward. The first report he made from Haydock was in 1777 when he informed Richard Orford about production levels: -

'Inclos'd you have six Bills value £192-4s-7d which I hope will come safe to hand the quantity of coal ship'd on bord the Navigation.

from May 1774 to May 1775 ——3,058 works
from May 1775 to May 1776 ——4,344 works
from May 1776 to May 1777 ——4,261 works

I can make shift to get the next reckoning over and hope to see you at Haydock before another, pray my compliments to the Ladys and Gentlemen of the stone parlor I am with the compliments of the season yr very humble Servant.'

His report gave the production levels of coals shipped on the Sankey Canal as 3,058 works, 4,344 works and 4,261 works for the three previous years. If we assume that a work was in the region of 3 tons, this gives the output of Florida Colliery as 9,174 tons, 13,032 tons and 12,783 tons respectively. Besides those amounts there would be also the landsale from Stocks Colliery.

Within five years Samuel Rigby had established himself as agent or manager of Haydock Colliery. Although not a good speller he possessed the great attribute of attention to detail. All bills he received, all payments he made and the trips he made in connection with his job were priced and listed. His disbursement, or outgoings, ledger is a marvellous record of expenses incurred by the concern. It is an invaluable record of work and workers in Haydock.

Most of Samuel Rigby's letters are signed off in the same manner, referring to the Ladies and Gentlemen of the Stone Parlour. The Stone Parlour at Lyme, also known as the Steward's Parlour, is situated on the ground floor and has a fine stone fireplace. It was where the more important members of the staff carried on their business and congregated during the evening. Any servant who was allowed to sit and converse in the Stone Parlour had probably reached the pinnacle of their career.

Sometime in the 1770s James Grimshaw, who ran the agricultural side of the Haydock estate, appeared in the correspondence. He was to become a well-liked and trusted servant and carried on that work for over 50 years. Many of his letters still survive and they give an impression of a hard working man who was also a bit of a character. In October 1777 he informed Richard Orford that a delivery of livestock had arrived with comical results: -

'John Hall and Thomas Harrison came to Haydock on Sat. night about six o'clock and brought with them the two Mares and sixty sheep, and they themselves two swine for they was both drunk, the parcel that was sent for your daughter they have lost it but where they know not, but they say they lost it at supper or before they came there, I hope you make them to pay for it.'

1776		Florida Coal Disbursements	Days	£	s	d
Mar. 30	..	Benja Harrison Blacksmith this Mo.	24	2	–	–
...	..	John Winstanley do.	24	1	8	–
...	–	do. leting down Colliers 4 Whs.		..	10	–
..	..	Thom. Haselden taking care of the Waggon Horses do.	24	1	8	–
..	–	Wm Haselden do. at Coal Winding Horses	24	1	8	–
...	..	John Thomason Waggoning	23	1	3	–
...	...	Zach Thomason do.	23	1	3	–
...	..	Richd Thomason do.	24	..	16	–
...	–	Edward Eden do.	24	1	4	–
–	–	Robt Glave assisting Browman &c.	24	1	4	–
...	..	Willm Glave do.	23	1	3	–
...	..	Jos. Carry do.	23	1	3	–
...	..	Edwd Harrison do.	21	1	1	–
...	–	Peter Wood do.	7	..	7	–
...	–	Thom. Lowe do.	3	..	3	–
–	–	Willm Whitaker 4 Whs attending Engine		2	12	–
...	..	Jos Knowles underlooking 4 Whs.		1	4	–
...	–	Willm Smith filling 999 Waggons at 1½d		6	4	10½
...	–	do. 21 days Browing		1	1	–
			£	27	2	10½

Disbursements or outgoings for Florida Pits in March 1776.
The Winding Horses were used to raise the coal baskets by means of a Ginn.
The Wagon Horses were used to transport the coal to the canal, probably via a railed road.
William Smith was paid for Browing plus a rate for transferring coal from basket to wagon.
The Underlooker examined the underground workings and can be compared to the modern official of the mine.

COALS

To be SOLD by

WEIGHT,

Twenty Hundred to the Ton; and 120lb to the Hundred;

At the Proprietors Coal-Office, Oppoſite the *New Machine* on *Nova Scotia*; at the following Prices; *for Ready Money only:*

	Delivered to Houſe-keepers, per Ton.			Delivered to Shiping per Ton.		
	£.	s.	d.	£.	s.	d.
Peter Leigh, Eſq'rs Coal	0	7	2	0	6	6
John Mackay, Eſq'rs: do.	0	7	0	0	6	4
Thomas Case, Eſq'rs. do.	0	6	10	0	6	2
Sir *Thomas Gerrard's* do.	0	6	6	0	5	10

Any perſon taking a FLAT LOAD, may have any of the above ſaid Coal, paying the Coſt at the Pits, River Dues, Freight and Cartage. And to accomodate Poor Houſekeepers, or ſuch as cannot purchaſe a Ton at one Time, ſmaller Quantities will be delivered at the Yard, at *[illegible]pence halfpenny* per Hundred, of 120lb.

Sworn Agents will attend conſtantly at the ſaid Coal-Office; to whom the Public may apply.

By Order of the Proprietors.

Coal Advertisement in connection with the Sankey Navigation

A certain amount of sympathy must be given to the two men who had to drive sixty sheep and two mares from Lyme to Haydock.

In the late 1770s Richard Orford became involved in discussions with the other coal proprietors over shipping levels on the Sankey Canal. The four main shippers at that time were John

Mackay, the Cases, Sir Thomas Gerard and Peter Legh. Some of the local coal proprietors had made various agreements with each other to limit production, which indicates that the local mining industry was going through a difficult period. Richard Orford took a major part in the negotiations and for most of the time John Mackay agreed with him. In a letter written in 1778 John Mackay stated: -

'But for Mr Orfords acquainting you with what pass'd at our meetings, I should not have delay'd acknowledging the honor of your last letter. I am perfectly in opinion with Mr Orford, nor can I see any reason against our meeting.'

The agreement that Richard Orford made, or attempted to make, with Mr Mackay, Mr Case and the Gerards is contained in two lengthy reports that he wrote in the early months of 1778. The first began: -

'Suppose the Quantity of Coals sent down the Navigation amounting to 20,000 works, in that case
Mr Legh will be satisfied at——-3500
Sir Thomas Gerard———————3500

It is proposed Mr. Legh's should be sold at 5/3 per Ton
Sir Thomas's 4/8 per Ton
M . Mackay's 5/- per Ton
Mr. Case's 5/- per Ton

In the quantity of coals to be got by Sir Thos. 'tis meant his best coals, and not the bad ordinary coals which are unsaleable, and that Mr. Legh's works no delfs, but the present ones.

Should other Collieries be opened on the Navigation, in that case the quantity should be reduced from each party to bring such Colliery on a footing rather than lower the price of coals.

The quantity of coals sent down the Navigation for the three last years to be procured by Mr. Case and laid before the next meeting.

Sir Thomas and Mr. Legh ties themselves neither to open any New Works or let any Collierys to be worked during this agreement.

We agree to meet the 12th January, Monday, at Mr. Shaws, Prescot at 11 o'clock that morning provided Mr. Penswick can attend if not anyday that will be more convenient to him.'

This is the major part of the preliminary agreement made by Richard Orford. The group thrashed this out the following week at Prescot. It is interesting to see that out of the 20,000 works, which was equivalent to 60,000 tons, Mackay and Case were the major producers. Mr. Penswick was Thomas Penswick, the steward at Garswood Hall. His Master, Sir Thomas Gerard, was at that time mentally ill, so Thomas Penswick was virtually in charge at Garswood. He was known as a very tough negotiator as can be seen in the next report. After the meeting at Prescot Richard Orford wrote out a full report of the proceedings: -

'On my return from Prescot I called on Mr.Penswick and informed him what conversation had passed amongst us there, and that we had fix'd for to see that place again on the 26th. He gave me for answer that I had prevailed on him to offer such terms as he could not have thoughts of doing had not I assured him that I would prevail on Mr. Legh to accept of the same and desired I would write you and Mr. Case that his ultimate determination was, that he would accept of 3250 works of coals at 4/8 per ton to be guaranteed to him for 5 yrs by you and Mr. Case, or if you would guarantee to him 1/6 part of all coals that went down the River let the quantity to be more or less, either of which terms he would be satisfied with, his reason of the quantity being expected is the great concession of Covenanting not to work or let any other colliery during the agreement, also the additional quantity to be sent down by you and Mr. Case more than by Sir Thomas and Mr. Legh.

I mentioned your apprehension of the Northwich proprietors having some thoughts of engaging Mr. Eccleston's coal, his answer was to that, he would put a stop to it, for if this business did not go forward he would offer them such

a mine of Sir Thomas's and at a lords part, that they might afford coals put on board (and they have a profit) at 10/6 per work or he would contract with them for to supply them at that price, if either of these should be the case I am certain coals on the Navigation will not have a sixpence advance for 10yrs next to come, provided Sir Thomas Gerard lives and Mr. Penswick continues as agent there, you was not as well acquainted with Mr. Penswick as I was at the time the misfortune of lowering coals on the Navigation last happened, or you would then have known what would have been the consequence for he at that time say'd he would lower 1/- per ton which was the case, and if things cannot be made agreeable to him, I am certain what I say will be put into execution.

I have made my Master acquainted with every part that has been taken over and to reconcile all parties he will give up the 250 works a year and put himself on the same guarantee as Mr. Penswick proposes and accept of 3250 works which you know is much less than our present sale.'

This clarified the character of Thomas Penswick, who was prepared to cut his profits to the bone before he would be beaten. Richard Orford also made a remark about the agreement of the late 1760s. This was when Peter Legh and Richard Orford wanted to keep the price of coals high but were undercut by the other proprietors.

Later that month Thomas Penswick made a closer agreement with Mackay and Case. It did not save the Cases and Sarah Clayton for they became bankrupt that year.

Within five years all the early coal magnates were dead. In their place appeared a series of smaller concerns that carried on the work. The only remaining major shippers of coal on the Sankey Canal were the two landowners, the Leghs and the Gerards.

Meanwhile, back at the collieries, Samuel Rigby had a dispute on his hands: -

'I received the favour of yours am glad to here you are well, we have made the alteration of twenty one Baskets to the lode at Florida and attempted to do it at the Stocks likewise but the Colliers gave over work and as we wanted coal verry ill was obliged to let them go on in the old way at present as the Stocks Mine is full of faults and obliged to take their drifts narrower they could not so well afford to do it.'

The colliers were probably paid by the load and Mr.Rigby was increasing the number of baskets per load for the same money. A load was equivalent to 1 ton, so a basket at the Legh collieries was approximately 1cwt.

Samuel Rigby's right hand man was Shaw Allanson. He worked for many years at Haydock and later took over the running of the Edge Green Colliery. Shaw Allanson was quite literate and was allowed to make his own reports to Richard Orford and Peter Legh. Here he reported in 1779 about a sough in Florida Colliery: -

'I can now with great pleasure tell you we have got our great difficulty over in the Sough we have been so long about, last night about 6 o'clock we got through the place where it fell in and we have got it set with bricks and today we shall let the water of its right course the dam we made and the pump was our mean security in the geting it through.'

The next important letter from Samuel Rigby was in October 1779, when he reports about 'mobs' in the area: -

'Inclosed have sent you a Bill value £40 which I hope will come to hand we have nothing but mobing in this neighbourhood, they are distroying all the Carding Engens and last night they distroyed Nedeys they have not done any damage to the Buildings but the Engen. I hope to see you here in a short time to have a meeting of the Coal Proprietors for if things must go on as they do the Stocks colliery will not be able to seport the others. Mr. Mackay has ten large flatts of his own which is constantly imployed in carrying coal to Liverpool which he sells so lowe that no other person can afford, so that we cannot sell a lodeing in a quarter of a year to that place therefore desire you will come and see what can be done.'

The remarks in the letter are an early example of the type of behaviour that culminated in the Luddite riots between 1811 and 1816. Samuel Rigby sounded very despondent in the latter half of the letter. It is obvious that John Mackay was up to his old tricks of undercutting his competitors. Richard Orford must have complained to John Mackay for in November he received a letter from James Orrell with a promise: -

'Mr.Mackay has been so much out of order, that I could not see him before yesterday. He desires me to accquaint

Mr Jas Robinson

HAYDOCK COLLIERY, 3d Apr 1778.

Dr. to PETER LEGH, *Eſq.*

To 36 Tons of Coal, at 5/ 3 per Ton, - £ 9..9..0.

By the Flat Thomas & James

Thomas Bennett Maſter.

Sankey Canal Delivery Receipt

The older section of Haydock Lodge complex

1780	Ton	John Mort Esq.	£	s	d
Decr 1	33	at 5/ p Ann	8	5	..
5	33	do p Dolly	8	5	..
7	37½	do p Speedwell	9	7	6
12	30	do p Hawk	7	10	..
20	33	do p Ann	8	5	..
26	33	do p Hope	8	5	..
29	30	do p Hawk	7	10	..
	30	do p Diligance	7	10	..
1781 Jany 3	36	do p Speedwell	9	..	..
6	33	do p Dolly	8	5	..
8	33	do p Nancy	8	5	..
13	28½	do p Hawk	7	2	6
22	33	do p Ann	8	5	..
Feby 15	33	do p Hope	8	5	..
			114	..	..
Mar 3	28½	do p Diligance	7	2	6
13	31½	do p Dolly	7	17	6
16	30	do p Hawk	7	10	..
23	33	do p Ann	8	5	..
29	30	do p Diligance	7	10	..
April 2	30	do p Hawk	7	10	..
6	33	do p Dolly	8	5	..
9	33	do p Ann	8	5	..
May 8	30	do p Hawk	7	10	..
10	30	do p Diligance	7	10	..
24	30	do p do	7	10	..
			84	15	..
June 6	30	do p Hawk	7	10	..
7	31½	do p Dolly	7	17	6
11	33	do p Hope	8	5	..
..	30	do p Diligance	7	10	..
14	30	do p Hawke	7	10	..
23	30	do p Diligance	7	10	..
26	31½	do p Dolly	7	17	6
July 9	33	do p Hope	8	5	..
Augt 6	30	do p Hawke	7	10	..
			69	15	..
Sept 15	30	do p do	7	10	..
19	31½	do p Ann	7	17	6
24	36	do p Hope	9	..	..
26	33	do p Dolly	8	5	..
		Carried to page 147.	32	12	6

A page from the Canal shipment accounts for 1780 showing coal shipped to John Mort Esq. The amounts shown are in tons and the name of the Flat is given *you, that he will do everything that is fair proper and honourable and when you return to Haydock, he desires you will fix a day for meeting and settling the affairs.'*

At that time James Orrell was probably working as John Mackay's agent. Later in the century he became a coal owner in his own right and was a close associate of Richard Orford.

If Richard Orford required any secret information about Haydock he would ask James Grimshaw. Because he was on site James was in the ideal position to provide such information. In November 1780 he replied to one of those requests: -

'Thanks for your early intelligence of Master coming to Haydock, you say you rather think Mr. Rigby was displeased at your writing about the Navigation Coal but be assured he was for he mentioned it to me in such a manner that your letter was not pleasing to him. They have set more Pitts agate at Florida work and gets Day and night, I can say nothing of particulars but I think if they had coal they would sell a great quantity for this day there is 7 flats all waiting for your coal.'

This was certainly good news from the pits. The quality of the Haydock coal was well known in the salt fields and Northwich was still a major market for the coal. One of the Salt Proprietors, a Mr. John Hunt, wrote to Richard Orford in 1782 with an apology: -

'I have been making (little) Salt this few months past and have been obliged to have recourse to Sir Robert Gerard's Coals for what little I have wanted, but when my Pans go forward again which hope will be soon shall most certainly send my Flatts as usual to Mr. Legh's Pitts.'

And again in the same year: -

'We are at present engaged sinking a Brine shaft if we are fortunate we shall want a deal of Coals. We have traded with Mr.Legh upwards of 40yrs.'

This remark is an example of a long and trusted customer. Also in 1782, Samuel Rigby wrote with news about Florida Colliery: -

'I'me afraid you will think me negligent in not writing sooner but I put it off in hopes of haveing something better to send but Florida swallows up everything that I can get inclos'd have sent a bill value £40 which hope will be exceptable, should be glad to hear me Master is well tho' I have not had the pleasure of a line from him since he left Haydock am sorry if I have done anything to disoblige him but have not to me knowledge. John Yates is at Hesketh Bank and has been for three weeks pray my compliments to Mrs. Orford and the Ladys and Gentlemen of the stone parlor.'

It is worth noting his concern over Peter Legh's silence. In the following year he uncovered a plot by the colliery Banksmen: -

'I have every reason but a plain proofe to believe that James Atherton and the men that works in that pit, have agreed to keep part of the coals out of the reckoning and devide the money amongst them, as we wear obliged to leave off won of the pits by reason of the colliers going to work at Florida, I have given over that pitt, turned off the Banksmen, and devided the men amongst the other pits, I shall explain what I have learned about it when I have the pleasure of seeing you.'

Shaw Allanson also reported the same scam. He was renowned for having new ideas so it was typical of him to produce a remedy: -

'James Atherton and Thomas Lowe, two browmen both at one pit, as the report goes has been guilty of cutting of coals after the old custom, as was in practice when Edward Cundley was underlooker, which I think cannot be done but who ever is in that place must have a knowledge of it, and he took pains in the summer to burn coaks in the night and sell coals in the morning from that Brow, John Atherton I mean. John Davies, George Cundley senior, George Cundley junior, William Abbott and Issac Atherton son of John Atherton, was five getters in that pit, the browmen Mr.

Rigby has turned of but the getters are not because the coals are so wanted. I think a scheme might be adapted to overcome all the Browmens projects, which they have many, if a weighing machine was erected near to the pits so that all the coals might be weighed and paid for at the machine, it would be of service to the publick and our master also.'

Shaw Allanson's scheme was taken up by Richard Orford and a weighing machine was erected close to the Haydock pits. At the beginning of 1784 Samuel Rigby lost one of his underlookers in an amusing way: -

'John Atherton is gone off with George Cundliffs wife on friday morning he has attracted many debts in the neighbourhood, more than you can imagine in short everybody has suffered that had anything to do with him, as Abraham Naylor has been brought up in the coal pits and one that may be trusted, I have put him into Johns place at present if you approve of him he may stay in it, if not, hope you will appoint another.'

Shaw Allanson also reported upon it in his own dramatic manner:-

'This morning John Atherton and George Cundleys wife have packed up both their cloaths and gone of together and left Haydock, there will be an underlooker wanted, this strengthens the matter of his sons affair, that he must know of the matters being carried on in that clandestine manner, I was thinking of going to Richard Sharratt to see if he could recommend a man that has been acquainted with long work which would be of use at the works.'

The event must have been the talk of Haydock. Shaw's reference to *long work* may indicate that in some of the pits they were using the Longwall system for extracting the coal.

Samuel Rigby wrote both to Peter Legh and Richard Orford throughout his career. His letters to Peter Legh usually contained the accounts of the Haydock collieries. Here is the one for 11th July 1785: -

'Coal got at Haydock Stocks to 8th July 1785.

458.5 Loads at 5/3 per load—— £120-7s-1.5d.
Paid for getting—————— £47-14s-9.5d.
Disbursements———————-£36-16s-0.5d.

Profit————-£35-16s-3.5d.

Coal got at Florida to 8th July 1785.

119 Works at 15/9 per work————£93-14s-3d.
Paid for getting——————£45-11s-2d.
Disbursements———————£26-17s-9d.

Profit————£21-5s-4d.'

It can be assumed that a work was equivalent to 3 tons and a load to 1 ton of coal. The figures give the amounts raised over a fortnight. This was the usual period of accounting and continued for many years in the Legh coal business. If it is assumed that these outputs are maintained for a year allowing for seasonal differences, this means the annual output would have been over 15,000 tons per year for the two collieries.

During that year Samuel Rigby was having problems with one of his workers: -

'I have writ to our master to acquaint him of Roberts conduct for by all accounts he is seldom sober and some days never goes near the machine therefore as I recomended him thought it my duty to let both him and you know.'

The worker in question was in charge of the Warrington weighing machine, an important job in Samuel Rigby's eyes. Richard Orford must have replied that he would admonish Robert when he next went to Warrington but he failed to do so as the next letter showed: -

'We got the papers you left but expected to find you at the Machine instead of that you did not come near it, as you told Robert you would not, he was verry saucy but did not mind him nor say but little to him.'

It can only be hoped that saucy Robert did keep his job. A tragedy occurred at Haydock in August 1785. Samuel Rigby reported it sadly to Richard Orford: -

'George Allanson left Thomas Edlestons last tuesday was a weeke ago about half past eleven at night drunk and was found yesterday in won of the old coal pits in a chaten'd condition, is to be burid today at Winwick am sorry for his father, he is in great trouble, they had examined near thirty pits before they found him.'

The George Allanson who died in the shaft fall was the son of Shaw Allanson, the Edge Green manager. A significant fact was that there were at least 30 old pits to search in the Haydock area before they found him!

Baronial Style Hall at Haydock Lodge

Samuel Rigby takes a Holiday.

The year 1785 saw many reports on mining progress. In June Samuel Rigby informed Richard Orford that: -

'The Sutton Lime used in the coal pitts that are sinking in the Clipsley at Florida and that upon Haydock Green, answers tolerable well though it does not quite stop all the water, there is so much timber wanting for the new Raild Roade we have marked 770 trees for felling.'

Throughout Haydock's history of coal mining a number of railroads were laid from the collieries to the canal. Haydock must have been well wooded to stand such an amount of tree felling. Sutton Lime was used to seal off the water feeders. If used correctly it hardened when allowed to dry.

In July of the same year Samuel Rigby also stated that: -

'They have finished the pit on Haydock Green but say nothing about the colliery as we expect to see you in a little time.'

The area known as Haydock Green was a built up part of the town opposite the modern stable yard. In August he reported:-

'We have not begun of the Stocks Engen pitt it has been such wett wether as the days are going short it might perhaps be as well to let the Engen House be till after Christmas.'

An engine had not been required at Stocks Colliery because of its position at the top of Haydock. After all that activity Samuel Rigby must have decided to have a holiday. He asked permission from Peter Legh: -

'Desire you will give me leave to go to the salt water for a week, which will much oblige your most humble and obedient servant.'

It seems his visit to the seaside was probably taken at Blackpool because later in the year he wrote to Richard Orford with this remark: -

'Should be glad to know when you go to Blackpool agean if you come this way may perhaps go along with you.'

More serious work required his attention later in the year for it is obvious that Richard Orford had insisted that the sinking of the Engine Pit went ahead at Stocks Colliery. Here we have Shaw Allanson's report on the subject: -

'Our new Engine Pit was but about 12yds of marle and is now about 16yds sunk in red rock and not through it, it has taken all the water out of the by pit at the side of the lane which shows no fault betwixt them.'

Peter Legh must have been concerned about the Engine Pit because he ordered James Grimshaw to have a look how things were progressing. James Grimshaw sent a secret letter to Richard Orford with the following information:-

'I received a letter from our Master when he ordered me to go instantly down to the Coal Pitts and write to him to say how they went on with taking down the Old Engine and building the new one, I writ to him by the same post I write this, that they have not began to pull down the Old Engine nor to build a New one, and that they do not intend doing it till the spring, I only writ you this that you might be better prepared if he should say anything to you about it.'

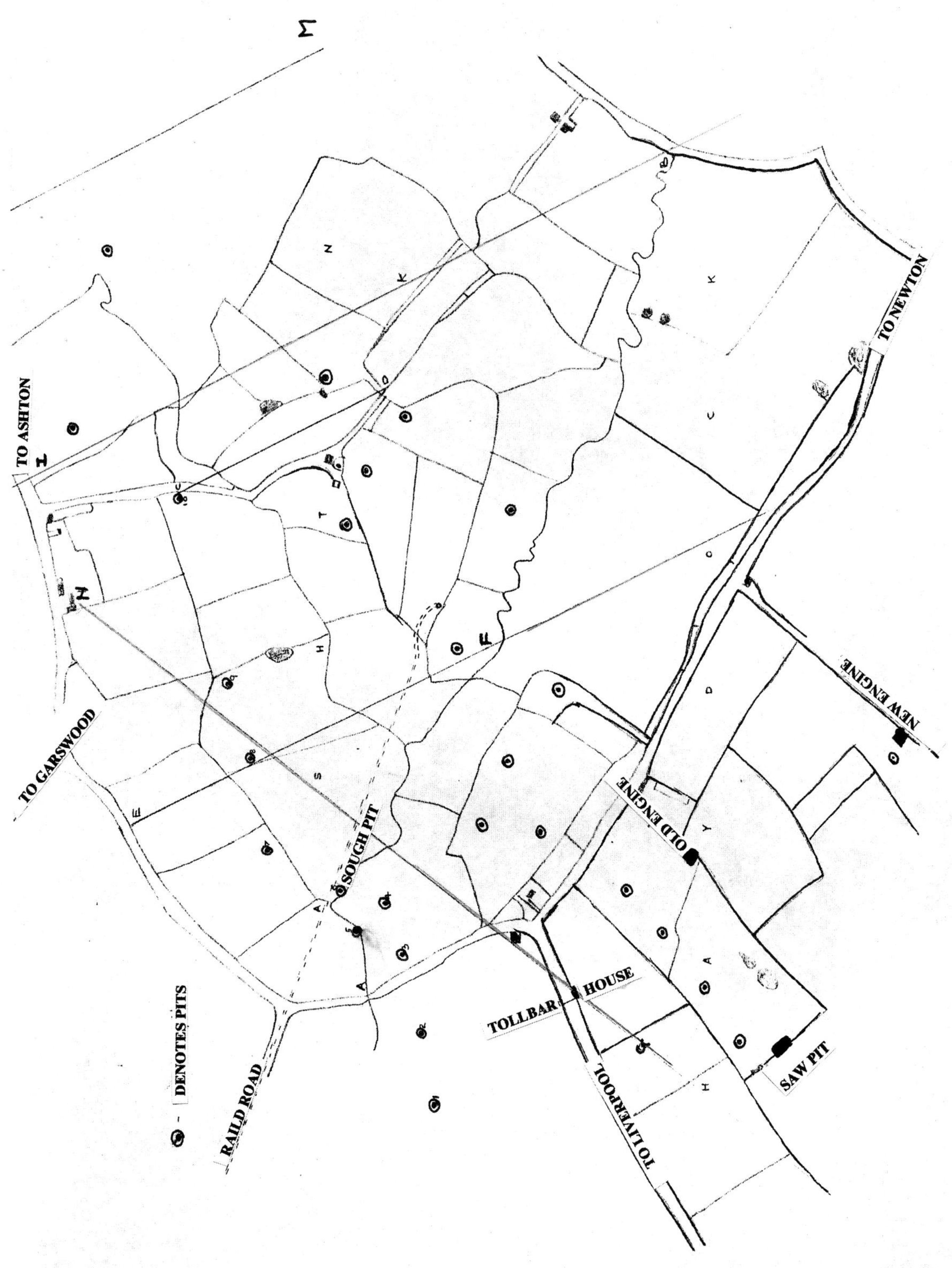

The earliest known map showing coal mining in the Haydock and Ashton area. The attached legend is shown below:-

Plan of the Coal works of Lord Robert Cansfield Gerard Bart. and Peter Legh Esq. lying in the Townships of Ashton and Haydock. Surveyed by J. Wallworth - 1783.
The Brook AB divides the Townships of Ashton and Haydock.
The line CD denotes a fault in the coal.
And also EF, GH, IK and LM
The mark O denotes where the coalpits are and the sough pits by the numbers 1, 2, 3, 4, 5, 6, 7, 8, 9, 10.

It's obvious from the above that the Legh Estate staff stuck together under pressure. He also said in the postscript, *'do not say a word of my writing to you.'*

Shaw Allanson provided a clue to the upsurge in activity when he informed Richard Orford: -

'I was told by Mr. Orrell's brother Saturday last that Stanley Copper Works are sold to St. Hellin Copper Work Company and they are going to erect new buildings to enlarge the works upon that they will want a great many more coals from Sir Roberts Works and will do a great deal more damage to Haydock side in the lands its much if Mr. Penswick dont give us a push to get forward with our levels as their consumption will be considerably larger if they ship their share.'

Peter Legh was keen to get his share of a new market for his coals. By November of that year things had progressed at the Engine Pit:-

'They have let off the water from the old Engen yesterday, they go on verry well with sinking the engen pit are in hopes of getting it down without fixing the engen upon it, all things gose on tollerable well.'

The new Engine was working by the beginning of 1786 and was very successful. The next letter of interest from Samuel Rigby was in June 1787 when he informed Richard Orford of a dispute: -

'The colliers at Edge Green all give out working in order to raise their wages but we sound verry cool about it, they did not work for three or four days but are all gone to their work again on the same terms.'

This is an early example of an industrial dispute albeit short lived. Again in 1787 Shaw Allanson sent a very interesting letter to Richard Orford concerning one of the Edge Green Pits: -

'There is now wanted at Edge Green Colliery a waggon road, in the pit that was last sunk in the deep level it must be to fetch coals Dam Lane side, I have put the men by for some time, as you mentioned the work being stopped, they are now got so far they cannot draw them so it must be laid, or the men shifted elsewhere.'

It is obvious that the coal was some distance from the shaft and the men would have had to drag the baskets on small sleds, probably using a leather belt or chain. Shaw had decided that this was impractical. His solution was to lay an underground rail track and transport the baskets out on small trams.

Later in the letter he informed Richard Orford that the local coal trade was slack and gave his own solution to the problem. It sounds very dangerous indeed: -

'The sale at Edge Green has been slack for a week past and more so that we have piled coals there again as well as at Haydock.'

His solution being:-

'If the work must be stopt, it would be best to take the men out of the deep level first, and stop winding water, and keep shifting higher as the water rises, and get as long at them as they can, so that the coals on the brows may be lessening as there is too many on the brows at this time of year.'

In the late 1780s Shaw Allanson was concentrating most of his time at Edge Green Colliery, probably being in charge there.

The construction of so many railroads and the introduction of underground tracks would require large amounts of iron rails. Most of the rails for the Legh Pits were ordered from Corn & Reynolds of Brosely near Coalbrookdale. The next letter to Richard Orford gives an indication of the numbers required: -

'Your favour of the 30th was duly received ordering 960 Rails to same pattern as last, which I have the pleasure of aquainting you are now in hand and intend to forward them in quantities of about 200 at a time to Haydock which will I suppose suit you better than sending the whole together. Proper Sand Castings it is almost impossible to keep the Rails of the same thickness however we shall attend as much as possible to your request on that head.'

It seems surprising that so many rails were required by such an early concern. It is possible that they were constructing a long overland railroad. Another supplier of rails to Haydock Colliery, was John Wilkinson of Brosely, the famous Iron Master. One account showed Samuel Rigby paying £214 for iron rails.

The Wilkinson family became connected to the Legh family in the nineteenth century when William Legh married Mary the daughter of John Wilkinson. William and Mary Legh were the parents of William John Legh, the 1st Lord Newton.

It was in 1787 that James Orrell appeared again in the correspondence: -

'At the sale of the Parr Estates on Tuesday Mr Penswick produced the Old Coal Lease he mentioned to you, which put an entire stop to the sale of lot No.7 until another can be settled between the parties. Mr. Aflick refuses having any concern but there are I believe other gentlemen who will take his shares. I hope to have the pleasure of seeing you before the next sale, which will probably not be of some time, and we can then fix upon the plan we are to persue. You will be surprised when I tell you that I have bought Parr Hall Lot and Lot.3 and I think on very good terms.'

Mr Afleck had taken over the estates of John Mackay, who had died in 1783. James Orrell had purchased the old estate of Sarah Clayton at Parr Hall. He became a close associate of Richard Orford and they combined many times in various disputes.

In December of 1787 Shaw Allanson sent a dramatic report of an explosion at Edge Green: -

'Yours I received, and on account of Edge Green we go on but badly at present in geting coals. We had a fire the Tusday morning after you left Haydock. Mr Beven was going by to Manchester that instant, I thought you might have heard of it, for it was a surprising one; it went off by three contrary explotions, and fire came up at the pit eye the height of tops of trees they say, it blue up the head gear bricks and at the pit top burnt the rope that was down the pit. The blast of wind made rough work in the water pit, there was only one man in the pit John Greenough he said it fired in the opening betwixt the two higher levels it took him in the gust of wind before the fire as I suppose or he would a been worse burnt, he found himself at last he said in the water hole, it took all before its blast, and the men from Orrell have took their tools and left us who dares stand such fires. We are sinking a pit down on the Crop about ten yards above where Abbott was burnt, if crop air won't kill the fire I don't know what will, they dare not sink it night and day for fear of fire, we bord a hole in an old pit I found on the green the day you left Haydock to about 38ft deep, and there came up at the augre hole a very bad smell we tryed it and it fired, and will at any time fire now, we are getting a few coals at the water pit, the pit above it no one will go into with light till we get the crop down and air it down brow, it will be about six or eight weeks yet before it can be done, then I shall be able to give a better account if we can have men that will stay with us, I was with Mr. Orrell last Friday he told me all Laffack coal was gone and when you and he meet he has 93 pounds for you, which is better news than from Edge Green at present'

They were very lucky that there was no loss of life in the explosion. Their method of sinking another shaft upbrow of the other workings, to kill the fire with crop air, created a ventilation system that provided fresh air thus freeing the workings of gas.

A month later Shaw Allanson requested a small pump for one of the collieries: -

'A fire Engine to raise water about 8ft high and a working barrell 5in diameter, To raise 30 or 40 gallons per minute will be of a small construction. A working barrell 5in diameter Cylinder 8in diameter, a 7ft stroak, eight stroaks in one minute will raise about 46 gallons in a minute but the 8in cylinder would work a larger bore therefore do its work in less time. who ever is imployed to erect it will follow their own construction. Bateman of Manchester has fixt a small Engine at Warrington Glass house upon a well that serves them with house water and turns the Machine for grinding their glass, That over Warrington Bridge at the Cotton Manufactory will be a patent one and I am imformed the patentee is to have £70 per year for saveing of fire.'

The engine would only be small compared with the massive pumping engines used to free the pits of water. The term patent one refers to the policy of Boulton & Watt, the famous steam engine builders, of patenting their beam engines. James Watt held the patents on all his designs. People who attempted to copy them without paying, were pursued through the courts with great vigour. Boulton & Watt engines were more efficient and that allowed them to demand a percentage of the coal saved.

Richard Orford must have written to Bateman's of Manchester almost immediately, because they replied in February of that year: -

'In reply to your intended favour I would complete and fix up an Engine, with a Rotation motion thereto, readyto turn any kind of Machinery required, the same fixt as that at the glass house at Warrington for £250, provided it was at no great a distance from my works. If it is, it would be something more on account of carriage, this sum is exclusive of any brickwork or building, what is understood to be done for the above sum is the Engine completed and fixed up, also the first mooveing powers which consists of two double cogged Iron wheels with shafts, headstocks, steps and then we also fix up ready to join or fix to any sort of machinery what was that may be wanted. I herd you or any of your friends be wanting anything of this sort I am certain I could complete it to their intire Satisfaction.

Warrington Engine is a 20inch Cylinder the Brick Work for Engine only is very triffeling, other Buildings for works will intirely depend on the nature of the business to be done.'

James Bateman sounds quite the salesman but there is no evidence to show that Richard Orford purchased his engine. In June 1788 a breakdown occurred at Florida Colliery when the beam of the fire engine broke. The first report was from Samuel Rigby: -

'I writ to you as soone as the engen beame broke down, but Molly forgot to give it to you before, I have paid John Duckworth £50 in Bills which sum I rec'd from Mr. Blackburn for the Bill you return'd, canot say anything of the fault in Clypsley, as the water prevents anything being done in that pit, they hope to have the Beame up next weeke sometime of it should be much oblig'd if you will get my accounts signed, if you think it necessary shall come to Lyme rather than not have them finished pray my complements to you famaley and Mrs. Crew from your obedient servant.'

In such an early colliery the fire engine breaking down was a drastic occurrence. All production would have stopped eventually as they lost control of the water situation. Mrs. Crew would have been the head cook and a servant of some note. Shaw Allanson was next to report about the beam engine: -

'As the Engine Beam yesterday was a week broke down quite in two near to the centre and we have fallen two trees for arches and they answer very well we have sawn the arches and stabalised the beam I expect we shall have it at work by the weeks end.'

In the same letter Shaw Allanson decides to take advantage of the redundant colliers: -

'Edge Green is now ready air'd and fit for men to work there if we had them, I expect the By pits men at Florida will be drown'd out and to have some of these men to Edge Green till water is got out again in the meantime some others will be droping in to succeed them I expect.'

The last remark shows that the colliers were very flexible in their employment and were prepared to travel great distances for work. Their problems with the beam engine were evidently not over for Samuel Rigby later reported more damage in the shaft: -

'I recv'd the favour of yours last night, the engen beame breaking in the midle went down with such a force, that it broke pump rods and burst the working barrell at the first lift, as such it must stand still, then there is a new one got. Shaw as writ to Coalbrookedale to know when he may depend of one being ready that he may send a cart for it that there may be no time lost.'

It is obvious that no-one locally could produce that type of pump part. It can be imagined how long and arduous the journey to Coalbrookedale and back would have been. The engine was repaired by the end of July 1788 and production restarted. Samuel Rigby sent a short report in August about a pit they were sinking near Clipsley Lane: -

'The amount of the two Bills for iron rails is £323-8s-0d, the level in the Clipsley is just the same to all appearance the stone is so hard, they get but verry sloly forward desire you will not forget to send me some cash.'

Further reports from Samuel Rigby on Clipsley Colliery show that its main task was to raise water to keep the pits upbrow of it clear.

Beam Engine with Wooden Beam

A Whim Gin

Problems with the Salt Proprietors.

In the late 1780s an attempt was made by the salt proprietors of Liverpool to gain control of some of the coal mines in the St. Helens area. Their aim was to govern the price of their coal supplies. They bought any available coal bearing land in the district and immediately opened up coal works on the site. To combat this the coal proprietors formed themselves into a group or cartel to keep prices high and oppose any moves by the salt men.

In 1788 one of those groups consisted of James Orrell, who was mining in Blackbrook, Thomas Speakman, who was mining in Parr, Thomas Penswick, steward to the Gerard estate and Richard Orford, steward to the Legh estate. These letters, from James Orrell to Richard Orford, give a clear and sometimes amusing view of the battle between the coal and the salt proprietors.

The first letter, written in November 1788, shows the coal group had become very concerned. James Orrell had been to Liverpool to bid for land in Parr and it's obvious that the salt proprietors were prepared to pay extravagant amounts for coal bearing land: -

'I duly rec'd your favour and sit down at present to give you an account of the proceedings at Liverpool on Tuesday - The Great Coal Lot was bid at by Mr. Ashton and others to £5,000 no further bidding being offer'd the Sellsman (Mr. Richmond) declar'd his price 6,000 guineas of course it remained unsold. The Laffog Land was first bid at by myself £500 Mr Ashton immediately bid £2,100 I thought it was not prudent to cope with a gentleman who bid £1,600 at one bidding, more than the former, so I declined the contest, Mr. Richmond then declar'd, his price £3,500 if such prices as these are given we (would) not fear the undetakers of such concerns. All the other lots except one small farm were not sold but I hear since that two or three more are disposed of by private contract.'

The next letter in December 1788 showed that James Orrell was so worried that he called a meeting of the coal group. One solution was that the group would put in a bid for the Parr Lot: -

'I have had an application from Mr. Ashton (as I expected would be the case) to take my coals lying above his, in his new purchase, but fearing it might break into our general plan on the navigation, and perhaps not sail my other Engagements in the Coal Trade, I declin'd giving an answer till I had made my friends acquainted with the matter. I have seen Messrs Penswick and Speakman, who with myself, wish to have a meeting on the Business and leave it to you to fix the time so as to make it convenient to yourself either the begining of the week after the 28 instant or the begining of the week following. Mr. Ashton is determined to begin getting coals immediately, the particulars of the business shall be stated to you when we meet, and the probable mischief he may do us. The Ashton's Green lot is not sold as yet.'

Nicholas Ashton had been successful in buying the Laffack land near to James Orrell and had opened a colliery. It is obvious that James Orrell was very cagey and upset about Mr. Ashton's attempts at coal mining. That fact is confirmed in a letter from Thomas Billinge to Richard Orford on the 18th December 1788. It is clear that Nicholas Ashton had little knowledge of coal mining as he was already attempting to hire experts: -

'Sir, Mr. Ashton has bought the piece of Land late Mrs. Clayton's that lys between Laffock and Mr Orrells and is for opening the colliery, he wants a man to superintend the same he would have one that understands something of the bottom as well as the top and can be trusted with the money to pay the men he is not for seling coales unles to a perticular Flat and no money to be received. He ordered Mr Berry to get me to enquire for such a man, and as I go now from home does not know of any. Now I desire you it you know of any such you will let me know and Mr. Ashton will take it a perticular favour, he will likewise want a carpenter but that will be easier found.'

The meeting mentioned in James Orrell's letter of the 14th December must have taken place about Christmas 1788. Certainly a decision was made at that meeting and Thomas Speakman was dispatched to Liverpool to acquire the Ashton's Green Lot. James Orrell wrote with the bad news on the 15th January 1789: -

'I presume you have often been told that delays are dangerous. Our friend Speakman went to Liverpool as he was bidden yesterday, but to his great Mortification, and our great loss, the Parr Coal Lot was sold the very Evening we were deliberating matters at Mr. Penswicks, to Mr. Heywood the Banker of Liverpool and who has with him I presume Mr. Blackburn, the price £5,500. The colliery is to be opened immediately, it is a sad business for the Proprietors of Collieries on the Navigation, I expect Messers Penswick and Speakman here this afternoon, and intend to propose to them to raise coals immediately to 5/6 per ton, provided we have your concurrence and in order to do that, a meeting must be called as soon as you can be over with us, I have wrote to Mr. Ashton to inform him that I can say nothing to him about my coals.'

James Orrell was devastated by the news and had begun to suspect that the salt proprietors were behind the deal. Their first, albeit hasty, reaction was to attempt to raise the price of coals. James Orrell remarked later in the letter: -

'Our great satisfaction in the opening of these two collieries will be the disorders it will occasion amongst our Workmen, as they will be determined to have them upon any terms.'

He was concerned that the new coal owners would poach their best workmen a worry which later proved to be correct. In the postscript James Orrell asked Richard Orford to agree to a rise in coal prices: -

'Messers Penswick and Speakmen are now here and think the proposal of raising the coals a very proper one, if you cannot take a journey over your letter signifying Mr. Legh's consent with orders to Mr. Rigby to raise the price when we raise ours will be efficient. Will it be neccessary that you should inform Mr. Gilbert of the scheme.'

Mr. Gilbert was Richard Orford's contact with the Staffordshire coal proprietors. The next letter informs us why he had to be consulted: -

'Holden brought me your favour, and found here Messers Penswick and Speakman, we are much at a loss to know what to do in regard of advancing the price of Coals, as from Mr. Speakman's account who has been over at Northwich this week there is some danger in attempting it, if we are not certain of Mr. Gilbert and the Staffordshire people; They therefore desire you, if possible, to see Mr. Gilbert and confer matters with him, and as you must be over at Haydock to receive the rents on the 20th of next month, we hope to see you at Whittle's on Thursday the 19th our years account will then be looked over, and a determination made as to the scheme of raising the Coals. I shall be at Northwich next week and will make every enquiry I can. I suppose Mr. Gilbert will not think of less than 4d or 6d per ton. It is near certain that Mr. Blackburn and a Captain Smith are partners with Dick Heywood in the purchase. Mr. Ashton is begining in a few days on the crop of our present mine where he has about an acre of coals which he refused on Wednesday to leave to me. The more I think of the Blander we have made the more I blame the conduct of some of the parties.'

The worry was, of course, that the Staffordshire men would refuse to raise their coals and gain a larger slice of the market. Mr. Blackburn was a member of the Liverpool family of saltwork proprietors. When James Orrell used the term mine he meant an actual seam of coal. Richard Orford thrashed out a deal with the Staffordshire proprietors. James Orrell referred to it in March 1789: -

'The business with Mr. Gilbert ended as I suppos'd it would do, that the Staffordshire gentlemen would not raise their Coals 6d per ton; were we to do it, I fear it would throw too much of the Trade into their Hands, which we might find it difficult to regain.'

James Orrell sounded disconcerted and went on to hope that the opposing parties would be in some way paid back: -

'I look upon the purchase of the Ashton's Green Colliery (from something I have heard lately) to be a plan of the Navigation Proprietors, as at a meeting thay had it was proposed to purchase it, and divide it in shares; I hope the owners of the Coal incomes on the River will remember it, and one time or other make them a proper return for the compliments.'

Meanwhile back at the Haydock coal works, Samuel Rigby reported to Richard Orford in April 1789: -

I recv'd yours this morning the Navigation sale is good but we have stop'd two pits at Florida, which is better than paying 5s per work the Stocks sale is tollerable but there is coals upon the Brow, as we have brought some of the Florida men to the stocks work makes more coal to be got hope it will not be long before you come to Haydock as the town is willing to joyne our Master in slagging the roade down to Florida think it would be the best thing that we can do as it would make it all in one work for sometimes we have been without coals at the top and this winter, and then it gets all over the country that they cannot get loading which halts the sale for sometime, and we likewise could get more coals at Florida as there would be great deal more land sale.'

This extract makes plain that the two collieries were reasonably close together and that Stocks Colliery was north of Florida Colliery.

James Orrell's prophecy, regarding the danger of workmen being poached, came true in the latter half of 1789. Samuel Rigby reported the news in September: -

'Shaw has now declared he is engeaged at Ashton's Green Coalery and intends to leave this work in a short time.'

James Grimshaw dramatically reported on the same date: -

'Have you heard that Shaw Allanson is leaving your coal works he is going to the new coal work at Ashton's Green I think you had better come to Haydock for Shaw is coming to Lyme next Saturday and he says he will see Mr. Legh but you are the best judge in that.'

Shaw Allanson had been an excellent agent at Florida and Edge Green and would surely be missed. Shaw's last letter to Richard Orford was written on the 25th September 1789, so we can assume that he left soon afterwards:-

'As to our loading place is very bad and the pond we ship our coals in is to be let off tonight for us to repair our loading place therefore we shall have it to bottom and pile and plank the sides to hold them up its the bank I mean that slips in so that flats cannot come under of frame to load so we shall be obliged to work Sunday also to get it done as Mr. Orrell's pond is to be let off at after we have done ours, for Mr. Ashton to put down a frame for to load off so it will be Sunday following before I can come to Lyme.'

The letter is of interest because it indicates what they had to do before any big job was attempted on the canal. A pond meant a basin in the canal where the flats could load and turn round. Sections of the canal could be emptied between locks to allow work to be carried out. The last letter from James Orrell was in December 1789. In it he reported to Richard Orford on the amount of coal held by the other proprietors on their brows in the area. He also commented on Nicholas Ashton's attempts at Laffack: -

'Mr. Ashton is trying what he can do in the Laffog Land, I think he will not be hard enough to keep doing, as the water is already growing very heavy.'

Clearly James Orrell thought Mr. Ashton was an inexperienced man with little hope of success in coal mining. When it came to Ashton's Green Colliery James Orrell did have the last laugh. In the 1790s he acquired shares in that concern. He worked it with Thomas Claughton, John Blackburne, John Fitchett and John Leigh.

By the beginning of the 19th century James Orrell had become one of the more prosperous of the local coal owners. He lived at Blackbrook House, a fine Georgian building very close to the Sankey Canal, near Blackbrook Basin. It still stands today as part of the St. Mary's Convent complex. During his career James Orrell worked collieries at Blackbrook, Gladehill and Ashton's Green. The 1820 sale notice on page 59, shows some of the shares in his Blackbrook Colliery became available in Northwich. This again indicates the close connection between the Cheshire Salt Works and the coal industry in the St. Helens' area.

TO BE

Sold by Auction,

AT THE HOUSE OF

WILLIAM GARFT,

KNOWN BY THE SIGN OF THE SPORTSMAN'S INN,

IN NORTHWICH, IN THE COUNTY OF CHESTER,

On Friday, the 29th Day of December inst.

AT THE HOUR OF SIX O'CLOCK IN THE EVENING OF THE SAME DAY,

4 Thirtieth Parts or Shares

OF AND IN CERTAIN

COAL MINES,

And the Appurtenances thereunto belonging, situate in Parr, in the County of Lancaster, called the Black Brook and Gladehill Collieries, now carried on under the Name and Firm of JAMES ORRELL & Co.

The above Coal Mines are held under Lease from James Orrell, Esq. for 31 *Years, commencing the 2nd Day of February,* 1792.

For particulars apply at the Office of Mr. Hostage, Solicitor, in Northwich.

Northwich, 12th December, 1820.

Coal Mines Sale Notice

Death of Master and Servant.

For many years different groups connected with shipping on the Sankey canal had complained about dealers loading short measures onto the flats. Eventually full measure marks were fitted to all flats in use on the canal network. The system was further strengthened because only authorised persons could fit the marks. As far back as 1774 the General Advertiser of Liverpool reported: -

'Many and (it is to be feared) just complaints having been made by housekeepers and others of impositions and unjust dealings by delivery of short measure, and other unfair practices of the common dealers in that most useful article Coal, where by the coal coming down Sankey Canal may have fallen into disrepute to obviate all such complaints, and to secure to all persons a certainty of having the full quantity and true quality of all such coal which they may hereafter pay for, the proprietors of Sankey Navigation have come to a resolution of delivering coal by sworn agents in whom the public may confide.'

The article concluded with the promise: -

'sworn agents will attend constantly at the coal office adjoining the weighing machine on Nova Scotia, to whom the public may apply.'

The practice of short measuring carried on intermittently for some time. For instance in May 1789, Henry Wilckens & Co, one of the major shippers on the canal, sent a very strong letter to Samuel Rigby: -

'Our agent Mr. Davies writes us, that the Flatt Stagg, James Molineux Master loaded from Mr. Leghs pitts with Coal, and on weighing the same out proved 2 tons 15 short. He further informs us, that when he remarked to your people, he was not loaded to his marks, and that he had not got the quantity charged, they replyed, 'If the coals were not liked at their weight, the Flatts might stay away, and others would come in plenty'. We are sensible such an answer could not originate from you Sir, yet we think it hard to be left to the mercy of people who can make such a speech, and are capable to act us to it, by giving really short weight.'

He stated later in the letter: -

'This matter is of such serious consequence to the proprietors of Salt Works, that if we find that you or other dealers in coals approve of these misconducts of the servants, we think it high time to have a meeting of the proprietors to put a stop to these proceedings, on purpose to know for the future what we get, and what we have to pay for. You will likewise inform us if you prefer our flatts staying away or coming to your pitt, which will depend on your answer and the weight we get in future.'

The letter was so serious that Samuel Rigby did not reply but sent it to Richard Orford. He replied at the end of the month with an apology: -

'Your favor of the 2nd Inst only got to me by this mornings Post,— I am very sorry any person belonging to Mr. Legh's works should be guilty of any expressions your Captain tax them with, as I am certain they are not encouraged in any such thing, and should be very glad to have them pointed out who say'd it,— the instructions given, is to use every one of our friends the same, and am certain that on examination our Waggons will all be found full Navigation measure, as to the weight, I believe that the same measure will be heavier from other delfs on our Navigation, but cannot help saying that we flatter ourselves that no other Coal on the Navigation will do more business in the Salt making I assuredly will write by this post to have this complaint looked into and you may depend you shall have the same measure as all others our friends have, and hope they are as good as any of our Brother Colliers are.'

This letter though had arrived too late. The delay had caused Henry Wilckens to stop loading at Legh's pits. He wrote to Richard Orford in June 1789: -

'In answer to your letter of the 26th part Mr. Rigby's long silence to our letter and complaints there in contained, caused us to think that it was not his wish to clear the matter up, or could not do it, to his own satisfaction. In consequence we have directed all our flatts not to load at Mr. Leghs pit, and we don't know any have done so, and indeed it is so serious a matter we must abstain taking any, and we can only go by weight and nothing else.'

He again complained about the workmen: -

'We know full well that the Gentlemen who are proprietors don't approve of such conduct but their lower servants and coal getters have too much power to cheat, as when they please, and do it very effectually to our cost.'

He concluded with the statement: -

'As soon as we know what you conclude respecting the deficiencies complained of, and what we may depend on in future, we shall do accordingly. In which expectation we remain with due regard.'

Richard Orford probably replied with assurances for the future. Woe betides the workman who tried it on again. There was no mention of it in Samuel Rigby's report in September so all must have returned to normal:-

'I got the reckoning over, had two guineas and a half left and one of them that you sent is light, desire you will let me have cash against the 10th of next month it will take above £70 as the sinking pit will be finished by that time and the carpenters to pay a months wage, they are now got into the coal in the tunnell that should loose Sir Roberts water, hope they will not be long before they finish it. They are likewise got through the fault in won of the deep levels they have been a long time in it as it is a verry hard burrstone, but are in hopes they will now get fast forward, the 10th of next month comes into this quarter so it will be sometime before I can collect for the quarters coal.'

Sir Robert was Sir Robert Gerard of Garswood. Samuel Rigby must have been driving a tunnel that would drain the Gerard coal seams, which where upbrow of his - a clear case of co-operation between the two estates.

Throughout 1790 there was little reference to coal mining in the reports. The last report from Samuel Rigby was in June 1790 when he informed Richard Orford of his intention to reduce the price of coal: -

'I recv'd eighty four pound 9s by the Butcher which have placed to your credit it came just in time, have got the reckoning over, we have dropped the coals yesterday to 2d per hundred as they have lane so long thought a farthing would not answer to get them off, hope it will not be long before you come to Haydock.'

The term reckoning meant when all the outstanding bills were paid, usually quarterly. Hundred meant hundredweight, which was the approximate weight of a basket.

James Grimshaw had been looking after things at Edge Green in 1790. He reported in much the same manner in September: -

'Coals go of very poorly at Edge Green and slower at Haydock. I have spoke to John Astley to make some alterations at Edge Green as there is but seven men to get Coal and there are seven men on the brow, what is your opinion of it.'

This tells us that there were seven Getters or Colliers at Edge Green Colliery, a seemingly small number when compared with modern manpower levels.

It was at the end of 1790 that Richard Orford suddenly died. As Steward of Lyme he had run the Legh estates for thirty years. At the end of his days his power seemed complete, his position in the district secure. His master, in his will, had settled a large amount of land upon him. However it was to be Orford's children who saw the benefit of the gift. Even in death Richard was better remembered than his master was. There were three memorials erected in his memory: one at Disley, one at Prestbury and one at St Oswald's, Winwick, where he is buried.

Peter Legh the Younger, Lord of Lyme, survived his illustrious servant by only 15 months. He died on the 20th May 1792. He had been Lord of Lyme for 48 years. A distant member of his family later mentioned

Peter in the nicest terms: -

'Old Mr. Peter Legh died May the 20th 1792 aged 85 his benevolent mind justly entitled him to rank amongst the best of men —- his numerous tenants had to lament a mild and good landlord —- his servants a kind and generous benefactor —- his houses were for many years the few remaining examples of old English hospitality.'

Haydock coalfield had lost two of its major influential characters. As the end of the century approached it was going to be other men who were to lead the collieries into the 19th century.

Exterior View of Haydock Lodge

Transition.

The Haydock coal works had now entered a period of transition. The loss of Richard Orford, quickly followed by Peter Legh probably caused a certain amount of disruption. Samuel Rigby also left the collieries at about the same time. The new Lord of Lyme was Thomas Peter Legh who was known as a sporting and military man and had little interest in coal mining. During his tenure Thomas Peter Legh delegated most of the estate business to associates and agents. The estates accounts showed that the coal production did not cease and the rents were still collected but the time of detailed documentation had passed. The steward at that time was a Mr. Hayes, an indistinct character possessing little power. Never again would a steward of the standing of Richard Orford be in charge.

The accounts for 1794 showed that the Leghs were working 5 pits: -

No.2 - James Taylor's Brow
No.4 - William Higham's Brow
No.5 - John Greenough's Brow
No.6 - William Thomason's Brow
No.21 - Zackery Thomason's Brow

The name was that of the Banksman who was virtually in charge on the surface. For the fortnight ending 22nd February 1794 the men working in the various pits were as follows: -

No.2 Pit -	**Banksman** -	James Taylor
	Colliers -	William Abbot, Henry Makin, Thomas Dierden & John Makin.
	Waggoning -	Joseph Glave & Thomas Baley.
No.4 Pit -	**Banksman** -	William Higham
	Colliers -	Henry Twiss, Joseph Knowles, Thomas Twiss & Thomas Glave.
	Waggoning -	James Winstanley & James Twiss.
No.5 Pit -	**Banksman** -	John Greenough
	Colliers -	Ralph Fairhurst, Thomas Fairhurst, John Cundliff & Bart Cundliff.
	Waggoning -	Turton
No.6 Pit -	**Banksman** -	William Thomason
	Colliers -	John Forshaw & sons, Thomas Knowles, John Makin & Job Lee.
	Waggoning -	Perter Ashton & John Houghton
No.21 Pit -	**Banksman** -	Zackery Thomason
	Colliers -	William Hughes, Thomas Hughes, Timothy Winstanley & James Naylor
	Waggoning -	James Leatherbarrow & son

The colliers were paid 4s per work for coal and 1s for slack, a term used for small coal. The waggoners were paid 22d per day and the working period was 12 days per fortnight. The Banksman was paid 18d per day plus money for letting down the colliers. Coal at that time was worth 18s-4d per work. During this fortnight the

21 colliers listed above had produced 163 works of coal equivalent to 489 tons. The total production for the six months covering the first half of 1794 was 2057 works equivalent to over 12,000 tons per year. By 1798, which was a good year for output, six pits were producing over 19,000 tons per year.

The early death of Thomas Peter Legh in 1797 could only have caused extra concern and trouble in the running of the estates. His will had stated that Richard Cross and George Heron were in total charge of the estates until Thomas Legh reached the age of 21. Richard Cross was a distant relation of the Leghs of Adlington and assumed the name Legh when he succeeded to the Adlington estate. From then onwards he was known as Richard Legh or Richard Legh Cross. George Heron was a vicar and many times he officiated at baptisms and weddings in the Legh family.

The task left to the two men was to raise money from the estates to settle Thomas Peter Legh's debts and provide money for the education of his children. But as the end of the century approached it was evident that a Haydock man, Thomas Claughton, was to have a great influence on the Legh estates.

Interior View of Haydock Lodge

Thomas Claughton and Thomas Legh.

Thomas Claughton was born in 1774 at the Hayes in Haydock. The Claughtons had lived there since the 1740s and were tenants of the Legh family. Thomas was initially educated as a lawyer, a profession that assisted him in the legal wrangling of his later life. In 1806 he married Maria Legh the eldest daughter of Thomas Peter Legh. Although she was illegitimate it must have been quite a catch for Thomas Claughton to marry the sister of the young Lord of Lyme. Over the next 15 years the couple produced 12 children and Thomas advertised his connection to his wife's family by naming most of them after people and places associated with the Leghs. During the first two decades of the 19th century Thomas Claughton's aspirations grew. He became a salt manufacturer, coal proprietor, land speculator, dealer, MP for Newton and took over the running of the Legh estates. His coal works were situated at Orrell, Pemberton and Wigan and in 1822 he built the Wigan Pier that has acquired such fame in the present day. He purchased large amounts of land throughout the district, consolidating his inheritance of the Myddleton estate, near Winwick, with the Southworth Hall estate and the Houghton estate. He also acquired estates in Sankey, Penketh and Sutton. His greatest attempts at land acquisitions were the Hafod estate in Wales and Newstead Abbey, the home of Lord Byron, for which he offered £140,000. However, both of these deals fell through due to a lack of ready money. In the 1820s he was involved in a whirlwind of land dealings, buying estates and immediately mortgaging them to buy others. Thomas Claughton was made bankrupt in March 1824.

Thomas Legh gained control of his estates in 1813. He was still travelling in Europe so he was greatly assisted by Thomas Claughton for a number of years in the running of the family businesses, notably the coalmines. It was only in the 1820s that the two men fell out. It was actually Thomas Legh who made Thomas Claughton bankrupt by calling in a large number of outstanding bills. Thomas Claughton was most aggrieved by this action. He thought he had served his brother-in-law well over the years. At his bankruptcy examination he told of how he had saved the estates from ruin by the mis-management of Richard Cross and George Heron. The fact was that Thomas Legh had found out his brother-in-law was untrustworthy and had to be brought down. A Legh family story tells of a wayward uncle who nearly ended up in the debtor's prison. The reputed cause was over indulgence and becoming part of the Prince Regent's set.

Thomas Legh, after the turbulent period surrounding his brother-in-law's bankruptcy, began a programme of improvements to his lands, estates and businesses. For a hereditary landlord Thomas Legh had an excellent insight into the problems that industrialists had and this ability allowed him to improve and expand the industry on his property.

One of Thomas Legh's greatest achievements was the modernisation of Haydock Colliery. During the 1820s he radically altered the running and technology of the colliery concern. On all of the major shafts he fitted new steam engines to improve winding of coal. A large pumping engine was erected over the Engine Pit in the centre of the Haydock coalfield to drain all the surrounding strata. He up-rated the baskets that were in use at the pits, discarding the small 1cwt ones and fitting 3 and 4 cwt baskets in most of the larger pits. The transport system to the major markets was modernised and new railways were designed and constructed. His manpower, of course, had to increase to keep up with the greatly increased production.

The table below gives an indication of how the manpower and output changed from the beginning of the nineteenth century to 1830: -

YEAR	No. of PITS	No. OF COLLIERS.	OUTPUT (approx)
1809	7	14	24,000 tons
1812	7	14	20,000 tons
1818	6	12	19,000 tons
1821	8	16	19,000 tons
1828	8	38	39,000 tons
1830	10	80	66,000 tons

VALUABLE

Estates, Collieries and Mines.

PARTICULARS

OF SEVERAL

Valuable Estates, Collieries and Mines,

SITUATE IN

PARR, GOLBORNE, GREAT BOLTON, SUTTON AND WARRINGTON

In the County of Lancaster,

AND IN LATCHFORD AND APPLETON

IN THE COUNTY OF CHESTER,

WHICH

WILL BE SOLD BY AUCTION,

By order of the Assignees of

MR. THOMAS CLAUGHTON A BANKRUPT,

At the ***RED LION INN****, in* ***WARRINGTON,***

IN THE COUNTY OF LANCASTER,

On Thursday the 23rd, *and Friday the* 24th, *Days of June,* 1825,

AT THREE O'CLOCK IN THE AFTERNOON OF EACH DAY

In 17 Lots, or in such other Lots as may be agreed upon at the time of Sale.

The respective Tenants will shew the Premises: Printed particulars may be had Gratis, at the principal INNS in *Liverpool, Warrington, Manchester, St. Helen's, Bolton, and Wigan,* and at the Offices of Messrs. TAYLOR and ROSCOE, *Kings Bench Walks, Temple,* and Mr. GEORGE BARKER, 8, *Gray's Inn Square, London,* Messrs. A. & W. KEIGHTLEY, Solicitors, *Liverpool;* Messrs. DUCKWORTH and DENISON, Solicitors, *Manchester,* Mr. W. P. MORRIS, Solicitor, *Wigan,* and from Mr. JOSEPH WAGSTAFF and Mr. GEORGE WORTHINGTON *Warrington,* joint Solicitors to the said Assignees, from whom also further Information may be obtained.

WARRINGTON: PRINTED BY J. & J. HADDOCK, MARKET-GATE.

Sale Notice for Thomas Claughton's Mines

The figures clearly show the improvement in production after the re-organisation of the colliery. The year 1831 was the last year that was documented and the same output was maintained. Besides the colliers listed per pit there would have been waggoners, hookers-on, underlookers and labourers working underground. In most collieries workmen tended to use members of their family as waggoners and drawers to keep the money earned in the same household.

Thomas Legh was certainly the entrepreneur of the Legh family and attempted many projects during his lifetime. He also went some way towards ridding the Legh family of the stigma created by his father. The country was entering the Victorian era with its different ideals and protocol and it is possible that his illegitimacy did impede him during his lifetime.

In the first quarter of the nineteenth century a series of coal strikes, over pay, disrupted the South Lancashire coalfield. At that time the early unions were forming and competing with the coal owners over wages and conditions. Thousands of colliers were beginning their struggle against oppression by some coal owners by attending meetings throughout the country. Of course during some of the meetings, as will happen in such cases, violence and rioting erupted. In 1831 it reached such a level of disorder that the militia was called in to suppress the rioters and protect property. This petition shows that Thomas Legh, because of worries for his property, offered Haydock Lodge as a temporary barracks: -

'That in the months of January, February and March in the year of our lord 1831 certain disturbances took place in the Coal Districts of Wigan, Bolton and St.Helens and the Coal Pits on the Sankey Canal in the said colliery adjoining near to which last mentioned place the said House or Mansion of the said petitioner is situate and great numbers of the workmen engaged in the working of the Collieries in the district aforesaid were in a state of open tumult and insubordination.——That in consequence of representations made by certain Magistrates and others to the Government of your Majestys Royal Predecessor his late Gracious Majesty King William the 4th touching the matters aforesaid a body of Troops and soldiers of his said late Majestys 43rd Regiment of Foot acting under the orders of his said late Majestys Government to the District aforesaid for the purpose of quelling of the said disturbances and preserving the public peace. And the Petitioner sheweth to your Majesty that it having been thought expedient by the Government of his late Majesty that a certain Military Force should be stationed and quartered for a certain time in the said District for the purpose of maintaining the public peace there but there not being in the District aforesaid any Barrack or other Building or Buildings in which the officery, soldiery and troops constituting such said force could be conveniently or safely lodged and quartered the Petitioner permitted the said House or Mansion of the Petitioner called Haydock Lodge with the said stables Coach houses and premises to be occupied as a Barrack by the said officers soldiers and troops of his said Majesty for the use and service of his said late Majesty by way of temporary accommodation for as long a time as the said disturbances should exist or until other quarters could be provided.—And the Petitioner further sheweth to your Majesty that in pursuance of the said permission and consent of the Petitioner 4 Companies of his said late Majestys 43rd Regiment of Foot and a half troop of his said late Majestys 10th Regiment of Hussars on or about the 5th day of March in the year of our Lord 1831 entered into possession of and began to occupy the said house or mansion and premises and that from thenceforth continually until the 9th day of January 1841 when the same were restored and delivered up to the Petitioner.'

Thomas Legh's petition was delivered because, during the ten years that Haydock Lodge had been occupied by the troops, he had not received a penny of rent or compensation. Moreover the building required over £2,000 worth of restoration after the occupancy. He had to wait for some time before he received any remuneration and the amount did not come up to his expectations.

By the 1830s the re-organisation of Haydock Colliery was complete. Thomas Legh was working 9 or 10 pits in the centre of Haydock and producing over 65,000 tons of coal per year. The workforce was comprised of men with many local names that are still present in Haydock today. The following are a list of the Haydock Colliery workmen with their wages for the fortnight ending March 25th 1831: -

No.1 Pit.

Peter Greenall	£2 - 12s - 11d
John Greenough	£1 - 13s - 0d
John Forshaw	£1 - 19s - 2d
John Naylor	£ 1 - 18s - 11d
Abraham Naylor	£2 - 3s - 6d
Thomas Naylor	£2 - 12s - 10d
George Naylor	£1 - 0s - 3d
John Taylor	£1 - 3s - 1d
James Winstanley	£1 - 5s - 5d
George Greenough	£2 - 15s - 11d
Thomas Lievesly	£0 - 17s - 4d
Joshua Lievesly	£1 - 8s - 9d
Mathias Dierden	£1 - 15s - 7d
Thomas Dixon	£1 - 10s - 7d
Thomas Naylor	£0 - 17s - 9d
William Bailey	£0 - 11s - 9d
John Holton	£0 - 13s - 6d
Hooking on night & day	£7 - 1s - 6d
Driving ponies night & day	£4 - 5s - 0d
James Naylor & Co - Browmen	£5 - 3s - 4d
F. Beatmen & Co - Derby men	£3 - 14s - 10d

No. 2 Pit.

John Waterworth	£0 - 11s - 10d
John Dierden	£0 - 8s - 10d
Abraham Lievesly	£2 - 3s - 9d
Henry Dierden	£1 - 9s - 10d
William Cunliffe	£3 - 2s - 9d
John Cunliffe	£2 - 16s - 1d
James Cunliffe	£2 - 8s - 5d
George Cunliffe	£1 - 0s - 8d
Edward Cunliffe	£1 - 4s - 9d
Thomas Owen	£1 - 6s - 8d
John Millington	£0 - 17s - 11d
Henry Waterworth	£0 - 17s - 4d
John Cunliffe	£1 - 2s - 7d
William Cunliffe	£0 - 14s - 9d
James Fairhurst	£3 - 12s - 7d
Thos & Will Twiss	£4 - 18s - 2d
John Waterworth	£1 - 1s - 1d
John Unsworth	£0 - 10s -5d
John Battersby	£2 - 4s - 2d
David Lievesly	£1 - 9s - 4d
William Lievesly	£1 - 10s - 2d
Thomas Cunliffe	£3 - 1s - 6d
Peter Naylor	£0 - 17s - 4d
John Dierden	£0 - 13s - 4d
Ralph Dierden	£0 - 9s - 0d
Browmen	£4 - 19s - 2d
Hooking on	£3 - 4s - 6d
Driving Ponies	£1 - 3s - 0d

No. 3 Pit.

Peter Hughes	£0 - 3s - 8d
James Greenall	£1 - 10s - 1d
David Bane	£1 - 10s - 9d
William Bane	£1 - 9s - 1d
John Bane	£1 - 13s - 8d
Daniel Lathom	£1 - 19s - 5d
Waggoning	£0 - 10s - 6d
Browman	£1 - 8s - 0d

No. 4 Pit.

William Gretan & Co - Derbyshire Men	£2 - 17s - 5d
John Harrison	£0 - 6s - 9d
William Battersby	£0 - 11s - 0d
Browmen	£1 - 8s - 0d

No. 5 Pit.

William Unsworth	£1 - 17s - 5d
Robert Winstanley	£1 - 7s - 3d
James Winstanley	£1 - 13s - 8d
Zach. Thompson	£1 - 8s - 5d
Peter Abbott	£1 - 9s - 2d
Waggoning	£0 - 12s - 0d
Browmen	£1 - 0s - 0d

No. 6 Pit.

Joshua Gratrid & Co Derbyshire men	£2 - 13s - 6d
Henry Cunliffe	£0 - 8s - 6d
Henry Unsworth	£0 - 9s - 10d
Ralph Unsworth	£0 - 7s - 9d
Ralph Dierden	£0 - 6s - 3d
H. Winstanley Waggoning	£1 - 2s - 0d
Browmen	£2 - 4s - 0d

No.7 Pit.

Naylor Greenough	£0 - 5s - 11d
Henry Unsworth	£0 - 12s - 8d
James Bailey	£1 - 2s - 5d
James Owen	£2 - 1s - 7d
Thomas Knowles	£1 - 9s - 3d
Henry Cunliffe	£0 - 18s - 6d
Waggoning	£0 - 15s - 8d
Browmen	£1 - 4s - 0d

No. 9 Pit.

Joseph Glave	£1 - 19s - 11d
William Glave	£0 - 18s - 7d
John Glave	£2 - 0s - 5d
Waggoning	£1 - 6s - 0d
Browmen	£1 - 0s - 0d

No. 11 Pit.

Robert Winstanley	£0 - 15s - 11d
William Dierden	£0 - 14s - 7d
Thomas Hilton	£0 - 5s 0 3d
John Harrison	£0 - 2s - 4d
Waggoning	£0 - 14s - 0d
James Twiss	£1 - 8s - 0d

The amounts are for two weeks work and consisted of money per coal and a yardage rate which varied between 1s-9d and 6s-6d depending on difficulty of job. The wages list showed that the largest pits by far were No.1 and No.2 Pits. Here 42 men were producing over 60% of the total output. No.2 Pit also seems to have been a family pit. Out of the 25 workers eight were Cunliffe, four were Dierden, three were Lievesly and three were Waterworth. At No. 9 Pit, one of the smaller pits, only members of the Glave family are listed as workers.

The Derbyshire men would have been outside labour brought in to combat the organised unions that had begun to appear about that time. Employing outside labour in itself caused problems within the coalfield and the resident workforce.

New Boston Colliery & Tipples c. 1930

The Sale of Haydock Colliery.

In 1833 the Haydock Colliery concern, which consisted of nine main shafts, was split into three groups. No.1 Pit, No.2 Pit and Engine Pit were situated south of Church Road, on the site of the modern Haydock Foundry and Office complex. King Pit, Ellen or Queen Pit and Chelsea Pit were situated north of Clipsley Lane. No.3 Pit and No.4 Pit or South Florida Pits were south of Clipsley Lane, at the side of the modern Cooper Lane. King and Queen Pits formed the basis of the Haydock Colliery run by Richard Evans throughout the Victorian era.

The colliery concern had excellent transport facilities with connections to the Sankey Canal, the Liverpool and Manchester Railway and major roads for landsale. The connection to the Sankey Canal was via an inclined plane railway of 4ft gauge running from the pier head on the canal along Cooper Lane to the various pits. Motive power was provided by a stationary steam engine, which was positioned at the top of Cooper Lane behind Florida Pits. The railway had previously run down Wagon Lane but had been moved to give easier access to the pits. The colliery was connected to the Liverpool and Manchester Railway by a 4ft 8ins gauge, wrought iron railway, which ran from the pits in Haydock to the junction of the Liverpool-Manchester and Warrington Railways at the place that eventually became Earlestown. It was known for many years as the Haydock mineral line. In 1833 Thomas Legh was running three of his own locomotives on that line - Black Diamond, Shrigley and Viaduct. Overall the concern was an attractive business with a guaranteed coal production and good market outlets with coal yards at Liverpool and Warrington.

The decision to sell the Haydock Colliery was probably taken after much thought on the part of Thomas Legh. To release one of his most successful concerns would have been a hard decision to make. His family had been in charge of coal mining in Haydock for over 130 years and he himself only a few years previously had organised the modernisation of the colliery. What had brought him to that momentous decision? Could it have been the uncertainty of the coal trade at that time? Or was it the appearance of unions and the accompanying riots and disturbances in the area. Only Thomas Legh himself could have provided the answer.

The Haydock Colliery was sold in November 1833 and the lease began in the following way: -

'This Indenture made the fourth day of November in the year of our Lord One Thousand eight hundred and thirty three Between Thomas Legh of Lyme in the County of Chester Esquire and William Legh of Brymbo in the County of Denbigh Esquire of the one part and Richard Evans of Liverpool in the County of Lancaster Coal Proprietor and William Turner of Shrigley Hall in the said County of Chester Esquire of the other part. Whereas under and by virtue of the last Will and Testament of Thomas Peter Legh Lord of Lyme aforesaid Esquire deceased bearing date on or about the twenty sixth day of April which was in the year of or Lord One Thousand seven hundred and ninety seven All and every the Messuages Land Mines and hereditaments late of the said Thomas Peter Legh are and stand limited to the use of the said Thomas Legh for life with remainder to the heirs male of his body and in default of such heirs to the said William Legh for his life with a like remainder to his issue male And Whereas the said Thomas Legh and William Legh according to their respective Interests and rights they have agreed to let to the said Richard Evans and William Turner who have consented and agreed to take the Mines, Beds of Coal and premises hereinafter described for the term and subject to the Covenants, restrictions and conditions hereinafter contained.'

The first section of the lease sets the scene for the sale. Thomas Legh, the Lord of Lyme and William Legh, his younger brother, allowed Richard Evans and William Turner to mine coal under their land. In 1829 Richard Evans bought the Edge Green Colliery from William Turner and Thomas Legh. William Turner was the father-in-law of Thomas Legh and was involved in mining in parts of South Lancashire.

'Thomas Legh and William Legh doth grant demise lease and to farm let unto the said Richard Evans and William Turner All those three several beds or seams of Coal called the Earthy Delf the Higher Delf and the Lower Delf lying and being under lands of the said Thomas Legh situate in Haydock,——— being bounded on the Northerly side thereof by the Old Works on the Crop, on the Easterly side thereof by a fault supposed to rise East One hundred yards on the Southerly side thereof by a Stratum of Red Rock and on the Westerly side thereof by another fault supposed to be cut off and ranging in the whole under a surface of about One hundred and seventy Cheshire acres of land.———And also

the Mines called the Potato Delf now getting at a Colliery called the Wicken Edge Colliery and also such a part of the Earthy Delf as shall be gettable to a profit at the Wicken Edge Colliery. And also all the said mines called the Earthy Delf and the Lower Delf on the Western boundary shewn by the said plan and between such boundary and the Sankey Canal. Together with full free and uninterrupted liberty license power and authority for the said Richard Evans and William Turner to dig sink work drive delve bore search sink for and get the seams or beds of Coal.'

This sets out the extent of the coal workings and the type of seams to be mined. Turner and Evans, as the new company was to be named, were to be allowed to mine four seams under Haydock: Potato Delf, Earthy Delf, Higher Delf and Lower Delf. The area of extraction was to be bounded by three faults and the outcrop to the north. The Potato Delf, or Crombouke, was one of the shallowest seams in Haydock and was mostly worked out, the only section was near Wicken Edge Colliery, which was at the east end of Haydock, south of Penny Lane. Earthy Delf, better known as Ince Seven-Foot or Brassey Mine, was a thick seam of average quality. The Higher and Lower Delf seams were known throughout the area as the Florida seams. They were of top quality and the coal was much prized.

'And also to take, lead and carry away with Carts Waggons Locomotive Engines and other Carriages all the Coals raised and got out of the said Mines and the same to sell and dispose of from time to time. And also to raise clay and make bricks on such part of the said Lands as shall be agreed upon. And also to get stone gravel sand or clay in or upon any part of the Land described in the said plan for the purpose of repairing all necessary roads to and from the said Coal Mines.'

This relates to transport details and the permission to mine clay. It was a profitable sideline that most colliery concerns took part in during the 19th century.

'Together with the use and enjoyment of the present fire and other Engines at work at the said Mines which shall be selected by the said Richard Evans and William Turner with all the Utensils Machinery Railways Tram-roads Underground Railways and appurtenances to the said Coal Mines.'

'And also the full and uninterrupted privilege to use all the railways except as hereinafter is excepted to and from the said mines and all branch railways belonging to the said Thomas Legh including the Branch Railway to the Newton Crown Glass Works hereinafter covenanted to be made by the said Richard Evans and William Turner and to receive tonnage for all goods coals and merchandise carried along the present Colliery Branch to the Liverpool and Manchester Railway and the said Branch there from hereinafter covenanted to be laid down to the Newton Crown Glass Works at the rates follows namely for all Materials and goods except Coals at the rate of One Penny per ton per mile for all coals not brought from the said hereinafter demised mines. And also on the branch from the Warrington and Newton Junction Railway to Mr. Muspratts Chemical Works at the rates following namely for all Materials and goods except Coals at the rate of one penny per ton for all Coal not brought from the said hereinafter demised Coal mines.'

This relates to the railways that Thomas Legh had constructed throughout Haydock. The branch line to James Muspratt's chemical works, which were near the Sankey Canal, was already constructed. They also had to construct a branch line from the mineral railway to the Crown Glass Works. The lease was very specific on this point: -

'And also the said Richard Evans and William Turner shall within six months lay down construct and make a railway or tramroad from some part of the Branch Railway leading from the Liverpool and Manchester Railway to the Newton Crown Glass Works in the occupation of Messrs Ackers Davies and Company.'

This railway, when constructed, ran from the mineral line at Vista Road along the side of Crow Lane to the coal yard that was opposite the present Library.

'To require to remove build and set up again any Engine Whimseys Wheels Fire Engines or other Engines Machines Smithies Stables Houses Cabins Huts and other buildings or proper and convenient works.'

Turner and Evans were not limited to the buildings and machinery already constructed but were allowed to make their own.

'The said Richard Evans and William Turner shall not for the purpose of getting the Mines between the Western boundary and the Sankey Canal drive through the fault called the Twenty Acre fault without the express permission and consent in writing of the said Thomas Legh and William Legh.'

The Twenty Acre Fault was at the western end of the village. The strata on the other side of that fault were fragmented and Thomas Legh could have been worried by that fact.

'The said Richard Evans and William Turner shall not get the coal as shall lie or be under or near the House and outbuildings in the occupation of Henry Critchley Esquire called Heyes Green or within 15yds thereof and also under any other buildings now built or hereinafter to be erected and built upon any of the said land shewn by the said plan in respect of which the said Thomas Legh shall give notice to the said Richard Evans and William Turner to preserve and protect the same from any sinking or damage to be done to such buildings.'

Thomas Legh was concerned about subsidence affecting his property in Haydock. He was insisting that Turner and Evans leave in panels of coal to support buildings.

'Thomas Legh reserving to himself the liberty to use any of the Old Pits which shall not be worked by the said Richard Evans and William Turner.——- and to make use of any of the existing courses and waterways for the purpose of getting any fire clay or any other Metals Minerals or Materials except Coal which may be found and lie under the said land.'

Even though he was to sign over all rights to mine in Haydock, Thomas Legh still reserved the right to extract minerals himself.

'Also save and except and reserving out of this present demise the building containing the Bone Mill at Florida with the Mill itself as well as the privilege of having the Mill worked by the Incline Engine for the purpose of grinding bones for the said Thomas Legh at such times as will not interfere with the business of the Collieries without any charge being made by the said Richard Evans and William Turner.'

The Bone Mill was situated near Cooper Lane, probably in the same building as the Incline Engine. It was used to crush animal bones to provide fertiliser for the estate.

'Thomas Legh reserving to himself the Branch Railway constructed by the said Thomas Legh from Crow Lane to the Newton Race Course.——— as well as the privilege of making use of the Colliery Railway from the Liverpool and Manchester Railway for the purpose of conveying Passengers during the Newton Race Week and also on such days before and after the Races as well as on any other occasions as may be required for the conveyance of Goods and Passengers to and from the Race course free of Tonnage.—— the said Thomas Legh making good any loss which may arise in the use of such Colliery Railway by breakage of Rails, Sleepers or Fences through the conveyance of such goods and Passengers.'

The Mineral Railway had a short branch line near Crow Lane that ran to the Newton Racecourse sidings at the top of Newton Common. The racecourse was situated between the present Swan Hotel and the canal. On Newton Race Week, in townships as far afield as Wigan, Warrington and St.Helens, work would come to a virtual stop. Horseracing was a favourite pastime of Thomas Legh so he had written into the lease permission to use the line during race week and other times, as long as it did not interfere with coal transport.

'Thomas Legh or assigns to enter upon the said demised premises and to view the state thereof and to inspect, examine and measure the said Mines, Pits and Shafts for the purpose of measuring the quantity of Coal gotten thereout and of examining and reporting whether the said Mines are worked in the most proper workmanlike and advantageous manner.'

Thomas Legh or his agent was to be allowed to check the amounts of coal extracted, the type of coal, the

King Pit in the 1930s

An Haydock beam engine in use in the 1930s

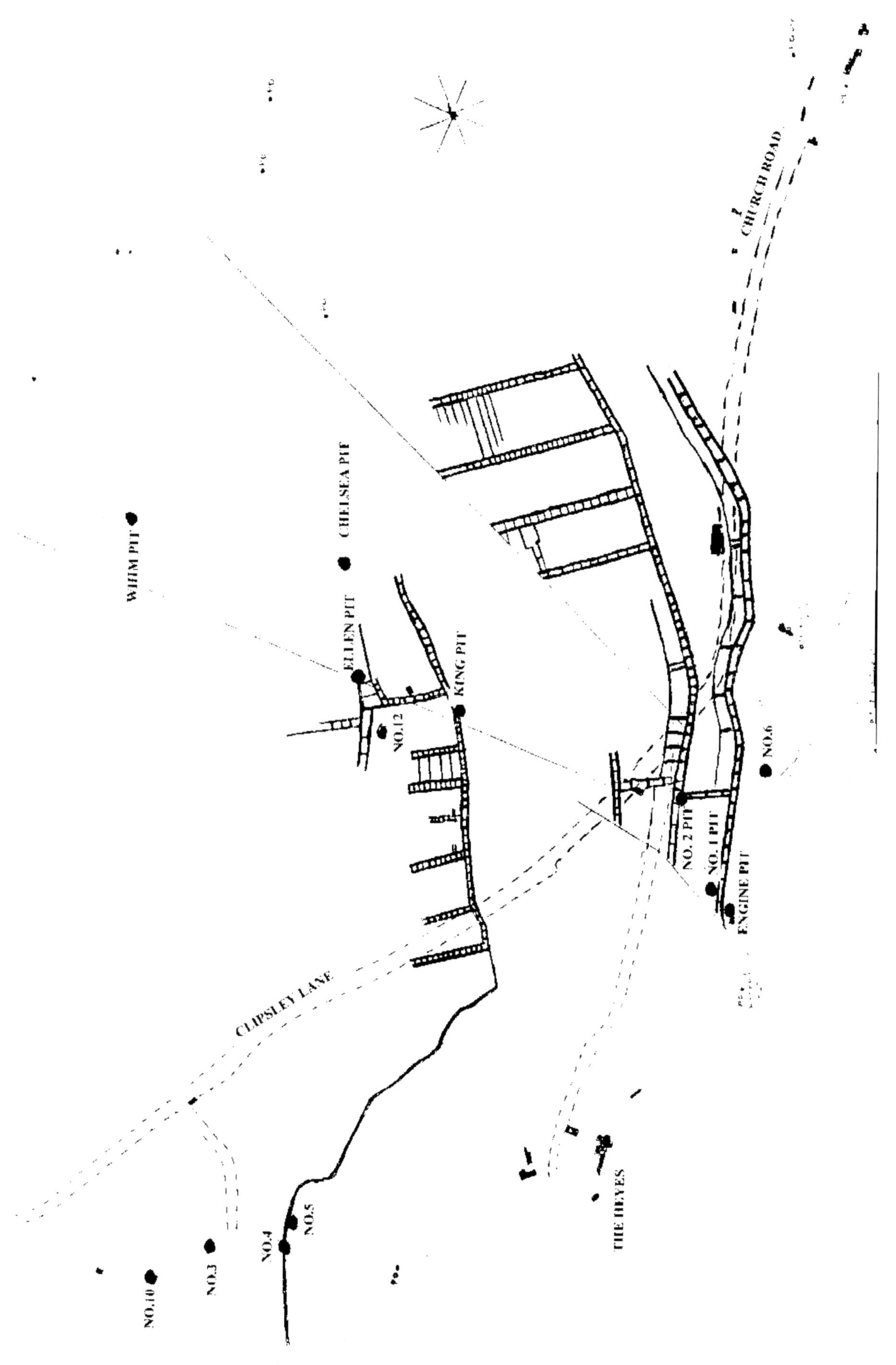

Coal workings under Haydock for Higher Florida seam

thickness of the coal and whether the work was being carried on correctly.

'Richard Evans and William Turner yielding and paying therefore yearly and every year during the said term unto the said Thomas Legh the yearly rent or sum of Four Thousand Pounds of lawful money.——-Also yielding and paying unto the said Thomas Legh the sum of one hundred and fifteen pounds per foot per Cheshire Acre for all the Coals which shall be gotten raised or sold out of the two seams called the Higher Delf and the Lower Delf and the sum of fifty pounds per foot per Cheshire Acre for all the Coals which shall be gotten raised or sold out of the two seams called the Earthy Delf and the Potato Delf.———— hereby expressly declared and agreed that in case the said rents shall not amount to the sum of four thousand pounds, the said rent or yearly reserved sum shall be fully paid.'

This section relates to the rents and payments that Turner and Evans had to pay. The charges for the four types of coal show the difference in quality of the Higher and Lower Delfs when compared with the Earthy and Potato Delfs.

'Richard Evans and William Turner yielding and paying the yearly rent or sum of two hundred and forty pounds four shillings and three half pence for the coal yards at Liverpool and Warrington and the use thereof being the sum of two hundred and ten pounds for the Liverpool yard and the sum of thirty pounds four shillings and three half pence for the Warrington Coal Yard.'

The two coal yards that they were renting were at Bank Quay in Warrington and Crown Street in Liverpool. Richard Evans & Co. continued to use these yards until nationalisation.

'Also the said Richard Evans and William Turner shall and will keep a book or books to be extracted from the pay chest in which shall be entered the true and exact quantity of all the Coals gotten or raised at the said Collieries hereby demised and shall and will at all times permit and suffer the said Thomas Legh or William Legh to inspect and examine the same for the purpose of ascertaining the exact quantity of Coals which shall be gotten or raised out of the said Mines.'

Thomas Legh insisted that account books were kept to enable checks to be made by his agents.

'And also shall not at any time bring or cause or suffer to be brought by or through the said Mines Beds and Veins of Coal or up at any eye or eye pit or pits any Coal other then what shall be dug or gotten except with the consent of the said Thomas Legh and William Legh.——— And also shall not get or work any part of the mines called the Higher Delf and Lower Delf on the dip side of the levels at present driven from No.1 Pit as laid down on the said plan except driving the levels and upbrows until the whole of the Coal lying on the Crop of the said No.1 Pit shall be gotten and worked.'

This section specified the type of coal to be extracted and limited Turner and Evans to a certain area.

'The said Thomas Legh and William Legh to let to Messrs Eccles and Stock or any other Company similarly situated any small portion of the said Mines not exceeding in the whole Two Acres to any one Company adjoining their Collieries which can be worked by them but could not be worked or gotten to profit by the said Richard Evans and William Turner.'

Eccles and Stock were coal mining to the north of Haydock and could possibly reach some seams from their workings.

'Total value of the Utensils, Machinery, Railways, Tramroads, Underground Railways and other matters referred to in the foregoing Indenture of Lease .———— £21,560-7s-5d.'

The asking price was for all the machinery and equipment, it did not include any buildings or land. Within a matter of years Richard Evans was paying a yearly coal rent of £4000 to the Legh family.

Typical Coalfield Scene - 19th Century

Endings.

So ended the Leghs direct involvement in Haydock coal mining. For many years after 1833 the revenue from coal rents partly funded their estates and supported the family. During their time as coal proprietors they had been involved in many changes. Technologically they had improved their coalmines from the primitive days of bell pits to the age of steam and they had taken part in the canal era and welcomed the railway age. Historically, their mining era had commenced during the reign of Queen Anne and finished just before the Victorian age.

The dominant purchaser of Haydock Colliery, Richard Evans, went on to do great things in Haydock. When William Turner died in 1842 Richard and his sons, Joseph and Josiah, expanded Haydock Collieries into a very profitable concern.

The Legh family, with the help of a series of inheritances, had over the years increased their estates in Lancashire and Cheshire to over 13,000 acres. In the Victorian era their estates were worth £45,000 per year in rents.

In the present day the Leghs appear separated from their many estates and solicitors carry out most of their business. But the Rams Head and the Hand & Banner can still be found in local schools, outside pubs and in books although their connection to coal mining is forgotten.

Bibliography.

Primary Sources: -

John Rylands Library - Legh Collection - Correspodence.
Cheshire Record Office - Tabley Collection - Correspondence.
Greater Manchester Record Office - Legh Collection.

Secondary Sources: -

W. Beamont, A History of the House of Lyme (1876)
Lady Newton, The House of Lyme (1917)
T.C.Barker, 'Lancashire Coal, Cheshire Salt and the Rise of Liverpool', T.H.S.L.C., 103
T.C.Barker and J.R.Harris, A Merseyside Town in the Industrial Revolution: St.Helens 1750-1900 (1954)